काण्वशतपथब्राह्मणम्
Kāṇvaśatapathabrāhmaṇam

कलामूलशास्त्र-ग्रन्थमाला
(12)

KALĀMŪLAŚĀSTRA SERIES
(12)

General Editor
Kapila Vatsyayan

काण्वशतपथब्राह्मणम्

Kāṇvaśatapathabrāhmaṇam

Volume I

Edited and Translated
by
C.R. Swaminathan

INDIRA GANDHI NATIONAL CENTRE FOR THE ARTS
NEW DELHI
and
MOTILAL BANARSIDASS PUBLISHERS PVT. LTD.
DELHI

First Published 1994

Published by
INDIRA GANDHI NATIONAL CENTRE FOR THE ARTS
Central Vista, Janpath, New Delhi-110001

in association with

MOTILAL BANARSIDASS PUBLISHERS PVT. LTD.
Bungalow Road, Jawahar Nagar, Delhi-110007

ISBN : 81-208-1126-7 Vol. I)
81-208-1128-3 (set)

Photocomposed by Neographics
1811, Gyani Bazar, Kotla Mubarakpur
New Delhi-110003
Printed in India at Shri Jainendra Press
A-45, Naraina Industrial Area, Phase-I
New Delhi-110028

FOREWORD

As is now well-recognised, the Indira Gandhi National Centre for the Arts through its diverse programmes of research and publications, field work an documentation, seeks to recontextualise the arts within the larger dynamics of the natural and human environment. The methodology is interdisciplinary and multidisciplinary. As a primary prerequisite is the need to make accessible, in original and translation, texts that lay the foundations of the Indian artistic traditions and those others that are specific to particular arts. The *Kalāmūlaśāstra Series*, thus, concentrates on the 'textual' in relation to the traditions of oral transmission, as also contemporary practice. In the *Series*, early fundamental texts on music, such as, *Mātrālakṣaṇam, Dattilam, Bṛhaddeśī* as also comparatively late texts, e.g., *Śrīhastamuktāvali* and *Nartananirṇaya,* have already appeared. Also, *Śilparatnakośa* and *Mayamatam, vāstu* and *śilpa* texts of the Orissan and Tamilian traditions have been published. Two texts belonging to the category of *Āgama* and *Purāṇa*,viz. *Svāyaṃbhuvasūtrasaṃgraha* and *Kālikāpurāṇe mūrtivinirdeśaḥ*, have also been published. Now, we have pleasure in introducing the first volume of the *Kāṇvaśatapathabrāhmaṇam*, as twelfth in the *Series.* The present volume comprises only the first Kāṇda of the Brāhmaṇa. Subsequent volumes will present the remaining Kāṇdas.

While the texts on particular arts or a group of related arts, provide details of the principles of form and delineate intricacies of techniques, the foundations of these lie in the articulation of a world-view in the Vedas, the speculative thought of the Upaniṣads and the elaborate system of rites and rituals enumerated in the Brāhmaṇas. The theory and technique of the particular arts is but a specific branch and flowering of a single unified vision. The world-view is embedded in the recognition of ceaseless movement of the universe where the parts are related to the whole, matter and energy are reciprocal and 'man' is only one amongst all living matter. Vedic hymns are considered as 'revelations' (*Dṛṣta*) because they are inspired by an intuitive insight and 'flash'. Little wonder while the *Śruti* (the Vedic corpus) has remained immutable, its interpretation at the level of thought, intellection and systematised concretisation, have been many.

While the Upaniṣads speculate on the nature of the universe, and the relationship of the one and the many, the immanent and transcendental, the Brāhmaṇas make concrete the world-view and the concepts through a highly developed system of ritual–*yajña.* This functions as a strategy for a continuous reminder of the inter-relatedness of man and nature, the five elements and the sources of energy. The rituals (*yajñas*) yoke together the different orders of time and space in specific duration, and thus establish a system of correspondences between the micro and the macro, the finite and infinite, the specific and the universal, the physical and the metaphysical. Physical space is demarcated and consecrated, the *śālā*, altars are made, Sky, Earth, Sun and the Moon are invoked, fire is kindled, verses of *Ṛg*, *Sāman* and *Yajuṣ* are chanted, sung and recited, by different people, oblations are made of diverse substances through stylised movement and gestures. Through the ritual a spatial and temporal order is restored, individual identities are submerged in a collective purification. The Brahmanic ritual also is, in our contemporary language, a multimedia performance of a very high order. In this performative act lie the seeds of later temple architecture, musical forms, dance and drama. It is not without significance that the writer of the *Nāṭyaśāstra* acknowledges debt to all the Vedas and states that the theatrical performance is a *yajña*.

Aesthetics and artistic practices are rooted in the functionality of ordinary and everyday life but its goal and ultimate objective is to evoke a state of bliss and experience, analogous but not identical, to the supreme mystical *ānanda*. The ordinary is transubstantiated to the extraordinary, the *laukika* to the *alaukika*. For this purpose,at the level of structures, methodologies and techniques, the Brāhmaṇa texts and the practice of the *yajña* and its *viniyoga* serve as a model. The Brāhmaṇa texts thus serve as the foundation of artistic practice, as much as being texts of theology and liturgy or litany. The texts on the specific arts tacitly accept this as is evident from a reading of the early texts on the arts and an examination of the actual survivals.

So far, the Brāhmaṇa texts have been looked at and studied by those whose primary concern has been with cosmology, religion and ritual. It is only in the last decade that there has been a new and fresh interest in the study of art as ritual and ritual as artistic practice. In this context the re-edited publication of this fundamental text on ritual --- the *Śatapathabrāhmaṇam* — is both timely and relevant.

Julius Eggeling, Caland and other pioneers, had edited and translated the text. While Eggeling translated the Mādhyandina recension, Caland carried on the work of editing and translating eight Kāṇḍas of the *Kāṇvaśatapathabrāhmaṇam*. Julius Eggeling who spent many decades of his life on this particular Brāhmaṇa, in an erudite introduction, says –

".... In the whole range of literature few works are probably less calculated to excite the interest of any outside the very limited number of specialists, than the ancient theological writings of the Hindus, known by the name of Brāhmaṇas. For wearisome prolixity of exposition, characterised by dogmatic assertion and a flimsy symbolism rather than by serious reasoning, these works are perhaps not equalled anywhere; unless, indeed, it be by the speculative vapourings of the Gnostics, than which, in the opinion of the learned translators of Irenaeus, 'nothing more absurd has probably ever been imagined by rational beings'. If I have, nevertheless, undertaken, at the request of the Editor of the present Series, what would seem to be a rather thankless task, the reason will be readily understood by those who have taken even the most cursory view of the history of the Hindu mind and institutions."

As Eggeling continued the work, gradually but surely he began to recognise the value of the work. Not only was he impressed with the ritual (then called 'sacrifices') practices, but began to see the philosophic and mystical significance. He recognised that through the ritual (*yajña*), the 'cosmos' was being renewed. The *yajña* in essence is refuelling the depleted energies — a resurrection of the dead elements. He began to appreciate why in the etymology of the Brāhmaṇas it is born through movement. Hence it is *yañ + ja* which is as much *yajña*. Eggeling then remarked that "............. the periodical sacrifice is nothing else than a microcosmic representation of the ever-proceeding destruction and renewal of all cosmic life and matter." – (Introduction to Part IV).

At the end of his arduous task requiring extraordinary patience, perhaps, Eggeling himself changed, for no longer was it a thankless task. The Brāhmaṇas were no longer just a series of highly artificial system of sacrificial ceremonies, but were, instead, both mystical and concrete. Understandably, he concluded :

"And now my task is done, and I must take leave of this elaborate exposition of the sacrificial ordinances of Indian theology. For well-nigh a score of years the work has 'dragged its slow length along,' and during that time it has caused me — and, I doubt not, has caused some of my readers, too —not a few weary hours.

.... but for Professor Max Muller's timely exhortations and kindly encouragement, the work might perhaps never have been completed. 'I know,' he once wrote to me, 'you will thank me one day for having pressed you to go on with your work;' and now I do indeed thank him most sincerely and with all my heart for the kindness and patience he has shown me these many years. But, strange to say, now that the work is completed, I feel as if I could not do without working at it; and certainly, if a second edition could ever have been required of a work of this kind, it would have found me ready once more to work my way through the bewildering maze of rites.." – (Introduction to Part V)

The IGNCA undertook to look at the text, once again, taking into account the valuable work done by Eggeling and Caland, in order to contextualise the text within the larger discourse of the Indian tradition, specially its system of developing multilevelled and multilayered structures of thought, meaning and form. Also, because the *Śatapatha* is a fundamental text of the formal aspects of ritual traditions relevant for identifying the principles of form and the methodology of establishing correspondences between the idea and the 'image', the concept and the symbol and of course, myth and ritual in the Indian arts. As is well recognised, the conception of the 'Puruṣa' is fundamental and pervasive in the Vedas, Brāhmaṇas and the Upaniṣads. While the Puruṣa Sūkta of the *Ṛg Veda* may be revelation, it is the Brāhmaṇas which identify the ritual (*yajña*) with Prajāpati. The physical construction of the altars, the essence of the piling up of bricks is essentially symbolic. It has the purpose of carrying out in ritual form the essential act of reconstruction of Prajāpati whose sacrifice as Puruṣa has resulted in the creation of the universe in all its parts. The ritual is not restricted to a definite act in time; it is a constant process. Therefore, the dismembered Prajāpati must be ever and again renewed. The renewal is brought about by the construction of Prajāpati in the shape of a fire altar. The concepts of Prajāpati, Puruṣa and Agni coalesce. The *Śatapatha* develops the theme in the tenth Kāṇda philosophically and identifies its symbolic significance in terms of space and time. Indian architecture, likewise, conceives of the temple as Puruṣa and assembles the architectural members as in a ritual. So far, art-historians have not paid adequate attention to this relationship, except a few like Stella Kramrisch in her monumental work "The Hindu Temple".

The publication of a new edition with text and translation will, it is hoped, facilitate access to a primary text of fundamental importance for the student of both ritual as well as the arts.

The *Śatapathabrāhmaṇam* belongs to *Śukla Yajurveda* and as has been pointed out by the editor, is available in two recensions known as Kāṇva and Mādhyandina. The Mādhyandina text was edited by Weber in the year 1923 and its English translation was rendered by Eggeling. In the case of

Kāṇvaśatapatha, Prof. Caland published the critical edition only of the first seven Kāṇḍas; of the remaining ten Kāṇḍas he included only the difference in reading in the two recensions.

The present edition includes the full text with translation. No doubt, the work of Caland and Eggeling has been considered primary. However, the learned editor, Dr.C.R. Swaminathan has consulted other manuscripts, specially one in Telegu script and another in a private collection from Karnataka. These are based on the oral transmission of the text.

A careful re-collation of the text has thus been done by checking original manuscripts used by Caland and others, now located in Nasik, Belgaum and Pandarpur and the orally transmitted text. Consequently, the text has been culled out by a most comprehensive search, collation, editing and translation. Also, naturally, the view point differs from the European scholars. No longer is the fundamental concern to trace Indo-Iranian sources and make comparisons with the Romans, etc. Dr.C.R.Swaminathan — our editor – critically assesses the text in *Vimarśa* section. With a command on both language and contemporary practice, he comments and elucidates certain technical aspects of the performance of *yāgas* connected with this Brāhmaṇa. Besides, he alludes to other *yāgas* and the relevance of the *Kāṇvaśatapatha* as textual authority. A Glossary of technical terms related to objects used in performing *yāgas* along with their illustrations, has been added. All this material, it is hoped, will be an invaluable source of knowledge on a much partially quoted and discussed but infrequently read text, in original or translation. The contents would be of interest both to theologists as also to those interested in the foundations of artistic traditions, architecture, music, dance and theatre and those interested in the study of ritual as a discipline.

IGNCA is deeply indebted to Dr.C.R.Swaminathan for undertaking this enormous and highly specialised project. With his command on the subject, he has accomplished a very difficult task, with erudition, patience and rare understanding. I should also like to acknowledge and appreciate the work of Dr. Advaitavadini Kaul for seeing this complex text through the press.

NEW DELHI KAPILA VATSYAYAN
14.11.1994

CONTENTS

ABBREVIATIONS

B	Manuscript from Belgaum got through the good offices of Sri Pimplapure.
C	Manuscript in the Calcutta Asiatic Society Library, described by Caland as codex 3.
Ca	The reading adopted by Caland in his edition.
CL	Calcutta manuscript described by Caland as codex 10.
Co	Colebrooke's manuscript described under codex 4.
H	Paper manuscript in possession of Sri Marthanda Dikshit, Hubli, Karnataka.
K	Incomplete palm-leaf manuscript of Sri Kumaraswami Dikshitar, Illippai, Tamil Nadu.
L	Manuscript in the India Office Library, described by Caland as codex 9.
M	Madras manuscript—Government Oriental Manuscripts Library, Madras, described by Caland as codex 1.
MD	The Mādhyandina Śatapatha Text.
Ms	Manuscript.
Mss	Manuscripts.
My	Paper manuscript of Oriental Institute, Mysore, described by Caland as codex 8.
N	Manuscript from Nasik compared by the good offices of Sri Pimplapure.
Ne	Nepal manuscript described by Caland as codex 11.
P	Manuscript in the Paris Library referred to by Caland as codex 4.
P.1	Paper manuscript from Poona University Library, complete.
P.2	Paper manuscript from Poona University Library, incomplete.
Pa	Manuscript from Pandarpur, compared through the good offices of Sri Pimplapure.
Po	Oxford University Manuscript described by Caland as codex 5.
SB	*The Kāṇva Śatapatha Brāhmaṇa.*
T	Palm-leaf manuscript of Saraswati Mahal Library, Tanjore, described by Caland as codex 2.
TE	Printed edition of the *Kāṇva Śatapatha*, edited by Bhagavatulu Lakshmipathi Sastri, printed at Tripurasundari press, Tenali, published by Yajñavalkya Mahajana Sangha in 1923 in 2 Vols.
V1	Banaras manuscript numbered by Caland as codex 6.
V2	Paper manuscript belonging to Sri Lakshmikant Ramacharya Purohit of Varanasi.
W	Manuscript from Wai, Maharashtra, compared through the good offices of Sri Pimplapure.

INTRODUCTION

The Vedas form the earliest literature available to humanity, handed down by an unbroken oral tradition, throwing light on the religious, social and cultural life and aspirations of the people who inhabited the south and south-east Asian regions. The word 'Veda', is derived from the root *vid,* to know. The Veda refers to that group of expressions which enables us to know the ways and means of achieving the fourfold aims of human existence, namely *dharma* (righteousness), *artha* (prosperity in material terms), *kāma* (physical and mental happiness) and *mokṣa* (unmitigated spiritual bliss of ever-lasting nature). Another definition of the Veda is that which throws light on those means of emancipation or on those superhuman agencies who can help in the emancipation, which cannot be known or identified by the other two means of knowledge, viz. *pratyakṣa* (perception) and *anumāna* (inference). It is, in other words, a collection of sounds that reveal super-mundane matters or that which enables us to perceive the supra-sensual phenomena, अलौकिकार्थवेदकशब्दराशिर्वेदः.

The Vedas consist of the *mantras* (also called Saṁhitās) and the Brāhmaṇas. *Mantras* include prayers to divine beings and also deal with the super-natural powers of those divine entities which have a sway over the living beings in this Universe, both in their genesis and in their behaviour. The *mantras,* by virtue of the potency of their sounds, are themselves believed to influence the atmospheric conditions and also divert the physical, psychical and metaphysical activities of living beings and bring about peace and harmony among human beings themselves and between human beings and nature.

The Brāhmaṇas are in a sense, the earliest annotations of the *mantras* also called the Saṁhitā portions. They contain some etymological derivations of words found in the latter, serve as manuals for the performance of Vedic sacrifices involving the usages of the *mantras,* dilate on some narratives and anecdotes to drive home the significance of particular statements of the Saṁhitā and their usages in particular contexts, etc. In short, the Brāhmaṇas reveal to us the nature of *dharma* (that unseen moral and spiritual merit or *adṛṣta* produced by such mental and physical activities that fall within the purview of righteousness), which would lead to the other three *puruṣārthas* or human goals, viz. *artha, kāma* and *mokṣa*. The Saṁhitā, on the other hand, reveals to us the divine entities to be propitiated for the earning of *dharma,* their nature and the various offerings that go to propitiate them.

Indian tradition holds both the Saṁhitā and the Brāhmaṇa equally sacrosanct revelations of non-human origin. They are eternal collections of sounds revealed from time to time due to divine will. Jaimini, who, according to

Indologists, antedates the Christian era, in his *Mīmāṃsā-sūtras* that lay down the guide-lines for the interpretation of the Vedas, has treated the Saṁhitā and the Brāhmaṇa at par. He has not only accepted both as authentic Vedic texts but laid at rest all speculations regarding the *apauruṣeyatva* of the Brāhmaṇa part. He refers to an earlier scholar, by name Kāśakṛtsna, on whose lines, he claims to have planned his own *sūtras*. That means, much earlier to Jaimini, the *apauruṣeyatva* of both the Saṁhitā and Brāhmaṇa had come to stay as an accepted fact and both together had been held as the uncontrovertible source of the entire spectrum of valid knowledge, the sheet-anchor of later metaphysical speculations.

Of the four Vedas, the first three are considered specially important and are collectively called the *Trayī vidyā*. This is because these three are indispensable for the performance of sacrifice or *yāga*. The hymns of the *Ṛgveda*, totalling 10,424 *mantras* are distributed over one thousand *sūktas* (hymns) that are divided into ten *Maṇḍalas*. These *Ṛks* are used in the chanting of *śastras* or invocatory prayers in honour of deities like Indra, Agni, Varuṇa, etc. and in the uttering of *yājyas* and *puronuvākyas* at the times of actual offerings. The *Yajus* formulae in prose, refer to the details of the performance of the various *iṣṭis* and *yāgas* and to the process of pressing Soma juice,etc. While collecting the pressed Soma juice in different cups or *grahas* for different gods, the *Ṛk* hymns set to music called *Sāmans* are sung. These *Sāman* chants are called *stotras*. Both *śastras* and *stotras* (in *Ṛks* and *Sāmans* respectively) are in praise of the qualities and characteristics of various deities for whom the *grahas* are collected. The priests who handle these three Vedas and perform the rituals connected with these are respectively called Hotṛ, Adhvaryu and Udgātṛ. Besides these, there is the Brahmā who is to monitor the entire sacrificial rituals and is supposed to be well-versed in the functions of the other three categories of priests. Each one of these four priests have three assistants, forming four *gaṇas* or groups. Thus the Hotṛ-gaṇa includes (1) Hotṛ, (2) Maitrāvaruṇa, (3) Acchāvāka (4) Grāvastut. The Adhvaryu-gaṇa consists of (1) Adhvaryu, (2) Pratiprasthātṛ, (3) Neṣṭṛ and (4) Unnetṛ. The Udgātṛ-gaṇa comprises of (1) Udgātṛ, (2) Prastotṛ, (3) Pratihartṛ and (4) Subrahmaṇya. The Brahma-gaṇa includes (1) Brahma, (2) Brāhmaṇācchaṁśin, (3) Āgnīdhra and (4) Potṛ.

The *Yajurveda*, which is most important from the point of view of sacrifice, is concerned with the techniques of conducting the *yāgas* and its Brāhmaṇa parts explain the rationale behind each one of the technical details. The priest handling the *Yajus* part is called Adhvaryu denoting his role in the *adhvara* or sacrifice. The *Yajurveda* has two main divisions, namely the *Śukla* or white and the *Kṛṣṇa* or black. There are three *śākhās* or schools of recitation of the *Kṛṣṇa-Yajurveda*, called the Kāṭhaka, the Maitrāyaṇīya and the Taittirīya. The Brāhmaṇa portions of the first two are not available now. The Taittirīya śākhā has two divisions of Mantra and Brāhmaṇa but they are not exclusively of

Mantras and Brāhmaṇas respectively. There is an intermixture of the two and that is perhaps the reason for its being named *Kṛṣṇa* or black.

Two recensions of the *Śukla-Yajurveda* have come down to us and each of them has the Saṁhitā and the Brāhmaṇa clearly separated and exclusive of each other. The Brāhmaṇa texts of both are called by the same name of *Śatapatha,* which literally means 'The hundred paths'. In the Mādhyandina version, the order in which the topics are dealt with, is the same as they appear in the Saṁhitā text of that *śākhā,* except for the *Piṇḍa-pitṛ-yajña* which appears after *Darśapūrṇamāsa* in the Saṁhitā and after *ādhāna* in the Brāhmaṇa. In the Kāṇva version, the Saṁhitā starts with the *Darśapūrṇamāsa* and the Brāhmaṇa deals with *ādhāna* first. Hence the first and second Kāṇḍas of the *Mādhyandina Śatapatha* are in the reverse order in the Kāṇva recension. The Mādhyandina Brāhmaṇa is divided into Kāṇḍas, Adhyāyas, Prapāṭhakas, Brāhmaṇas and Kaṇḍikās; whereas in the Kāṇva, all the divisions except the Prapāṭhakas are found. The contents of each division vary in the two versions and are as follows:

Divisions	**Mādhyandina**	**Kāṇva**
Kāṇḍas	14	17
Adhyāyas	100	104
Prapāṭhakas	68	Nil
Brāhmaṇas	436	435
Kaṇḍikās	7179	6806

The names of the Kāṇḍas also vary between the two and the sequence in which they appear is as below:

Name of the Kāṇḍa	**Serial no. in Kāṇva**	**Serial no. in Mādhyandina**
Ekapāt Kāṇḍa	1	2
Haviryajña Kāṇḍa	2	1
Udhāri Kāṇḍa	3	—
Adhvara Kāṇḍa	4	3
Graha Kāṇḍa	5	4
Vājapeya Kāṇḍa	6	—
Sava Kāṇḍa	—	5
Rājasūya Kāṇḍa	7	—
Ukhāsaṁbharaṇa Kāṇḍa	8	6
Hastighaṭa Kāṇḍa	9	7
Citi Kāṇḍa	10	8
Sāgniciti (Sāciti) Kāṇḍa	11	—
Sañciti Kāṇḍa	—	9

Agnirahasya Kāṇḍa	12	10
Aṣṭādhyāyī Kāṇḍa	13	11
Madhyama Kāṇḍa	14	12
Aśvamedha Kāṇḍa	15	13
Pravargya Kāṇḍa	16	—
Bṛhadāraṇyaka Kāṇḍa	17	14

Generally, the division of Kaṇḍikās is more rational in the Kāṇva text than in the other. The sequence of the Adhyāyas in the former recension is also less erratic than in the Mādhyandina. The name '*Śatapatha*', as Eggeling has suggested, might have been based on the number of Adhyāyas in the Mādhyandina which is exactly one hundred. But the Kāṇva recension, which has one hundred and four Adhyāyas is also known by the same name. In Indian tradition words like '*śata*' and '*sahasra*', indicating numbers, do not always stand for the exact numbers. They are often approximate indications. When they name a work as *Sahasranāma-stotra* (a prayer with 1000 appellations of gods) it is not unusual to find 1008 names in it.

The first half of the *Mādhyandina-Śatapatha* ending with Sañciti Kāṇḍa consists of sixty Adhyāyas distributed among nine Kāṇḍas and the corresponding portion of the *Kāṇva-Śatapatha* ending with Sāgniciti or Sāciti Kāṇḍa consists of sixty-five Adhyāyas distributed among eleven Kāṇḍas. There are some evidences to show that only this first part in each of these Brāhmaṇas was in vogue in the oral tradition of learning, i.e. *adhyayana-paramparā*. It is perhaps due to the fact the Kāṇḍas from 10 to 13 in Mādhyandina and from 12 to 15 in Kāṇva deal with sacrificial rituals not usually practised and the 14th Kaṇḍa in Mādhyandina and the last two Kāṇḍas in Kāṇva (16 and 17) deal with metaphysical matters comprising the *Bṛhadāraṇyakopaniṣad*. However, it should be remembered that the *Bṛhadāraṇyakopaniṣad* has been in *adhyayana-paramparā* separately as an *Upaniṣad*, though not as a part of the Brāhmaṇa text. The text of the Mādhyandina school has already been critically edited by Weber and an English translation of the same by Eggeling has also come out. Prof. Caland prepared and published the critical text of the first seven Kāṇḍas of the *Kāṇva-Śatapatha*. In respect of the remaining Kāṇḍas, he has only indicated the main differences in readings between the Mādhyandina and the Kāṇva recensions.

Here an attempt has been made to present the critical text of the entire *Kāṇva-Śatapatha-brāhmaṇa* with all the 17 Kāṇḍas and also an English translation side by side.

It would be a repetition to describe the details of the manuscript material consulted by Caland in the preparation of his critical edition of the seven Kāṇḍas. The present edition, however, besides the variations in readings assiduously collected by Caland and carefully consulted here, has the added advantage of consulting the following materials:

(1) One imporant material that has been availed of for the preparation of this edition, which Caland has not mentioned, is the printed text of the *Kāṇva-Śatapatha* in Telugu script in two volumes. Despite many printing mistakes and typical characteristics of Telugu pronunciation, this printed edition has been very useful in sorting out some of the problems which Caland faced in deciding the correct textual passages. In the absence of a living oral tradition of the *Kāṇva-Śatapatha*, this edition, which was prepared at a time when the *adhyayana-paramparā* of the Brāhmaṇa was still in vogue, serves as a useful guide to understand how it was actually being chanted. In other words, it enables us to peep into the unbroken oral tradition upto a point of time when it was still a *śruti* and not a written document. We naturally attach maximum importance to this edition in keeping with our age-old practice of accepting greater credibility to what is an unbroken oral transmission than to what has been preserved in the form of written record.

(2) Out of the manuscripts collated by Caland, the following were rechecked in respect of the entire text. The reason being that Caland had to depend upon handwritten copies of Mss supplied to him by the concerned libraries and hence were likely to carry scribal errors.

(a) The manuscript designated as M (Madras) and numbered as Codex-1 by Caland has been rechecked with the original. This manuscript, as already described by Caland, is in Grantha script partly and Telugu script in some Kāṇḍas. It has no accent.

(b) The manuscript T (Tanjore) and numbered as Codex-2 by Caland is again unaccented and is a palmleaf manuscript which was described by Burnell and is available in the Tanjore Saraswati Mahal Library. The first three books of this manuscript which could not be consulted by Caland have also been collated for the present edition.

(c) The manuscript B (Benares) referred to by Caland as Codex-6 is the paper manuscript of the Sampurnanand Sanskrit University, Varanasi. This was also rechecked.

(d) The manuscript My (Mysore) described as Codex-8 by Caland belongs to the Oriental Library, Mysore and is again unaccented. A xerox copy of the entire manuscript in Telugu script, instead of a Devanagari transcript, was obtained for collation purposes.

(e) Besides the above, the paper manuscripts belonging to Sri Lakshmikant Ramacharya Purohit of Varanasi with accent, was obtained through the good offices of Pandit Rajahans Ghanapāṭhī, a disciple of Sri Purohit. This manuscript has been designated as V 2 indicating Varanasi-II.

(f) My good friend Dr. T.N. Dharmadhikari, Director, Vaidika Samsodhana Mandala, Pune, helped me in getting a xerox copy of each of the two manuscripts deposited in the Pune University Library. Both are paper manuscripts with accent. The first one is complete and is given the symbol P.1 in our references. The second one which seems to be only a copy of the former, covers the first three Kāṇḍas only and it is designated as P.2.

(g) One of the most valuable manuscripts which we could procure and which was not available for Caland, is the one in possession of Pt. Marthanda Dikshit of Hubli, Karnataka. It is a paper manuscript well accentuated and complete in every respect. It was got prepared by the late Chidambara Dikshitar of Hubli and he belonged to the last generation of *svādhyāyins* who maintained the oral tradition of *Śatapatha adhyayana*. The value of the manuscript is, for reasons stated earlier, of high order since it was recorded by a person himself well-versed in the oral recitation.

Hubli seems to have been a very well-known centre of Kāṇva studies in Karnataka and the name Chidambara is appearing in that line of scholarship almost in every alternate generation. All the five manuscripts including the two in Pune, that are found in south Maharashtra have somewhere or other the mention of Chidambara Dikshitar. My good friend Sri G.W. Pimplapure, who has been working on this text for quite some time, brought to my notice four manuscripts from Nasik, Belgaum, Wai and Pandarpur—all these four manuscripts from the region of north Karnataka and south Maharashtra have been partially collated with the help of copies made available by Sri Pimplapure. They are given the symbols N, B, W and Pa respectively. Although we may not attach individual importance to each of these four, because they all appear to be copies of the text of Hubli tradition but their utility in solving the riddles, particularly in the matter of accentuation cannot be under-estimated.

THE NEED FOR THE FRESH EDITION

Caland's edition is limited to the first seven Kāṇḍas;in respect of subsequent Kāṇḍas, he only gives main deviations in the *Kāṇva-Śatapatha* from the *Mādhyandina-Śatapatha*.

Caland has made some emendments either on the basis of the Mādhyandina readings or on his own conjecture.In many such instances we found that the transcripts of the manuscripts which were consulted by Caland and which were fortunately made available to us in original, provided the clues to solve the riddles instead of resorting to conjectures. In some other cases, Caland's emendments were found to have been induced by imaginary grammatical defects. In a few cases,consultation with other Brāhmaṇa texts was found useful to solve problems of the readings without resorting to arbitrary amendments.

There are certain instances where the Kāṇva recension is more elaborate than the Mādhyandina or the *vice versa*. In such cases doubts about readings could be solved either by referring to the Mādhyandina Brāhmaṇa text or its commentaries by Sāyaṇa and Harisvāmin. No doubt, Sāyaṇa has meant only a brief gloss to the Mādhyandina text and has skipped over many passages presuming that the reader would have understood them from the other Brāhmaṇa texts and their commentaries. Harisvāmin's commentary, though little more elaborate, is less helpful when the merit of variant readings has to be decided on etymological or grammatical grounds. In spite of these drawbacks, both Sāyaṇa and Harisvāmin have come to our rescue in quite a number of places.

Of course, it is intriguing to find Sāyaṇa interpreting the same expression in one way in the *Mādhyandina-Śatapatha* and in a different way in some other texts. In such instances, it becomes difficult to decide the text and the meaning of such expressions found in the Kāṇva recension. This is not mentioned with a view to questioning the credibility of Sāyaṇa's scholarship. It would only mean that Sāyaṇa himself has acknowledged the possibility of variation in the interpretation or it may be that the entire Bhāṣya literature attributed to Sāyaṇa was not from the same pen. They might have been the products of individual efforts of a synod or consortium of scholars under the supervision of Sāyaṇa—an inference which has widely been accepted by scholars.

The manuscripts in Grantha or Telugu scripts which were obtained by Caland for collation in the form of Devanagari transcripts, have obviously carried some human scribal errors causing some difficulties for Prof. Caland. These are rectified by directly rechecking the original manuscripts, as in the instances of misspelt letters like *dha* and *tha*.

The Telugu printed edition in two volumes, mentioned earlier, was published by Tenali Sambhasivaraya in the year 1923. This edition has the following drawbacks:

(1) It is non-critical in nature, since the manuscripts outside the peninsula do not seem to have been consulted.

(2) Being in Telugu script, there are some obvious spelling mistakes caused by the different pronunciation of Sanskrit letters by the Telugu-speaking people as indicated above.

(3) The printing is of very poor quality.

In spite of these drawbacks, this edition has the credit of having been produced at a time when oral tradition of *Śatapatha* study was alive.

Besides, the manuscripts got from Hubli has also indication that it was written down by those who were themselves preserving the oral tradition and hence were in a position to make corrections in the manuscripts, wherever there were errors.

In conclusion, with all due respect to the western scholarship that has brought to the limelight some of the most valuable Vedic texts, I would like to submit that the preparation of critical editions of Vedic texts cannot be and should not be on the same lines as preparing the critical edition of any other classical Sanskrit text. Insofar as the Vedic literature is concerned, the oral tradition is the most dependable basis and the sources where the oral tradition was alive till the recent past will be more dependable than the manuscripts which are copies of the copies. In other words, the validity of the recorded evidence of Vedic text is directly proportionate to its proximity in time and space, to the oral tradition. This principle has been kept in view while preparing this edition.

A detailed textual note is appended at the end of each Kāṇḍa where our preferences to a particular reading needed justification or inclusion of a particular alternate reading called for reasoning.

In the case of translation, Prof. Eggeling's rendering of the *Mādhyandina-Śatapatha* has been taken as a guiding light, not only because that great scholar has maintained a high level of excellence, but also because he has made it a readable translation despite the repetitive nature of the Brāhmaṇa text. His cross references to other texts on occasions where the translation of a passage is difficult, has helped us in no small measure. I have no hesitation in recording my dependence on Eggeling's translation.

A section entitled Vimarśa has been appended to discuss certain technical topics connected with the *Śatapatha-brāhmaṇa*. Incidentally it also contains a bird's eye view of all the *Somayāgas* which are elaborately dealt with in the *Śrauta-sūtras* and for the performance of which this Brāhmaṇa text provides the basic material. This section also includes certain titles, with a view to throwing some light on the ritualistic significance of some specific rites prescribed during the course of performance of *yāgas*.

We have also appended an almost exhaustive glossary of technical terms relating to the utensils used in the sacrifices and pictorial representations of these utensils and instruments are also given separately. An alphabetical Kaṇḍikā index with Kāṇḍa, Adhyāya and Brāhmaṇa numbers is included to facilitate quick reference. At the beginning, a descriptive list of contents of each Brāhmaṇa has also been provided for the benefit of scholars.

Originally it was proposed to give an English translation of Kaṇḍas I to VIII only where there are major differences between the Kāṇva and Mādhyandina recensions. It was even felt that giving an English translation for Kāṇḍas

IX to XVII may be redundant while the translation by Eggeling is available. In fairness to Eggeling, it must be mentioned that his translation does not call for much improvement. Despite this, a fresh translation has been attempted also for the latter half of the *Kāṇva-Śatapatha* even though the readings of Mādhyandina and Kāṇva have very little difference. This fresh attempt is justifiable on the grounds that it is in the interest of continuity of the methodology adopted for the first eight Kāṇḍas and it would also help to present a homogeneous independent translation of the Kāṇva recension. I have no hesitation to acknowledge my dependence on the translation of Eggeling and at the same time I would like to assure the readers that the alterations in the language of Eggeling are not introduced only for the sake of alterations and not in the least as a camouflage. The changes introduced are mostly to maintain continuity in the usage of English equivalents adopted in the earlier Kāṇḍas.

Therefore, to the extent my translation agrees with that of Eggeling, the gratitude to Eggeling is obvious. To the extent they differ from Eggeling, it may be ascribed to the compulsions which were felt to bring about homogeneity and uniformity with my translation of the first eight Kāṇḍas.

A colossal work like this, which was undertaken without fully realising its vastness could not have been completed without the unreserved co-operation of friends and institutions who lent or provided copies of manuscripts in their possession, team of scholars with knowledge of various scripts who helped in getting the manuscripts collated word for word and above all the unflinching help that was received from a group of scholars in editing and translating the text. Particular mention should be made of Prof. K.V. Seshadrinath Sarma, Sri T.K. Chayapati Sarma and Prof. A.V. Nagaraja Sarma who provided the academic co-operation for this monumental work. Sri S. Ranganatha Sarma, Sri G.W. Pimplapure and Sri A.S. Subbukrishna Srautigal have helped me in collating the various manuscripts. Last but not the least in importance, Sri H. Subramanian was very helpful in doing the typing work of the translation.

I cannot find adequate expression to convey my gratitude to the IGNCA and particularly to its dynamic Academic Director Dr. (Smt.) Kapila Vatsyayan for the confidence she reposed on these weak shoulders of mine when this project was entrusted to me.

C.R. Swaminathan

काण्वशतपथब्राह्मणम्

Kāṇvaśatapathabrāhmaṇam

एकपात्काण्डम्

प्रथमोऽध्यायः

प्रथमं ब्राह्मणम्

ॐ स वै संभारान्त्संभरति यद्वा एनानितश्चेतश्च[1] संभरति तदेव संभाराणाꣳसंभारत्वꣳ स यत्र यत्राग्नेर्यक्तं भवति ततस्तत एनꣳ संभरति यशसेव त्वदेनꣳ समर्धयन्पशुभिरिव त्वन्मिथुनेनैव त्वदेनं प्रजननेन समर्धयति संभरे[2]ꣳस्तस्माद्वा व संभारान्त्संभरति ॥ १ ॥

स यत्राग्नीं३[3] आधास्यन्भवति तत्स्फ्येनोल्लिखति बहु वा अस्याः पृथिव्या अमेध्यं यदभिष्ठ्यूतं वाऽभिष्ठितं वा तदेवैतत्स्फ्येनोल्लिखत्यथ मेध्यायामेव यज्ञियायां पृथिव्यामाधत्ते तदद्भिरवोक्षति सोऽपाꣳसंभारोऽन्नमु वा आपोऽन्नꣳ हि वा आपस्तस्माद्यदेहाप आगच्छन्त्यथेहान्नं जायतेऽन्नाद्येनैवैनमेतत् समर्धयति योषा उ वा आपो वृषाग्निस्तन्मिथुनं प्रजननं मिथुनेनैवैनमेतत् प्रजननेन समर्धयत्यद्भिरु वा इदꣳ सर्वमाप्तमद्भिरेवैनमेतदाप्त्वाधत्ते तस्माद्वा अ[4]पस्संभरति ॥ २ ॥

अथ हिरण्यꣳ संभरत्यग्निर्ह वा अपोऽभिदध्यौ मिथुन्येनाः[5] स्यामिति तास्संबभूव तासु रेतः प्रसिषेच तद्धिरण्यं तस्माद्धिरण्यमग्निसंकाशमग्नेर्हि रेतस्तस्मादेनदप्स्वेवानुविन्दन्त्य[6]प्सु पुनन्त्यप्सु ह्येनत्प्रासिञ्चन्नैनेन धावयन्ति न किंचन कुर्वन्त्यथ यशो देवरेतसꣳ हि यशसैवैनमेतत्समर्धयति[7] सरेतसं कृत्स्नमग्निमाधत्ते तस्माद्धिरण्यꣳ संभरति ॥ ३ ॥

१. एनानित्थाच्चेत्थाच्च C see Notes.

२. संभरꣳ TE.

३. यत्राग्नी३ P1, P2, H, TE., see Notes.

४. आप TE.

५. मिथुन्येना Ca., see Notes.

६. TE निन्दत्यप्सु; see Notes.

७. TE त्समर्धयति.

EKAPĀTKĀṆḌA

Chapter One

BRĀHMAṆA I

1. He (who is to perform the installation of the holy fires, *agnyādhāna*) gathers the requisite materials; he collects them from here and there (from various places). That verily constitutes the 'collectedness' of the materials. He gathers this (fire) from different places where there is inherence of fire. By that, he makes it flourish with glory, as it were, with cattle (wealth) and with a mate; thus he makes it grow with productivity. Therefore, indeed, he gathers the required materials.

2. That place where he is going to set up the two fires, he scrapes with a wooden sword. Much of this earth that has been spat upon and that has been trodden is indeed impure. That very thing he scrapes with the wooden sword and then he establishes (the fires) only upon pure ground that is fit for sacrifice. That (place) he sprinkles with water. That is the provision of water. Water is verily food; water, indeed, is food. Therefore when waters arrive here, then food grows here. This (sprinkling of water) makes it (the fire) flourish with (good) food. Water is, indeed, the female, fire the male. That makes a productive couple. This (sprinkling with water) makes this (fire) prosper with a procreative mate. All this (Universe) is verily pervaded by the (primordial) waters. Covering this (place) with water itself, he (the sacrificer) installs this (fire). Hence is it that he procures water.

3. Then he provides gold. (Once)Agni coveted the waters, thinking, "I shall be coupled with these." He united with them and deposited his seed in them. That (became) gold. Hence gold shines like fire; (for) it is indeed the seed of fire. So people find this (gold) only in waters. In waters do they purify (this), for he (Agni) deposited it verily in waters. People do not wash with this (gold), nor do they do anything (else). Now, splendour (glory) is the seed of gods. This (provision of gold) makes this (fire) grow with splendour. He (the sacrificer) sets up the entire fire with its seed. Therefore does he procure gold.

अथोषान्त्संभरत्यसौ ह वै द्यौरस्यै पृथिव्यै पशून्प्रददौ त [८]ऊषास्तस्माद्यत्रोषरं तत्पशव्यमाहुः साक्षाद्ध्येते पशवो यदूषाः पशुभिरेवैनं तत्समर्धयति स वा एषोऽमुष्या दिवो रसः सोऽस्यां पृथिव्यां प्रति[९]ष्ठितस्तमनयोर्द्यावापृथिव्यो रसं मन्यन्तेऽनयोरेवैनं[१०] तद्द्यावापृथिव्यो रसेन समर्धयति ॥ ४ ॥

अथाखुकरी[११]षँ संभरत्याखवो ह वा अस्याः पृथिव्या रसं विदुस्तस्मादधोऽध एव चरन्तः पीविष्ठास्ते ह यत्र यत्रास्या रसस्ततस्ततो हैतदुत्किरन्त्यस्या एवैनमेतत्पृथिव्या रसेन समर्धयति समानमु वै करीषं च पुरीषं च [१२]पुरीषीति वै स[१३]माचक्षते यः श्रियं गच्छति तस्याश्चैवावरुद्धये ॥ ५ ॥

अथ शर्करास्संभरति देवाश्च ह वा असुराश्चोभये प्राजापत्या अस्पर्धन्ताथ हेयं[१४] तर्हि पृथिव्ययतेवास यथा पुष्करपर्णं लेलायेदेवँ ह स्म लेलायति ताँ ह स्म वातस्संवहति सोपदेवाञ्जगामोपासुरान्त्सा यत्र देवानुपजगाम ॥ ६ ॥

तद्धोचुर्हन्तेमां प्रतिष्ठां दृँहामहा इति तां प्रतिष्ठां कृत्वाशिथिलां तस्यामग्नी आधाय द्विषतः सपत्नानसुरान्निर्भक्ष्याम इति तान्ह यत्रोपजगाम तदेनां यथा[१५] शंकुभिश्चर्म वितनुयादेवँ समन्तँ शर्कराभिः पर्यवृँहँस्तां प्रतिष्ठां कृत्वाशिथिलां तस्यामग्नी आधाय द्वि[१६]षतःसपत्नानसुरान्निरभजँस्तथो वा एष एतदिमां प्रतिष्ठां कृत्वाशिथिलां तस्यामग्नी आधाय द्विषतस्सपत्नान्निर्भजति ॥ ७ ॥

८. उषा TE, P1, P2, H. see Notes.
९. प्रतिष्ठित TE.
१०. रेवैनं Co.
११. करीषँ Co.
१२. पुरीषीति Ca.
१३. तमाचक्षते Ca.
१४. हेयं TE, P1.
१५. तदेनान्यथा Ca., see Notes.
१६. द्विषतः Ca.

4. Then he brings salts. Yonder sky (the resplendent region visible above) bestowed cattle (wealth) on this earth. That became the salts. Hence, where there is saltish ground they declare it fit for cattle. Verily, the salts are the visible wealth (cattle). Thus, this (provision of salts) makes this (fire) flourish with cattle (wealth). Such a thing (the salt) is the essence of the yonder divine region. It became established in this earth. They consider it (the salt) as the essence of Heaven and Earth. It (the provision of salts) makes this (fire) prosper with the very essence of these two—Heaven and Earth.

5. Then he secures (the earth from) a mole-hill. Moles, indeed, know the savour of this earth. Therefore moving down and (further) down they became fat. Wherever there is the essence of this (earth), from there they throw it up. This (provision of earth from a mole-hill) enriches it (the fire) with the essence of the earth. *Karīṣa* (what is scattered or thrown up) and *purīṣa* (what is cast off/wealth) are alike. (They are synonymous.) They call a person who attains wealth,*'Purīṣī'*; for the preservation (retention) of that (wealth) too (does the sacrificer provide the mole-hill).

6. Then he (the sacrificer) gathers pebbles. Devas and Asuras (gods and demons) both sprung from Prajāpati, contended (with each other). Then this earth was, as it were not restrained (fixed). It tossed about as a lotus leaf would toss about. The wind carried it along. It (the earth) then came near the Devas and then came near the Asuras.

7. When it approached the gods, they said, "Ah! Let us fasten this (to make it) steady. Having made it stable and tight and installing the two fires on it, we shall deprive the Asuras,our hateful rivals (of any share)." Where (when) it reached them, they fixed it all round with pebbles as one would spread out a hide with pins. Having made it firm and steady and setting up the two fires on it, they excluded the Asuras,their hateful rivals, from any share. In that manner, this person (sacrificer) keeps away (from any share) his inimical rivals by making this (ground) firm and steady and installing the two fires on it.

तान्वा एतान्पञ्च संभारान्त्संभरति पाङ्क्तो वै यज्ञः पाङ्क्ताः पशवः पञ्चर्तवः संवत्सरस्य तस्मादेतान्पञ्च संभारान्त्संभरति ॥ ८ ॥

तदाहुः षड्वा ऋतवस्संवत्सरस्येति यदि वै षळृतवस्संवत्सरस्य[१७] न्यूनमु वै[१८] प्रजननं न्यूनाद्वा इमाः प्रजाः प्रजायन्ते प्रजननमु वा अप्येतत्तर्हि [१९]श्वःश्रेयसमुत्तरावद्यद्यु वै षळृतवोऽग्निरेवैषाꣳ षष्ठो भवति तेनैव तं काममाप्नोति यस्तत्र कामः ॥ ९ ॥

तदाहुर्नैकश्चन संभरेदित्यस्या वा एतान् पृथिव्याः संभरत्यस्यामु वा आधत्ते स यदेवास्यामाधत्ते तेनैव तान्कामानाप्नोति ये संभारेषु कामा इति तदु समेव भरेद्यदाहास्यामाधत्ते तेन सर्वमाप्नोति यदु संभारैः संभृतैर्भवति तद्वस्य भवति स यश्च संभारेषु कामो यश्चास्यां पृथिव्यां तस्मा उभयꣳ समर्धयति तस्मादु समेव भरेत्[२०] ॥ १० ॥ इति प्रथमं ब्राह्मणम् ॥

द्वितीयं ब्राह्मणम्

कृत्तिकास्वग्नी आदधीतेत्याहुरेतद्ध वा अग्नेर्नक्षत्रं यत्कृत्तिकास्तद्वै सलोम यदग्नेर्नक्षत्रेऽग्नी आदधीताथो एकं द्वमिवं[१] वा अन्यानि नक्षत्राणि त्रीणि चत्वारीत्यथैष भूमा भूमानमेवैतदुपैति बहुर्हैव प्रजया पशुभिर्भवत्यथो इति च वा अन्यानि नक्षत्राणीति च व्युद्यन्त्यथैता एव प्राच्या दिशो न यन्ति प्राच्याꣳ हैवास्य दिश्याहितौ भवतः प्राचीमेवैतद्दिशमुपैति तस्मात्कृत्तिकास्वादधीत ॥ १ ॥

१७. षळृतवः TE.

१८. न्यूनमुवै P1, P2.

१९. Pa, P1 and Ca. श्वः श्रेयस other Mss श्वश्रेयस; see Notes.

२०. समेववभरेत् H.

१. त्वमिवा M; see Notes.

8. He verily collects these five requisite materials (described before). Indeed the sacrifice is fivefold and fivefold are the (sacrificial) animals and five are the seasons of the year. Hence he gathers these five materials.

9. Regarding that, they (some) say, "Indeed six are the seasons of the year." If the seasons of the year are six, surely deficient is the production . These creatures are indeed born of the deficient (lower part of the body). This is production too, then and the prosperity (of the future) has further improvement (for the sacrificer). If the seasons are six, then Agni himself becomes the sixth of these (materials) and he (the sacrificer) acquires (fulfills) with Agni himself, that desire (need for the sixth material) which is there.

10. About that (provision of materials) they (some) say, "One need not do anything at all. He (the sacrificer) indeed collects (all) these materials from this earth and installs (the fires) on this (earth). By the very fact that he sets up (the fires) on this (earth), he acquires (fulfills) those desires (needs) that are there in the matter of the materials."

But (in this matter) one must gather (the materials). Regarding what one says, "He (the sacrificer) sets up (the fires) on this (earth) and by that he obtains everything"; truly what occurs with the gathered materials come to him and there is the fulfilment of the desire for the materials and the desire regarding this earth (place). For that, he (the sacrificer) enriches both (by providing the materials). Therefore, he must verily gather (the equipment).

(First Brāhmaṇa Ends)

BRĀHMAṆA II

1. They say that one may set up the two fires under the constellation *Kṛttikā* (when the moon is in conjunction with the *Kṛttikā* stars). *Kṛttikās* are verily the asterism of Agni. It is but proper that one should install the two fires under the star of Agni. Moreover, the other stars (stellar groups) consist of one, two, three, or four (stellar bodies). But then, this *(Kṛttikā* group) is large. This (setting up of fires) verily attains largeness. And he (the sacrificer) becomes plentiful with progeny and cattle. Also, the other stars move away. Only these *(Kṛttikā* stars) do not move away from the eastern direction. His two (the sacrificer's two fires) become established only in the eastern quarter. That (setting up of the fires) reaches the eastern quarter only. Hence one should set up (the fires) under the *Kṛttikās*.

तदाहुर्न कृत्तिकास्वादधीतास्त्यासु परिचक्षेत्यृक्षाणाꣳ ह वा एता अग्रे[२] पत्न्य आसु-र्ऋक्षा इति ह स्म वै पुरा सप्तर्षीनाचक्षते ता मिथुनेन व्यानृधिरे अग्रेणोद्यन्तीहोत्तरेण सप्तर्षयः[३] कस्तास्वादधीत या मिथुनेन व्यृद्धा नेन्मिथुनेन व्यृद्धया[४] इति तद्वैव दधीताग्निर्वा[५] एतासां मिथुनमेतेन वा एता मिथुनेन समृद्धास्तस्माद्वैव दधीत ॥ २ ॥

रोहिण्यामग्नी आदधीतेत्याहू रोहिण्याꣳ ह वै प्रजापतिरग्नी आदधे प्रजाकामो बहुः प्रजया पशुभिस्स्यां प्रजायेयेति स[६] इमाः प्रजास्ससृजे तमिमाः प्रजास्सृष्टा रोहिण्य इवोपस्तब्धास्तस्थुरेकरूपा इवैव तद्रोहिण्या रोहिणीत्वं प्रजायते ह प्रजया पशुभिर्य एवं विद्वान्रोहिण्यामाधत्ते ॥ ३ ॥

रोहिण्यामु ह वाव पशवोऽग्नी आदधिरे मनुष्याणां कामे रोहामेति यथेमेऽद्यापि मनुष्याणां कामे रूळ्हाः[७] पशवो यथा ह वाव तत्पशवो मनुष्याणां कामेऽरोहन्नेवꣳ हैव पशूनां कामे रोहति[८] य एवं विद्वान्रोहिण्यामाधत्ते ॥ ४ ॥

मृगशिरस्यग्नी आदधीतेत्याहुः प्रजापतेर्वा एतच्छिरो यन्मृगशिरः श्रीर्वै शिरः श्रीर्ह वै शिरोऽथ योऽर्धस्य श्रेष्ठो भवत्यसौ तस्यार्धस्य शिर इत्याचक्षते श्रियꣳ ह यच्छति श्रेष्ठो ह भवति य एवं विद्वान्मृगशिरस्याधत्ते ॥ ५ ॥

तदाहुर्न मृगशिरस्यादधीतास्त्यस्मिन्परिचक्षेति प्रजापतेर्वा एतच्छरीरं यत्रैनमेष देव इषुणा त्रिकाण्डेनाविध्यत्तत[९] एतद्विद्धोऽजहात्तदेतद्वास्तु निर्वीर्यमयज्ञियं कस्तस्मिन्नादधीतेति तद्वैव दधीत न वै तस्य देवस्य वास्तु न निर्वीर्यं नायज्ञियमस्ति यत्प्रजापतेस्तस्माद्वैव दधीत॥ ६ ॥

पुनर्वस्वोः पुनराधेयमादधीत फल्ग्वोरादधीतैतद्ध वा इन्द्रनक्षत्रं यत्फल्ग्वावपि हास्य प्रतिनामानावर्जुनो हं वै नामेन्द्रो यदस्य गुह्यं नामार्जुन्यो नामैतास्तत्कोऽर्हति तस्य गुह्यं नाम

२. एतामग्रे Co; एता अग्रे V1, K, Ca.

३. सप्त ऋषयः M, Ca.

४. व्यृध्या Ca.

५. ग्निर्वै P1.

६. स्व इमाः TE.

७. रूल्हाः TE; रूळ्हाः Ca.

८. रोहंति P1, P2, H.

९. नाविध्यत एत TE.

2. About this they (some) say "One should not set up (the fires) under the *Kṛttikās*. There is rejection (disapproval) in their case". "At first (originally) these *(Kṛttikās)* were the wives of the *Ṛkṣas* (the Bears). Formerly they (people) called the seven sages (of the Great Bear constellation) *Ṛkṣas*. They *(Kṛttikās)* were deprived of pairing, because they rise here in the east and the seven sages rise in the north. Who will set up (the fires) under these stars that were deprived of copulation? If not (if one, on the contrary, sets up), it will lead to deprivation of intercourse".

One may well set up (the fires) under them. It is Agni that is their mate. These *(Kṛttikā* stars) prospered with intercourse with him. Therefore, one may surely set up (the fires under *Kṛttikās)*.

3. They say that one may install (the fires) under *Rohiṇī*. It was under *Rohiṇī* that Prajāpati who desired progeny set up (the fires), thinking, "I shall become plentiful with progeny and cattle. I shall be born (I shall create)". He created these creatures. The created beings were all of one form (similar), very much like herded red cows and they waited upon him. That is the red-cow nature *(Rohiṇītva)* of (the asterism) *Rohiṇī*. Indeed, a person who, realizing this, sets up (the fires) under *Rohiṇī* becomes rich (great) in progeny and cattle.

4. Thinking (wishing), "We should grow up (ascend) in the desire (love) of men" for cattle, did set up the two fires under *Rohiṇī*. Just as these (present) cattle even now have arisen in the wish of men and as those cattle arose in the desire of men, in the very same manner does a person who, understanding this, sets up (the fires) under *Rohiṇī* grows up in the wish (love) of cattle.

5. They say one may set up the two fires under (the asterism) *Mṛgaśiras*. What is called *Mṛgaśiras* is indeed the head of Prajāpati. 'Excellence' indeed is the head. Verily the head is 'excellence'! "He who is the best of a community (of people)—he is the head of that community" so they say. He who sets up (the fires) under *Mṛgaśiras*, knowing this surely attains excellence (wealth) and becomes the most excellent.

6. About that they (some) say, "One should not install (the fires) under *Mṛgaśiras*. There is rejection (disapproval) of this (asterism). This (star) is verily the body of Prajāpati wherein the god pierced him with a three-segmented arrow. Being struck, he (Prajāpati) gave it up. As such, this abode (body) (of Prajāpati) came to be without virility and unfit for sacrifice. Who will set up (the fires) under that (star)?

One may well install that (the fires) (under *Mṛgaśiras)*. That abode of God is neither lacking in virility nor is it unfit for sacrifice (unholy), as it belongs to Prajāpati. Therefore, one may certainly set up (the fires under *Mṛgaśiras)*.

7. Under *Punarvasu* one should perform *punarādheya* (re-kindling/ re-installation). One should set up (the fires) under the two *Phalgu* (stars). The

ग्रहीतुमिति परोक्षमिवाचक्षते फल्गुन्य इतीन्द्रो वै यजमानः स्व एवैतन्नक्षत्र आधत्त इन्द्रो यज्ञस्य देवता सेन्द्रमस्य भवति पूर्वयोरादधीत पुरस्तात्क्रतुर्हैवास्मै भवति न हैनमतिपद्यत उत्तरयोरादधीतोत्तरावद्धैवास्मै श्वःश्रेयसं[१०] भवति ॥ ७ ॥

हस्तेऽग्नी आदधीतेत्याहुर्यः कामयेत प्र मे दीयतामिति तद्वा अनुष्ठ्या यदिदꣳ सर्वꣳ हस्तेनैव प्रदीयते प्र हास्मै दीयते य एवं विद्वान्हस्ते आधत्ते[११] ॥ ८ ॥

चित्रायामग्नी आदधीतेत्याहुर्देवाश्च ह वा असुराश्चोभये प्राजापत्या अस्पर्धन्त ते होभये स्वर्गं लोकꣳ समारुरुक्षां चक्रुस्ततो हासुरा रौहिणमग्निं चिक्यिरे स्वर्ग्यमनेन स्वर्गं लोकꣳ समारोक्ष्याम इति त उ ह देवा बिभयां चक्रुरिमं चेद्वा इमे समाप्स्यन्त्यभि नो[१२] भविष्यन्तीति ततो हेन्द्र आर्केण दाम्नेष्टकां प्रबध्येयाय ब्राह्मणो ब्रुवाणः ॥ ९ ॥

स होवाचाहमपीमामुपदधा इत्युप हीति ताꣳहोपदधे स हाल्पकादिवासञ्चित आसाथ होवाचाहं तामिष्टकां दास्ये या ममेत्याहीति तामभिहायाबबर्ह[१३] तस्या आबर्हणमन्वग्निर्व्यव-शशादाग्नेरनु व्यवशादमसुरा व्यवशेदुः स ताभिरेवेष्टकाभिर्वज्रान्कृत्वैषां[१४] प्रजघान ततो देवा अभवन्परासुरा भवति हैवात्मना परास्य द्विषन्भ्रातृव्यो भवति य एवं विद्वाꣳश्चित्राया माधत्ते ॥ १० ॥

ते ह देवाः समेत्योचुश्चित्रं वा अभूम य इयतः[१५] सपत्नानवधिष्मेति तच्चित्रायाश्चित्रात्वꣳ हन्तीह[१६] सपत्नꣳ हन्ति द्विषन्तं भ्रातृव्यं य एवं विद्वाꣳश्चित्रायामाधत्ते तस्मादप्येतद्राजन्य-बन्धव उपेप्सन्ति ते ह जिघाꣳसन्ति[१७] वीव जिगीषन्त्येतद्वपि ब्राह्मण आदधीत पाप्मा वै

१०. See Notes on I-I-I-9.

११. आधत्ते P1, Co, B.

१२. न्त्यभितो भवि P1, P2, H.

१३. तामभिहयाबबर्ह TE; तामभिहायावबर्हं P1, P2, H.

१४. न्कृत्वैतान् M.

१५. इहतः VI My; इहतः Ca., P1, P2, H, TE.

१६. हन्ति ह Ca., P1.

१७. जिगाꣳसंति TE, L, H, P1, P2.

two stars called *Phalgu* form, indeed, the asterism of Indra and they have his corresponding names. Indra is also known as Arjuna, which is his secret (mystic) name. These (stars-*Phalgus*) are known as *Arjunis*. Who is fit to utter his secret name? So they indirectly call them (the stars) *Phalgunis*. The sacrificer is indeed Indra. He sets up (the fires) under this, his own asterism. Indra is the deity of the sacrifice. The installation is then connected with Indra. One may install (the fires) under the two prior stars *(Pūrva phalgunis)*. To him (the sacrificer) the sacrifice accrues even before (even at the outset). It does not go beyond him. One may set up (the fires) under the two later stars *(Uttara Phalguni)*. His future prosperity certainly acquires superiority (progression).

8. They say that one may set up (the fires) under *Hasta*. He who wishes, "May it (good things) be presented to me" may perform it. To him who, knowing this, sets up the two fires under *Hasta,* all that is given verily with the hand is given.

9. They say one may set up the two fires under *Citrā*. Devas and Asuras, both of them sprung from Prajāpati, contended. Both of them wished to ascend to the heavenly world. Then the Asuras kindled the fire (constructed the fire altar) *'Rauhiṇa'* (conducive to ascent) that would lead to heaven, thinking, "We shall ascend to heaven by means of this". The gods were afraid and thought, "If these (Asuras) will complete this (*Rauhiṇa* fire-altar), they will overpower us". Then Indra bound up a brick with a rope of lightning (a rope of *Ṛks*) and went there proclaiming himself to be a Brāhmin.

10. He said, "I too shall place this (brick). (The Asuras said). "Put it". He placed it. That (altar) seemed verily to be incomplete with very little (required very little for completion).

Then he said, "I shall take (back) that brick of mine". (They said), "Take it" He went towards it and pulled it. Following its pulling out, the fire became extinct. Following the extinction of the fire, the Asuras fell down. Making thunderbolts with their very bricks, he (Indra) killed (hit) them. Then the gods remained (safe) and the Asuras turned away (were afar). He who, knowing this, sets up (the fires) under *Citrā* remains by himself (unaffected) and his spiteful enemy goes far away.

11. Those gods got together and said, "We have become wonderful—we who have killed so many enemies". That is the wonderful nature *(Citrātva)* of *Citrā* (asterism). He who sets up (the fires) under *Citrā,* understanding this, destroys his rival and kills his spiteful enemy. Therefore, too, the Kṣatriyas want to take it

ब्राह्मणस्य सपत्नो हन्ति पाप्मानं परास्य द्विषन्भ्रातृव्यो भवति य एवं विद्वाꣳश्चित्राया-
माधत्ते ॥ ११ ॥

तानि ह वा एतानि क्षत्राणि नानैव तेपुर्यथासौ वा सूर्यश्चन्द्रमा वा तेषाꣳ होद्यन्नेवादित्यः
क्षत्रं वीर्यं तेजः प्रलुलोप तद्धैषामादधे[18] ते ह देवा ऊचुर्न वा इमानि क्षत्राण्यभूवन्निति
तन्नक्षत्राणां नक्षत्रत्वमा वा एषामदितेति तदादित्यस्यादित्यत्वं तस्मान्न नक्षत्रमाद्रियेत
यदेवैष कदा चोदिया[19]दथादधीतैष हि सर्वाणि क्षत्राणि यद्यु नक्षत्रकामस्या[20]दुपो आसीत
नक्षत्रमहा[21]स्य भवति नो एतस्यानुदयोऽस्ति तस्माद्वप्युपैवासीत ॥ १२ ॥ इति द्वितीयं
ब्राह्मणम् ॥

तृतीयं ब्राह्मणम्

वसन्तो ग्रीष्मो वर्षा एते देवा ऋतवोऽथ शरद्धेमन्तश्शिशिर एते पितरो य एवायमा-
पूर्यतेऽर्धमास एते देवा योऽपक्षीयते स पितरोऽहरेव देवा रात्रिः पितरस्समानस्याह्नः पूर्वाह्ण
एव देवा अपराह्णः पितर एते हैवर्तवो देवाः पितरः स य एवं विद्वान्देवाः पितर इति
ह्वयत्या[1] हास्य देवा देवहूयं यन्त्या[2] पितरः पितृहूयमवन्ति हैनं देवा देवहूयेऽवन्ति पितरः
पितृहूये य एवं विद्वान्देवाः पितर इति ह्वयति ॥ १ ॥

तान्वा एतानुभयानसावेवोद्यन्नभिरक्षति योऽसौ तपति स यत्रोदङ्ङेति तर्हि देवानृतू-
नभिरक्षति तर्हि देवेष्वृतुषु भवत्यथ यत्र दक्षिणैति तर्हि पितॄनृतूनभिरक्षति तर्हि पितृष्वृतुषु
भवति ॥ २ ॥

१८. माददे Ca.; see Notes.

१९. चोदीया TE, M, VI, P1, P2, H.

२०. कामः स्यादुपो TE, Ca.

२१. माहास्य P1, P2; see Notes.

१. ह्वयत्यास्य P.

२. यन्या TE.

up. They indeed wish to kill (their enemies) and desire to conquer. The Brahmin too may install this (the two fires under *Citrā*). Sin is verily the enemy of the Brahmin. He who knowing this sets up (the fires) under *Citrā* destroys sin and his hateful enemy goes far away.

12. Those stars that are (seen) shone variously just like the yonder Sun or the moon. The Sun, even (as he was) rising, destroyed their power, virility and lustre. He took that (power etc.) of these (stars). The gods said, "These are not powers (any more)". That is the 'powerlessness' *(nakṣatratva)* of the stars. He (the Sun) took away (cut off power etc.) of these (stars). That is the *Ādityatva* (the state of taker or cutter off) of the Sun. Therefore one need not mind the stars. Even when this (Sun), rises, one may then set up (the fires). For, this Sun is all the 'powers'. If one is desirous (mindful) of the stars (to set up the fires) (under any star) he may worship (the Sun) (set up the fires during day time). Indeed the (benefit of the) star comes to him. There is certainly no non-rise for this (Sun) (the Sun never fails to rise). Hence, too, one should verily worship (the Sun) (i.e. set up the fires during day time).

(Second Brāhmaṇa Ends)

BRĀHMAṆA III

1. 'Spring', 'summer', 'rains'– these seasons are (of) gods. And 'autumn', 'snow' and 'cold' (winter)'—these are (of) the manes. Verily this half-month (fortnight) that fills up (the fortnight of the waxing moon) is (of) gods. That which decreases (the fortnight of waning moon) is (of) the manes. The day itself is (of) the gods; the night (of) the manes. Of the day which is equal (uniform), the forenoon itself is (of) the gods and the afternoon is (of) the manes. These very seasons are the gods and manes. The gods surely come to the (ritual of) invocation of the gods and the manes come to the (ritual of) invocation of the manes, of that person who, knowing this, invokes them calling 'gods' and 'manes'. In the (ritual of) invocation of gods, the gods protect (please) him and the manes protect (please) him in the (ritual of) invocation of the manes, of that person who, knowing this, invokes them as 'gods' and 'manes'.

2. Verily, the yonder one (Sun) who shines protects both these (gods and manes), as he rises. Where (when) he reaches the north, then he guards the gods and (their) seasons; then he remains amidst the gods and (their) seasons. And where (when) he goes to the south, then he protects the manes and (their) seasons; then he remains amidst the manes and (their) seasons.

तस्माद्यत्रैवोदङ्ङ्[3]ङ्यात्तर्ह्येवादधीत तर्हि वा एष देवानुपावर्तते तर्हि देवानभिरक्षति तर्हि देवेषु भवत्यपहतपाप्मानो वै देवा अप पाप्मानꣳ ह तेऽमृता देवा नामृतत्वस्याशास्ति सर्वमेवायुरेति श्रीर्देवाः श्रियं गच्छति यशो देवा यशो ह भवति तस्मात्तर्ह्यादधीताथ यत्र दक्षिणैति न तर्ह्यादधीत तर्हि वा एष पितॄनुपावर्तते तर्हि पितॄनभिरक्षति तर्हि पितृषु भवत्यनपहतपाप्मानो वै पितरो न पाप्मानमपहते मर्त्याः पितरः पुरा हायुषो म्रियते तस्मात्तर्हि नादधीत ॥ ३ ॥

तद्वै ब्रह्मैव वसन्तः क्षत्रं ग्रीष्मो विड्वर्षास्तस्माद्ब्राह्मणो वसन्त आदधीत ब्रह्म हि वसन्तः क्षत्रियो ग्रीष्मे क्षत्रꣳ हि ग्रीष्मो वैश्यो वर्षासु भूमा हि विड् भूमा हि वर्षा यं तु ह कामं कामयेत तमभ्यादधीत ॥ ४ ॥

ब्राह्मणो यदि ह कामयेत ब्रह्मवर्चसी स्यामिति वसन्त आदधीत ब्रह्म वै वसन्तो ब्रह्मवर्चसी हैव भवति ॥ ५ ॥

यदि ह कामयेत क्षत्रस्य प्रतिमा स्याꣳश्रिया यशसेति ग्रीष्म आदधीत क्षत्रं वै ग्रीष्मः क्षत्रस्य हैव भवति प्रतिमा श्रिया यशसा ॥ ६ ॥

यदि हँ[4] पुष्टिकामः स्याद्वर्षास्वादधीत भूमा वै[5] विड् भूमो वर्षा बहुर्हैव प्रजया पशुभिर्भवत्येतन्नु यथर्तु ॥ ७ ॥

तद्वा आहुरपहतपाप्मानो वा ऋतव इत्यसौ वा एतेषामुद्यन्त्स[6]र्वं पाप्मानमपहन्तीति तस्माद्यद्दे[7]वैनं कदा चोपनमेदथादधीताथ यजेत न श्वः[8]श्वमुपासीत न वै मनुष्यः श्वस्तनं वेद को हि तस्मै मनुष्यो यः[9] श्वस्तनं विद्यात् ॥ ८ ॥ इति तृतीयं ब्राह्मणम् ॥

३. वोदङ्ङ्ङीया Ca.

४. यदि पुष्टि TE.

५. भूमा वै TE;भूमा वै Ca.

६. मुदꣳन्सर्वं TE;मुद्यन्सर्वं Ca.

७. तस्माद्यदैवैनं P2, H, Ca., see Notes.

८. श्व श्व TE; see Notes on I-I-I-9.

९. यत् H.

3. There one may set up (the fires) only when he (the Sun) moves to the north. Then indeed he returns (turns) to the gods, then does he protect the gods and remains amidst them. The gods have their evils dispelled. He (the sacrificer) dispels evil from himself. The gods are immortal. (But) there is no hope of immortality (for the sacrificer). He attains the entire (full span of) life. The gods are 'Prosperity'. He (the sacrificer) attains prosperity. The gods are 'glory'. He becomes (attains) glory. Therefore one should set up (the fires) there. When the Sun reaches the south, then one should not set up (the fires). Then indeed, this (Sun) returns (turns) to the manes; then he guards the manes and then does he remain amidst the manes. The manes do not have their evils dispelled. He (the sacrificer) does not (then) dispel his (own) evils. The manes are mortals. He (the sacrificer) dies before his (appointed) time (if he sets up the fires then). Therefore one should not set up (the fires) then.

4. Spring is the Brahman (Brāhmaṇa), summer is Kṣatra (Kṣatriya) and the rainy season is Viṭ (vaiśya). The Brāhmin should, therefore, set up (the fires) in spring; for Brahman, indeed, is the spring. The Kṣatriya (should set up the fires) in summer for Kṣatra (valour) is summer. The Vaiśya (should set up the fires) in the rainy season. Indeed, abundance (plenty) is Viṭ (Vaiśya); plentiful is the rainy season. What desire one may entertain, towards that, one may set up (the fires) (in the relevent season).

5. Should the Brāhmin wish, "I should become one having holy lustre *(Brahmavarcasa)*", he should set up (the fires) in spring. Brahman, indeed, is Spring and he (the sacrificer) verily becomes one endowed with holy lustre.

6. If one (a Brāhmin) should desire,"I should be equal to Kṣatra in splendour (wealth) and glory",he should set up (the fires) in summer. Kṣatra, indeed, is summer. He (the sacrificer) verily becomes the equal of Kṣatra (Kṣatriya) in splendour and glory.

7. If one is for nourishment (rich growth), he should set up (the fires) in the rainy season. 'Abundance' is verily Viṭ (Vaiśya) and 'abundance' is the rainy season. He (the sacrificer) becomes plentiful with progeny and cattle.(All) this is in consonance with the seasons.

8. They say (about this), "The seasons have their" evils dispelled. The yonder one (Sun), rising, destroys all evil of these (seasons). Therefore, one may set up (the fires) and perform sacrifice at any time it occurs to him. He should not look to the next day and the morrow. Indeed, man does not know of the thing of the morrow; which man is there who may know of the morrow for that (setting up of the fires).

(Third Brāhmaṇa Ends)

चतुर्थं ब्राह्मणम्

स वै यदहरस्य श्वोऽग्न्याधेयꣳ स्यात्तदहर्दिवैवाश्नीयान्मनो वै देवा मनुष्यस्याजानन्ति ते हैनमेतद्विदुरग्नी आधास्यमानमेषं[1] नः प्रातर्यष्टेति तस्य विश्वे देवा गृहानभ्यागच्छन्ति तेऽस्मिन्नेताꣳ रात्रिमुपवसन्ति तस्मादुपवसथस्तन्वा[2] अनवक्लृप्तं यो मनुष्यान्वसतौ[3]ऽत्यश्नादनवक्लृप्तमिदु तदसद्यो देवान्वसतोऽत्यश्नात्तस्मान्नाश्नीयादित्याहुस्तदु[4] काममेवाश्नीयान्न वै व्रतचर्यानाहिताग्नेरस्ति मानुषो न्वा एष तावद्यावदग्नीनाधत्ते तस्मादु काममेवाश्नीयात् ॥ १ ॥

तद्धैक एताꣳ रात्रिमजमुपबध्नन्त्याग्नेयोऽजोऽग्नेः सर्व[5]त्वायेति तदु तथा न कुर्याद्यद्यस्याज उपक्लृप्तः स्याच्छ्वोभूत एवैनमग्नीधे[6] सꣳस्थितौ दद्या[7]त्तेनैव तं काममाप्नोति यस्तत्र कामस्तस्मात्तन्नाद्रियेत ॥ २ ॥

तद्धैक एताꣳ रात्रिमेतमोदनं चातुष्प्राश्यं पचन्ति छन्दाꣳसीदं प्रीणीम इति वदन्तो यथा येन वाहनेन [8]स्यन्त्स्यन्त्स्यादिति तत्सुहितं कुर्यात्तत्सुहितं चिकीर्षेदेवमेतदिति तदु तथा[9] न कुर्याद्यद्वा[10]ꣳस्यर्त्विजश्चानृत्विजश्चास्मिन्वसन्तोऽस्य कुल एताꣳ रात्रिमश्नन्ति तेनैव तं काममाप्नोति यस्तत्र कामस्तस्मात्तन्नाद्रियेत ॥ ३ ॥

तस्य सर्पिरासेचनं कृत्वा सर्पिरासिच्याश्वत्थीस्तिस्रः समिधो घृतेनान्वज्य समिद्वतीभिर्घृतवतीभिर्ऋग्भिरभ्यादधति शमीगर्भमिदमाप्नुम इति वदन्तस्तदु तथा न कुर्यात्संवत्सरꣳ ह तथा पुराभ्यादध्यात्तेन ह तं काममाप्नुयाद्यस्तत्र कामस्तस्मात्तन्नाद्रियेत ॥ ४ ॥

१. मेष TE; Ca.
२. वसथस्तं वा My, Ca, Co.
३. न्वसतो Ca.
४. स्तस्मादु VI.
५. सर्वत्वायेति Ca., see Notes.
६. मग्नीध्रे TE.
७. तद्यत्तेनैव TE.
८. स्यन्स्यन्त्स्यादिति B.
९. यथा TE.
१०. यद्वा अस्यर्त्विजो Ca.; यद्वास्यर्त्विजो Co.

BRĀHMAṆA IV

1. He (the sacrificer) should take his food during the day-time itself on that day, on the morrow of which the *Agnyādheya* (setting up of the fires) is going to be. Indeed gods know fully well the mind of man. They know this about him who is going to install the two fires. "This person is going to worship us (perform sacrifice to us) in the morning." All the gods repair to his residence. There they fast that night. Hence it is called '*upavasatha*' (a day of fasting, a day of preparation, a day of remaining near). "It is indeed improper that a person takes his food while people remaining (with him) have not had their food. Surely, it is not right that a person should eat before the gods who remain (with him) have had their food. Therefore he (the sacrificer) should not take his food". So they say. But one may eat (at will). There is verily no observance of ritual restriction (abstinence) for one who has not set up the holy fires. As long as he does not set up the two fires, he is indeed a 'man' (a lay man). Therefore he may surely eat at will.

2. With regard to this, some tether a goat this night. The goat is intended for Agni and it is for the fullness of Agni. One need not do it that way. If a goat is meant (prepared) for this (fire), he (the sacrificer) may give it to the 'Agnīdh' the next day itself for (at) the completion (of the ritual). By that itself he secures that wish which is there (regarding the offering of the goat). Therefore, one need not favour it (the tying up of the goat,the previous night).

3. Here (in this matter) some (sacrificers) cook that night a (soft) rice-food sufficient for four (priests). "Cātuṣprāśya", saying, "with this we propitiate the *chandas* (Vedas)". "This is just as one would satisfy (with food,etc.) and wish to satisfy that (animal) by which he is going to move (ride/drive). This is so". One need not do it that way. For, he achieves the desire that may be there (of propitiating the metres or Vedas) by the very fact that the priests and non-priests staying in his house eat there that night. Therefore,he need not care for it (the practice of cooking special soft food for four priests).

4. Scooping out a depression in it (the soft rice-food) for *ghee*, pouring *ghee* in it and smearing three sticks of *Aśvattha* wood with *ghee,* they put them in the fire with (uttering) (three) *Ṛks* (metrical chants) containing the words *'Samit'* and '*Ghṛta* ', (specific *mantras*) and saying, "We obtain this (fire) that is within (in the womb of) the *Śamī* (wood)". One need not do that way. For, one should so put the kindling sticks on the fire, earlier for a year (daily, prior to the *ādhāna*) and by that indeed will he achieve that desire that is therein. Therefore one need not have concern for that (practice of putting the three special sticks).

तदु होवाचेन्द्रद्युम्नो भाल्लवेयो[११] यथान्यत्करिष्यन्नन्यत्कुर्यादिति यथान्यद्वदिष्यन्न-[१२]न्यद्वदेदिति यथान्येन पथैष्यन्नन्यं पन्थानं प्रतिपद्येतैवमेतद्य एतमोदनं पचादपरा[१३]द्धिरिव वै सा तस्मात्तन्नाद्रियेतेत्यनवक्लृप्तमु वाव तद्यद्यस्मिन्नृचा वा यजुषा वाहुतिं वा जुहुयुः समिधं वाभ्यादध्युर्[१४]यत्तं ततोऽनु वा गमयेयुर्दक्षिणा वा हरेयुरन्वाहार्यपचनो भविष्यतीति ॥ ५ ॥

तदाहुर्जागृयादेताꣳ रात्रिमिति जाग्रति देवा देवानेवै[१५]तदुपावर्तते सोऽभि[१६]श्रान्ततर-स्तपस्वितरः स देवतरोऽग्नी आधत्त इति तदु काममेव स्वप्यान्नै वै व्रतचर्यानाहिताग्नेरस्ति मानुषो न्वा एष तावद्यावदग्नीनाधत्ते तस्मादु काममेव स्वप्यात् ॥ ६ ॥

तद्धैकेऽनुदिते मथित्वोद्यन्तमुपासत उदिते प्राञ्चमुद्धरिष्याम इत्यहोरात्रयोः परिगृही-तये प्राणोदानयोर्मनसश्च वाचश्चेति तदु तथा न कुर्यादुभौ वा अस्यैतावनुदित आहितौ[१७] भवतोऽनुदिते हि मथित्वा[१८] तत एव प्राञ्चमुद्धरति य उ ह तमुदित आहवनीयं मन्थेत्स ह तत्पर्याप्नुयात् ॥ ७ ॥

तदु क उभौ निर्मन्थ्यौ कुर्वीताहर्देवा रात्रिः पितरोऽनपहतपाप्मानः पितरो न पाप्मान-[१९]मपहते मर्त्याः पितरः पुरा हायुषो म्रियते योऽनुदित आधत्ते[२०] ॥ ८ ॥

अथाहर्वै देवा अपहतपाप्मानो वै देवा अप पाप्मानꣳ हतेऽमृता[२१] देवा नामृतत्वस्या-

११. माल्लबेयो TE, P1, H.

१२. द्वदिष्यन्न वदेदिति TE.

१३. See Notes.

१४. वाभ्यादद्यु TE.

१५. देवानैवैत TE.

१६. सोविश्रान्त M.

१७. आहितौ TE, H, P1, Ca.

१८. मथित्वा V2.

१९. पाप्मानमुप TE.

२०. आधत्त V1, Po, L.

२१. ऽमृते P1, P2.

5. About this, Indradyumna Bhāllaveya said,"That one (the sacrificer) should cook this rice-food, surely seems to be a wrong thing and it is like this that one (actually) does something intending to do something else, intending to say something may say something else and intending to go along a (particular) path may go along a different way (with action and intention being at variance with each other). Therefore one need not care for it". It is indeed (improper) wrong that they (the sacrificers) should either extinguish (that fire) or take it to the south so that it will be *'Anvāhāryapacana'(Dakṣiṇāgni)*–that fire wherein they put the oblation or put a stick with (the utterance of) a *Ṛk* or *Yajus* (earlier). But really, they either extinguish or take it to the south that it may become (serve as) *"Anvāhāryapacana"*.

(The preparation of a fire for cooking of the soft rice-food the previous night itself and putting *ghee* and *Samit* in it with chants and extinguishing the sanctified fire is improper. Improper is it also to convert it into *Dakṣiṇāgni,* since it is a fire prepared before the actual *agnyādheya.*)

6. With regard to this (conduct on the previous night), they say, "He (the sacrificer) should keep awake during this (entire) night". The gods keep awake. This means that he approaches the gods by this and he sets up (the next day) the two fires becoming more subdued, more disciplined (with greater austerity) and becoming more godly. However, he may sleep as he pleases. For there is no observance of vow (ritualistic restriction) for one who has not (yet) set up the holy fires. He remains verily a man as long as he does not set up the two fires. Therefore he may sleep at will.

7. Now, some churn (the fire) (produce the fire by ceremonial churning of two prescribed pieces of wood) before sunrise and then worship the rising Sun, thinking, "After the Sun has risen we shall take it (the kindled fire) eastward, for securing (the benefit of) (both) day and night, the inhaled breath and the exhaled breath and the mind and speech." One should not do it that way. For both (the fires) of this (sacrificer) become set up (even at night) when the Sun has not risen. He churns before sunrise and then takes it to the east. (So the two fires are only nocturnal). Verily he who churns the *Āhavanīya* after the Sun has risen, will obtain that (benefit of setting up the fires).

8. Then who will make the two churned fires (before sunrise)? (Therefore one should make the two fires by churning (after sunrise only). The day is the gods, the night the manes. The manes do not have their evils dispelled. He (the sacrificer who kindles the fire before sunrise) does not dispel his (own) evil. The manes are mortal. He who sets up (the fires) when the Sun has not risen dies before his (normal) life-span.

9. Moreover, the day indeed is the gods and verily the gods have their evils dispelled. He (the sacrificer) dispels (his own) evil. The gods are immortal.

शास्ति सर्वमायुरेति श्रीर्देवाः श्रियं गच्छति यशो देवा यशो ह भवति तस्मादुदित एवाद-धीत ॥ ९ ॥

तदाहुर्यन्नर्चा न यजुषा न साम्नाग्निराधीयते केन त्वग्निराधीयत इति स ह ब्रूयाद्ब्रह्मण एव ब्रह्मणेति[22] वाग्वै ब्रह्म तस्याः सत्यमेव ब्रह्मता एताः सत्यमेव व्याहृतयो भूर्भुवः स्वरिति सत्येन हैवास्याहितौ भवतः ॥ १० ॥

भूरिति वै प्रजापतिरिमामजनयद्भुव इत्यन्तरिक्षꣳ स्वरिति दिवमेतावद्वा इदं यावदिमे लोकास्सर्वेण हैवास्याहितौ भवतः[23] ॥ ११ ॥

भूरिति वै प्रजापतिर्ब्रह्माजनयद्भुव इति क्षत्रꣳ स्वरिति विशमेतावद्वा इदं यावद्ब्रह्म क्षत्रं विट् सर्वेण हैवास्याहितौ भवतः[24] ॥ १२ ॥

भूरिति वै प्रजापतिरात्मानमजनयद्भुव इति प्रजाꣳ स्वरिति पशूनेतावद्वा इदं यावदात्मा प्रजा पशवः सर्वेण हैवास्याहितौ भवतः ॥ १३ ॥

स भूर्भुव इत्येतैस्त्रिभिरक्षरैर्गार्हपत्यमादधाति द्वे परिशिनष्ट्ययातयामतायै[25] केन ह्यमुमादध्याद्यत्सर्वैरादध्यात्ते एव द्वे इतराणि त्रीण्यन्वाप्यायन्ते तेनो तान्ययातयामानि भवन्ति तान्यष्टावक्षराणि[26] सम्पद्यन्ते त्रीणीमानि पञ्चामून्यष्टाक्षरा गायत्री गायत्रमग्नेश्छन्दः[27] स्वेनैवैनं तच्छन्दसाधत्ते ॥ १४ ॥

देवानु ह वा अग्नी आधित्समानान[28]सुररक्षसानि ररक्षुर्नाग्निर्जनिष्यते नाग्नी आधास्यध्व इति तस्माद्रक्षाꣳसि ततो ह देवा एतं वज्रं ददृशुर्यदश्वं तमुदयच्छꣳस्तेन

२२. ब्रह्मणैति TE, Ca, V1, P1, P2.

२३. भवतः Ca.

२४. भवतः Ca.

२५. परिशिनष्ट्य TE, B1, Ca, P1, P2, H.

२६. तान्यष्टाक्षराणि TE.

२७. श्छन्दस्वैनैवैनं TE.

२८. आधित्स Ca., आधित्स B; Ca, Po, TE; H.

There is no hope of immortality (for the sacrificer). He (the sacrificer) attains entire (full) life. The gods are wealth (prosperity). He attains prosperity. The gods are 'glory' (glorious). He becomes glorious. Therefore,one should set up the fires only after the Sun has risen.

10. They say, "As the fire is not set up with (the chanting of) a *Ṛk* nor with *Yajus* nor with *Sāman,* then with what is the fire set up?" He (the sacrificer) should indeed say, "Surely it is of *Brahman,* with *Brahman*"(it is set up) with *Brahman* (the symbolic formula of the *Brahman* only). Indeed "Speech is *Brahman*".Its truth itself is *Brahman.* These *vyāhṛtis* (mystic utterances) *Bhūḥ, Bhuvaḥ, Svaḥ* are only 'Truth'. His (the sacrificer's) two fires are verily set up with 'Truth'.

11. Indeed Prajāpati generated this (earth) by (uttering) (the mystic syllable) *'Bhūḥ'* the middle region (between earth and heaven) by *'Bhuvaḥ* and the sky by *Svaḥ'* As far as these worlds are thus far is this (Universe). The two fires become established with the whole of this (Universe).

12. Prajāpati created Brāhmaṇa(the Brāhmaṇa class/priesthood) by(uttering) *'Bhūḥ',* the Kṣatra(Ksatriya class) by *Bhuvaḥ* and viṭ (Vaiṣya)by *Svaḥ.* So much is this–as much as are Brāhmaṇa, Kṣatra and viṭ. Indeed the two fires are set up with the whole of this.

13. Prajāpati verily generated *Ātman* (the self) with *Bhūḥ*; the excellent creature(s) (human race) with *'Bhuvaḥ'* and the animals with *'Svaḥ'*. So much indeed is this,viz., as much as the self, humanity and animals.

14. He (the sacrificer) installs the *Gārhapatya* (fire) with (uttering) these three syllables *'Bhūrbhuvaḥ'* and (leaves out) keep (unused) two (syllables) for the sake of 'freshness' (the state of not becoming stale with lapse of time). With what will he set up that (the *Āhavanīya*) if he should establish (the *Gārhapatya*) with all (the five syllables)? He should set up (the *Āhavanīya*) with all (the five syllables). Those very two (syllables that were left out); the other three (once used) are strengthened (refreshed). Thereby they become fresh (not old and stale). They form eight syllables (for the two fires together)–these five and those three. Indeed *Gāyatrī* consists of eight syllables. *Gāyatra* is the metre of Agni. He (the sacrificer), thus sets up this (fire) with its own metre.

15. The Asuras and Rākṣasas verily kept away (prevented) the gods who wished to set up the two fires. (They said to the gods), "Agni will not be produced (be born); you are not going to set up the two fires". Therefore,they became (came to be called) 'Rākṣasas'(preventees). Then indeed did the gods see the thunderbolt, viz. the horse. They raised it up and on their destroying the

नाष्ट्रा रक्षाꣳस्यपहत्य तस्याभयेऽनाष्ट्रे निवातेऽग्निरजायत तस्माद्ब्रूयादग्निं मथिष्यन्[२९]नश्व-मानयेति ॥ १५ ॥

स पुरस्तादुपतिष्ठेत तथो वा एष एतं वज्रमुद्यच्छति तेन नाष्ट्रा रक्षाꣳस्यपहत्य तस्याभयेऽनाष्ट्रे निवातेऽग्निर्जायते ॥ १६ ॥

स पूर्ववाट् स्याद्वीर्यं वा अश्व एष वा अपरिमितं वीर्यमभिवर्धते यः पूर्ववाड्यदि न पूर्ववाळपि य एवं कश्चित्स्याद्यदि नाश्वोऽप्यनड्वान्त्स्यादेषो एवानळुहो बन्धुता ॥ १७ ॥

तं यत्र प्राञ्चमुद्धरि[३०]ष्यन्त्स्यात्तद्ब्रूयादश्वेन पूर्वेण प्रेहीति वज्रो वा अश्वो वज्रेणैवैतत्पु-रस्तान्नाष्ट्रा रक्षाꣳस्यपघ्नन्प्रभिन्दन्नेत्यथैतमभयेऽनाष्ट्रे निवाते हरति तं तथा हरेद्यथा प्रत्यङ्-यजमानमुपाचरेत् ॥ १८ ॥

एष वाव यज्ञो यदग्निः प्रत्यङ्हैवैनं यज्ञः प्रविशति तं क्षिप्रं यज्ञ उपनमत्यथ यस्मादेष पराङ्भवति पराङ्हास्मा[३१]द्यज्ञो भवति यो हैनं तत्रानुव्याहरेत्पराङस्माद्यज्ञोऽभून्नैनं यज्ञ उपनꣳस्यतीतीश्वरो ह तथैव स्यात्तस्मादेनं तथा हरेद्यथा प्रत्यङ् यजमानमुपाचरेत् ॥ १९ ॥

एष वाव प्राणो यदग्निः प्रत्यङ्हैवैनं प्राणः प्रविशति स सर्वमायुरेत्यथ यस्मादेष पराङ्भवति पराङ् हास्मात्प्राणो भवति यो हैनं तत्रानुव्याहरेत्पराङस्मात्प्राणोऽभूत्प्राण एनꣳ हास्यतीतीश्वरो ह तथैव स्यात्तस्मादेनं तथा हरेद्यथा प्रत्यङ्यजमानमुपाचरेद्योऽयं पवते ॥ २० ॥

एष उ वाव यज्ञः प्रत्यङ् हैवैनं यज्ञः प्रविशति तं क्षिप्रं यज्ञ उपनमत्यथ यस्मादेष[३२] पराङ् भवति पराङ् हा[३३]स्माद्यज्ञो भवति यो हैनं तत्रानुव्याहरेत्पराङस्माद्यज्ञोऽभून्नैनं यज्ञ

२९. मन्थिष्य TE. Ca

३०. मुद्धरि Ca. M, T, My.

३१. पराङ्ह स्याद्यज्ञो TE, see Notes.

३२. देव H.

३३. हस्मा TE.

destructive Rākṣasas, fire arose (was produced) in its safe shelter that was free from fear. Therefore, one who is going to churn the fire (produce fire by churning) should say, "Bring the horse".

16. It (the horse) should stand in front. Thus indeed does this (sacrificer) light up this thunderbolt (viz. the horse). (On his) Destroying the destructive Rākṣasas with it, fire arises (is born) in its fearless and safe (not destructive) shelter.

17. It (the horse) should be one that (moves ahead) (eastward) is a leader (foremost of horses). Indeed 'virility' is the horse. This (horse) is verily (represents) limitless vigour. He who is the leader (who goes in the fore front—who moves eastward) grows greatly. If there is no leader (leading horse) available, any one (any horse that is available) will do. If even (an ordinary) horse is not available, there may be an ox (an ox will serve the purpose). This indeed is the relationship of the ox (with the horse).

18. Where he (the sacrificer) is going to take it (the fires) on eastward, then he should say, "Move on with the horse ahead". Indeed the horse is the thunderbolt. Verily destroying the devastating demons (Rākṣasas) in front with the thunderbolt itself and breaking them up, he (the sacrificer) moves and then takes it (the fire) into the safe and fearless shelter. One should take it in such a manner that it will turn (westward) (backward) towards the sacrificer. (As the fire is taken forward towards the east, the smoke will move backwards towards the Yajamāna).

19. This fire is indeed the sacrifice. The sacrifice verily enters him (the sacrificer) (westward) backwards. Him the sacrifice quickly approaches. Moreover, the sacrifice turns away from him from whom this (fire) turns away. If one, there, should curse him saying, "May the sacrifice turn away from this person, may the lordly sacrifice not approach this person: lordly is it (the sacrifice). (The sacrifice will not approach this person)". It will surely happen so. Therefore, one should carry this (fire) so that it will turn (back) towards (facing) the sacrificer.

20. This fire indeed is the vital breath. Him (who takes the fire in such a way that it turns back towards him) verily the life-breath enters back. He attains the entire (span of) life. And from whom this (fire) turns away, vital breath also turns away from him. If one should curse him thus saying, "May life turn away from this person. Vital breath (life) is going to leave this person". Lordly is it (the vital breath) and it will surely happen so. Therefore, one should convey this (fire) in such a manner, that this (vital breath which blows or purifies) will move back towards the sacrificer.

21. This (fire) verily is the sacrifice. Indeed, him (the sacrificer) the sacrifice enters backward. Him the sacrifice reaches quickly. And the sacrifice turns away

उपनꣳस्यतीतीश्वरो तथैव स्यात्तस्मादेनं तथा हरेद्यथा प्रत्यङ् यजमानमुपाचरेद्योऽयं[34] पवते ॥ २१ ॥

एष उ वाव प्राणः प्रत्यङ् हैवैनं प्राणः प्रविशति स सर्वमायुरेत्यथ यस्मादेष पराङ् भवति पराङ् हास्मात्प्राणो भवति यो हैनं तत्रानुव्याहरेत्पराङस्मात्प्राणो ऽभूत्प्राण एनꣳ हारयतीतीश्वरो ह तथैव स्यात्तस्मादेनं तथा हरेद्यथा प्रत्यङ् यजमानमुपाचरेत् ॥ २२ ॥

तमश्वमाक्रमयति तं प्राञ्चमुत्क्रमयति तं पुनरावर्तयति वीर्यं वा अश्वो नेदस्माद्यजमानात्पराङ् वीर्यमसदिति तमुदञ्चं [35]प्राञ्चं प्रमुञ्चति तमश्वस्य पद आधत्ते वीर्यं वा अश्वो वीर्य एवैनं तदाधत्ते तमुपस्पर्शयति तमुद्यच्छति[36] तमुपस्पर्शयति [37]तमुद्यच्छति तं तृतीयेनैव भूर्भुवः स्वरित्याधत्ते त्रयो वा इमे लोकास्तदेनेनेमांल्लोकान्व्यश्नुते[38] इमांल्लोकान्व्याप्नोति ॥ २३ ॥

तदाहुः सकृदेवोपस्पृश्याथ द्वितीयेनैवादध्यादिति यो वा अस्यामप्रतिष्ठितो भारमुद्यच्छतीति नैनमुद्यन्तुꣳ शक्नोति समेनꣳ श्रृणाति स यत्सकृदुपस्पृशति तदस्यां[39] प्रतिष्ठायां प्रतितिष्ठति स प्रतिष्ठितो द्वितीयेनैव भूर्भुवः स्वरित्याधत्ते तथा न व्यथते तद्धासुरिः पाञ्चिर्माधुकिरिति दध्रिरे[40] सर्वं वा एतदन्यदियसितमिति प्रथमेनैवैनं वयं भूर्भुवः स्वरित्यादधामेति त उ ह ते तथा चक्रुरत एकतमेनाधाय[41] ॥ २४ ॥

३४. चरेद्यज्ञोऽयं TE.

३५. प्राञ्चमवर्जति Ca., and most Mss; see Notes.

३६. मुद्यच्छयति TE.

३७. तमुपद्यच्छति TE.

३८. न्व्यश्नुत Po. Ca.

३९. तदस्याः TE.

४०. दध्रिरे TE.

४१. नाधाय M, T, Ca.; नाधाय B.

surely from him from whom this (fire) turns away. Should one curse him therein, "May the sacrifice turn away from this person! The sacrifice is not going to reach him!" The sacrifice (fire) being powerful, it will surely happen so. Hence, one should convey this (fire) in such a manner that this (sacrifice) which purifies will move back towards the sacrificer.

22. This (fire), indeed, is the vital breath (life). The vital breath enters this person (sacrificer) backward. He attains the full (span of) life. And the vital breath turns away from him whom this(sacrifice/fire) turns away. If one curses him, "May life-breath turn away from this person! Life-breath will leave this person ", the sacrifice being lordly, it will surely happen so. Therefore, one should convey this (fire) in such a manner that it will approach the sacrificer back.

23. He (the sacrificer) makes the horse step on it (the fire-altar), then makes it move up towards the east and then makes it turn back again. Indeed the horse is (represents) virility. In order that virility may not run away from this sacrificer, he turns it (the horse) towards the north and east. He places it (the fire) at the foot (foot-print) of the horse. The horse is verily 'virility'. Therefore this indeed places it (the fire) in virility. He (the sacrificer) makes it (the fire) touch it (the horse's foot-print) and lifts it up (again); he makes it touch it and lifts it up. Only at the third time he establishes it (the fire) chanting *'Bhūrbhuvaḥsvaḥ'*. These worlds are indeed three. Therefore with this he enjoys these worlds; he pervaded these worlds.

24. They say, regarding this, "Touching (the horse's footprint) only once, then at the second time one should establish (the fire)". He who, without remaining established (well planted) on this (earth) lifts up a burden (tries to lift up) cannot lift it up. It crushes him. The fact that he touches once (means) he stays firm on this resting place (the earth). Being firmly established, he sets up (the fire) at the second time uttering, *'Bhūrbhuvaḥsvaḥ'*. Thus (thereby) he does not come to grief. *Āsuri, Pāñci* and *Mādhuki* thus set up (the fire), (saying), "All this else (on the altar) becomes troubled. So, we established it, chanting *"Bhūrbhuvaḥsvaḥ'* even at the first time". Indeed, they did so, establishing (the fire) then, even with one (even at the first) touching.

25. He (the sacrificer) touches the burning sticks saying, "Like the sky with abundance, like the earth with girth (in superiority)". He says verily this, "Just as the yonder sky is plentiful with stars, so may I become plentiful!" By "like the earth with girth"–he says verily this , "Just as this earth is big (vast) may I become big (great)". He (the sacrificer) establishes this (fire) on the back of this (earth). Chanting, "Oh Earth! the one fit for the worship of the Gods! On the back of

उल्मुकान्युपस्पृशति द्यौरिव भूम्ना भूमिरिव वरिम्णेति [४२]यथासौ द्यौर्बह्वी नक्षत्रैरेवं बहुर्भूयासमित्येवैतदाह भूमिरिव वरिम्णेति यथेयमुर्वी भूमिरेवमुरुर्भूयासमित्येवैतदाह[४३] तस्यास्ते पृथिवि देवयजनि पृष्ठ इत्यस्या ह्येनं पृष्ठ आधत्तेऽग्निमन्नादमन्नाद्यायादध इत्यन्नादोऽग्निरन्नादो भूयासमित्येवैतदाह सैषाशीस्तां[४४] यदि कामयेत जपेद्यद्यु कामयेतापि नैवाद्रियेत ॥ २५ ॥

अथ सर्पराज्ञ्या[४५] ऋग्भिरुपतिष्ठत आयं गौः पृश्निरक्रमीदसदन्मातरं पुरः । पितरं च प्रयन्त्स्वः । अन्तश्चरति रोचनास्य प्राणादपानती व्यख्यन्महिषो दिवम् । त्रिंꣳशद्धाम विराजति वाक्पतङ्गाय धीयते । प्रति वस्तोरह द्युभिरिति स यदेवास्याधानेन वर्तुभिर्वा संभारैर्वा नक्षत्रैर्वानाप्तं भवति तदेवास्यैतेन सर्वमाप्नोति तदु नाद्रियेतेयं वाव सर्पराज्ञी यद्धि किं च सर्पति तस्येयमेव राज्ञी स यदेवास्यामाधत्ते तेनै[४६]वास्यैष कृत्स्नः सर्वः समृद्ध आहितो भवति ॥ २६ ॥

इति एकपात्काण्डे प्रथमोऽध्यायः॥

४२. तथासौ P1, P2.

४३. मित्येव तदाह P1.

४४. बाशीस्ता P1, P2.

४५. सर्पराज्ञा M-B,Co.

४६. तेनेवा P.

"Yourself–, I set up Agni the eater of food, for the sake of good food". He says (means) verily this "Agni is the consumer of food. May I become the consumer of food!" This is (a prayer for) blessing. One may mutter it, if he wishes. If he so wishes he may ignore it.

26. Then he worships with the *Ṛks* pertaining to the 'Queen of serpents', (thus), "This spotted bull has come here and has lain down before the mother and before the father, too, on going up to heaven. She, shining (with liking) moves in, breathing out from his breath. The great one has illumined the sky. He shines much in his thirty abodes. Speech is bestowed on the winged one, Ah! with the lustres of everything!" Whatever has not been secured by the installation of this (fire) or by the seasons or by the (gathered) materials or the stars, that very thing, all that one secures by this. One need not care for it. This (earth) is indeed the Queen of Serpents (for) whatever creeps along of (all) that this (earth) verily is the queen. The fact that he sets up (the fire) on this (earth), verily by that itself, this (fire), entire and full and rich, becomes established.

(Fourth Brāhmaṇa Ends)

(Chapter One ends)

द्वितीयोऽध्यायः

प्रथमं ब्राह्मणम्

उद्धृत्याहवनीयं पूर्णाहुतिं जुहोत्यन्नादं वा एतं जनयत आत्मनो यदग्निं तस्मा एतदन्नमपिदधाति यथा वत्साय वा जाताय तरुणाय वा कुमाराय स्तनमपिदध्यादेवमस्मा[1] एतदन्नमपिदधाति तेन शान्तः प्रीत उत्तराणि[2] हवीꣳष्युपरमते श्रप्यमाणानि शश्वद्धाध्वर्युं वा यजमानं वा प्रदहेद्यदस्मिन्नेतामाहुतिं न जुहुयुस्तौ ह्यस्य नेदिष्ठमिव चरतः ॥ १ ॥

तां वै पूर्णां जुहोति सर्वं वै पूर्णꣳ सर्वेणैवैनं[3] तच्छमयति स्वाहाकारेण जुहोत्यनिरुक्तो वै स्वाहाकारः[4] सर्वं वा[5] अनिरुक्तꣳ सर्वेणैवैनं तच्छमयति यामु वा अदः प्रजापतिः प्रथमामाहुतिमजुहोत्स्वाहाकारेण वै तामजुहोत्सो स्विद्वा एषा निदानेन तस्मात्स्वाहाकारेण जुहोति तस्यां वरं ददाति सर्वं वै वरः सर्वेणैवैनं तच्छमयति ॥ २ ॥

तदाहुरेतामेवाहुतिꣳ हुत्वेत्यथोत्तराणि हवीꣳषि नाद्रियेतेत्येतयैव तं काममाप्नोति यस्मै कामायोत्तराणि हवीꣳषि निर्वपेतेति ॥ ३ ॥

स यदग्नये पवमानाय निर्वपति प्राणं वा अस्मिꣳस्तद्दधात्यन्नं वै प्राणोऽन्नमु वा एषाहुतिस्तदेतयैवास्मिꣳस्तद्दधाति ॥ ४ ॥

अथ यदग्नये पावकाय निर्वपत्यन्नं वा अस्मिꣳस्तद्दधाति प्रत्यक्षं वा एषाहुतिरन्नं तदेतयैवास्मिꣳस्तद्दधाति ॥ ५ ॥

अथ यदग्नये शुचये निर्वपति वीर्यं वा अस्मिꣳस्तद्दधात्येतद्ध वा अस्य वीर्यꣳ शुचि य एषोऽर्चिरुज्ज्वलति[6] तदेतस्यामेव हुतायामुच्चैस्तरामिवोज्ज्वलति[7] वीर्यवत्तर इव भवति

१. मस्या P1, P2, H.

२. उत्तराणि TE, My, Pa.

३. सर्वेणेवैनं P2, H.

४. From पूर्णꣳ upto स्वाहाकारः the text is missing in TE.

५. वा missing in K.

६. रुज्ज्वलति Ca.

७. रुज्ज्वलति Ca.

Chapter Two

BRĀHMAṆA I

1. Having taken out the *Āhavanīya* fire, he (the sacrificer) offers the full oblations, *'Pūrṇāhuti'*. Indeed,he (thereby) makes this Agni become a consumer of food for his own sake. To him (Agni) he offers this food. Just as one (the cow or the mother) would offer the breast to the (just) born calf or to the young child (son), in the same manner one offers this food to this (fire). Appeased and pleased by that, he (Agni) waits quietly for the subsequent oblations that are cooked. If they (the sacrificers) do not offer this oblation, in this (Agni), it (the fire) will soon burn up the *Yajamāna* or the Adhvaryu(for) those two move, as it were, nearest to it (the fire).

2. That (offering) he offers in full. Indeed, full is (means) 'all'. That (offering) appeases this (fire) with 'all'. He makes the offering uttering the sound *'svāhā'*. The expression *'svāhā'* is undefined (general). 'All' also is undefined (general). That, then, appeases this (fire) verily with 'all' (every thing). The first offering which Prajāpati offered, he indeed offered it with the utterance of the sound *'svāhā'*. That is indeed this, primarily. Hence he (the sacrificer) makes the offering, muttering *'svāhā'*. At (when) this (offering has been made), he (the sacrificer) presents a boon (gift) (to the priest). Everything is indeed a gift (a worthwhile thing). That (offering of gift) appeases this (fire) with every thing (all).

3. Here they (some) say, "Having made this offering *(Pūrṇāhuti)* one need not care for the subsequent offerings. He surely achieves even by this that wish for which he may make the subsequent offerings.

4. The fact that one makes an offering to *Agni Pavamāna* (the Blower) means that it puts life-breath, indeed, into this (sacrificer). Verily food is life breath. This offering is indeed food. Thus it puts into this (sacrificer) that (vital breath) by means of this (offering).

5. Then, the fact that one makes an offering to *Agni Pāvaka* (purifier) means that it indeed puts food into this (Agni). This offering (viz.,) food is directly visible. Therefore one puts that (food) into this (fire) by this very offering.

6. That one makes an offering for *Agni Śuci* (the Brilliant) means that it puts virility into this (fire). That this flame blazes up; it blazes up higher only when an offering is put into this (flame). It (the fire) becomes, as it were, more virile. Therefore, one puts it (virility) into this (fire) only by means of this (offering).

तदेतयैवास्मिंꣳस्तद्दधाति तस्मान्नाद्रियेतेत्याहुस्तदु निर्वपेदेवं[८] परोक्षमिव वा एतत्तदं[९]दस्तदि-दमितीव यावद्वा अजातो गर्भो मातुर्वैव तावत्प्राणमनु प्राणिति यथा वा ॥ ६ ॥

स यदग्नये पवमानाय निर्वपति प्राणो वै पवमानो जात एवास्मिंꣳस्तत्प्राणं दधाति ॥ ७ ॥

अथ यदग्नये पावकाय निर्वपत्यन्नं वै पावकं जात एवास्मिंꣳस्तदन्नं दधाति ॥ ८ ॥

अथ यदाग्नये शुचये निर्वपति वीर्यं वा अस्मिंꣳस्तद्दधाति यदो वा अन्नेन वर्धते[१०]ऽथ वीर्यं करोति तदेनमेतदन्नेनैव वर्धयित्वाथास्मिन्नेतद्वीर्यꣳ शुचि दधाति तस्मान्निर्वपेदेव तद्वा एतत्समानमेव सद्विपर्यस्तमिव यत्र ह वा अग्निर्देवेभ्यो मनुष्यानुपाववर्त[११] तद्धेक्षांचक्रे मैव सर्वेणैवात्[१२]मना देवेभ्यो मनुष्यानुपावृत्सीति स तिस्रस्तनूरपनिदध एषु लोकेषु तस्य यत्पवमानꣳ रूपमासास्यां तत्पृथिव्यां निदधे यत्पावकमन्तरिक्षे तद्यच्छुचि दिवि तदथ मनुष्यानुपा[१३]ववर्त तदु हर्षयः प्रतिबुबुधिरे ये तर्हि मनुष्याणामृषय आसुरसर्वो वै नोऽग्निरु-पाववृतीति[१४] तस्मादेतानि[१५] हवींꣳषि निरवपन् ॥ ९ ॥

स यदग्नये पवमानाय निर्वपति यैवास्यास्यां पृथिव्यां तनूस्तामेव तेनाप्नोत्यथ यदग्नये पावकाय निर्वपति यैवास्यान्तरिक्षे तनूः पावका तामेव तेनाप्नोत्यथ यदग्नये शुचये निर्वपति यैवास्य दिवि तनूः शुचिस्तामेव तेनाप्नोति तꣳ सर्वं कृत्स्नमग्निमनपनिहित-माधत्ते केवलबर्हिः[१६] प्रथमꣳ हविर्भवति समानबर्हिषी उत्तरे इमे वै लोका एतानि

८. निर्वपेदेवं P1.

९. एतत्तदद H.

१०. अन्ने वर्धते H.

११. नुपाववर्त TE, P1, H, Co; see Notes.

१२. सर्वेणेवात्मना Ca.

१३. नुपाववर्त TE, P1, H, Co; see Notes.

१४. रुपाववृतीति M; see Notes on 11 above.

१५. तस्मा एतानि Ca.

१६. बर्हिः Ca.

Therefore, they (some) say, "One need not care for it (the subsequent oblations)". One must certainly make that (subsequent offerings). This (fact) is, as it were, invisible (incomprehensible) that "this is that yonder thing and that is this". Just as, as long as the child (embryo) is not born , it breathes (lives) in consonance with the vital breath of the mother.

7. That one makes the offering for *Agni Pavamāna* (the Blower) means that *Pavamāna* is the breath and he (the sacrificer) puts that into him (the fire) even as it (the fire) is born.

8. Then he makes the offering for *Agni Pāvaka* (Purifier) for, food indeed is the purifier. As soon as this (fire) is born, he (the sacrificer) puts the food into this (fire).

9. Then he makes the offering for *Agni Śuci* (the Brilliant)and it puts virility into this (fire). For when he (the fire) grows with food, then,he builds up strength. Thus making this (fire) grow by means of food, thereby he (the sacrificer) puts this bright strength into this (fire). Therefore, one must make that offering. This being alike, it (the practice of not making the subsequent offerings after *Pūrṇāhuti*) appears to be reversed (wrong), in a matter where Agni approached men from the gods and thought, "Let me not go to the men from the gods with my full self (body)". He placed (his) three bodies in these (three) worlds; what was his *Pavamāna* (blowing) form he placed on this earth; what was *Pāvaka* (the purifier) (that he placed) in the mid region and that which was *Śuci* (bright) (he placed) in the sky. And then he came to the men. Those who were then sages among men realized that (and thought), "Agni has come to us not in his entire form". (Therefore) They made these offerings for him (Agni).

10. What he (the sacrificer) offers to *Agni Pavamāna,* by that he gets (reaches) that very body (of Agni) which is in this earth. And then what he offers for *Agni Pāvaka,* by that he gets at that very body (of Agni) which is in the mid region. And then what he offers for *Agni Śuci,* by that he verily gets at that very body (of Agni) which is in the sky. (Thus) He (the sacrificer) sets up the entire Agni who is not placed away (who is present in his fulness).The first oblation has an only (separate) seat of sacred grass and the subsequent two (oblations) have a common *barhis* (seat of sacred grass). These are the worlds, these are the

हवीꣳषि सोऽयमद्धातमामिव लोको बहुलतमं[१७] इव लेलयमिवेदमन्तरिक्षं लेलयेव द्यौरुभे चिदेनं प्रत्युद्यामिनी भवतामिति सभारतायै ॥ १० ॥

अष्टाकपाला आग्नेयाः पुरोळाशा भवन्त्यष्टाक्षरा गायत्री गायत्रमग्नेश्छन्दस्[१८]स्वेनैवैनं तच्छन्दसाधत्ते तानि चतुर्विꣳशतिः सम्पद्यन्ते चतुर्विꣳशत्यक्षरा वै गायत्री गायत्रमग्ने-श्छन्दस्[१९]स्वेनैवैनं तच्छन्दसाधत्ते गायत्र्यो याज्यानुवाक्या भवन्ति गायत्रमग्नेश्छन्दस्[२०]स्वे नैवैनं तच्छन्दसाधत्तेऽथैष एवादित्यश्चरुरु परिष्टाद्भवति प्रच्यावयत इव ह वा एषोऽस्मान्म-नुष्यलोकाद्देवलोकमभ्यात्मानं य एतानि हवीꣳषि निर्वपत ऊर्ध्व इव हि समारोहन्नेतीयमु वा अदितिरियं प्रतिष्ठा तदस्यामेव प्रतिष्ठायामन्ततः प्रतितिष्ठति ॥ ११ ॥

तस्य विराजौ संयाज्ये स्यातां विराड्ढीयमित्[२१]यथो त्रिष्टुभौ त्रिष्टुब्भीयमित्[२२]यथो जगत्यौ जगती हीयमिति विराजौ त्वेव स्थितं तस्य धेनुर्दक्षिणा धेनुरिव वा इयं मनुष्येभ्यः सर्वान्कामान्दुग्धे सर्वान्वै कामान्धेनुर्दुग्धे मातेव वा इयं मनुष्याणां च पशूनां च मातेव धेनुस्तस्मादस्य धेनुर्दक्षिणैतन्त्वेकमयनम् ॥ १२ ॥

अथ द्वितीयमग्नय एवाष्टाकपालं पुरोळाशं निर्वपति परोक्षमिव वा एतदग्नये पवमानायाग्नये पावकायाग्नये शुचय इत्यथास्यैवं प्रत्यक्षमञ्जसाग्नी आहितौ भवतस्तस्य मूर्धन्वत्यौ याज्यानुवाक्ये भवतोऽथैष एवादित्यश्चरुरुपरिष्टात्तस्यैषैव बन्धुतैषा दक्षिणा ॥ १३ ॥ इति प्रथमं ब्राह्मणम् ॥

१७. तर M.

१८. श्छन्दः स्वे TE, Ca.

१९. श्छन्दः स्वे TE, Ca.

२०. श्छन्दः स्वे TE, Ca.

२१. विराडीय H; विराड्ढीय Ca.; See Notes.

२२. त्रिष्टुभीय P2, B.

oblations. This world (earth) is, as it were, fine and dense; the mid region appears to be oscillating and oscillating seems the sky. For (imparting) equal weightiness, so that those two (worlds) may counterpoise (may come towards) this (earth), (the last two oblations are offered with a common *barhis*).

11. The sacrificial cakes (intended) for Agni are cooked on eight potsherds. *Gāyatrī* (metre) has eight syllables (in a *pāda* or foot). *Gāyatra* is the metre of Agni. He (the sacrificer), then, establishes this (Agni) with its own metre. They (the potsherds) amount to twenty-four. Indeed *Gāyatrī* has twenty-four syllables (on the whole). *Gāyatra* is the metre of Agni. He then , sets up (the fire) with its own metre. The *Yājyānuvākyas* (the offering formulas and the connected expressions) are in the *Gāyatrī* metre. *Gāyatra* is the metre of Agni and he then sets up (the fire) with his own metre. Then subsequently, occurs this (offering of) cooked food dedicated to Aditi. He who prepares (and offers) these (preceding oblations) seems to make himself slip away from this world of men towards the world of the Gods. Indeed he moves, as it were, ascending above. This (earth) is Aditi. This is (the firm) resting place. Therefore, ultimately, he (the sacrificer) rests firmly on this (firm) resting place.

12. Its two *Samyājyas* (inviting and offering formulas) are in *Virāṭ* (metre), for this (earth) is indeed vast (shining); and (or) two *triṣṭubh* verses for this (earth) is *triṣṭubh* indeed (three-propped) and (or) two *Jagatī* verses; indeed this (earth) is *Jagatī* (constantly moving). But anyway it remains that they are only two *Virāṭ* verses. For that (the offering to Aditi) the fee is a cow; for this (earth) like a cow, produces (fulfils) all desires for men. Indeed the cow fulfils all the desires (of men). This (earth) is indeed like a mother to men and animals, like the cow which is like a mother. Therefore the fee for this (offering) is a cow. This is one way (of performance).

13. Now then (is) a second (way), one offers the cake cooked on eight potsherds only for Agni. This (offering) is, as it were, indirectly (invisibly) for *Agni Pavamāna, Agni Pāvaka* and *Agni Śuci.* Then the two Agnis of this (sacrificer) become visibly and truly established. There are two *Yājyānuvākyas* (one offering formula and one connected expression) containing the word *'Mūrdhan'*, for that (offering). Then (is offered) verily this cooked rice offering for Aditi, subsequently. This is indeed the relationship to it. This (cow) is the fee.

(First Brāhmaṇa Ends)

द्वितीयं ब्राह्मणम्

घ्नन्ति ह वा एतद्यज्ञं यदेनं तन्वते यद्राजानमभिषुण्वन्ति तत्तं[१] घ्नन्त्यथ यत्पशुꣳ संज्ञपयन्ति यद्विशासति[२] तत्तं घ्नन्त्युलूखलमुसलेन दृषदुपलेन हविर्यज्ञं घ्नन्ति स एवꣳ हतो यज्ञो न ददक्षे तं देवा दक्षिणाभिर्दक्षयांचक्रुस्तस्माद्दक्षिणा नाम यदाभिरदक्षयꣳस्तस्मादु दक्षिणा दद्यात्स यद्दक्षिणा ददाति यदेव हतस्य यज्ञस्य व्ययते तदेवास्यै तद्दक्षिणाभिर्दक्षयत्यथ समृद्ध एव यज्ञः ॥ १ ॥

ताः षळ्दद्यात्षड्वा ऋतवः संवत्सरस्य संवत्सरो यज्ञः प्रजापतिः स यावानेव प्रजापतिर्यावत्यस्य मात्रा तावतीभिरेवैनमेतद्दक्षयति ॥ २ ॥

अथो द्वादश दद्याद्द्वादश वै मासाः संवत्सरस्य संवत्सरो यज्ञः प्रजापतिः स यावानेव प्रजापतिर्यावत्यस्य मात्रा तावतीभिरेवैनमेतद्दक्षयति ॥ ३ ॥

अथो चतुर्विꣳशतिं दद्याच्चतुर्विꣳशतिर्वा अर्धमासाः संवत्सरस्य संवत्सरो यज्ञः प्रजापतिः स यावानेव प्रजापतिर्यावत्यस्य मात्रा तावतीभिरेवैनमेतद्दक्षयत्येता आदिष्टाः कामं[३] यथाश्रद्धं भूयसीर्दद्यात् ॥ ४ ॥

द्वया उ वाव देवा देवा अहैवान्यद्देवा अथेमे मनुष्यदेवा[४] य इमे ब्राह्मणाः शुश्रुवाꣳसोऽनूचानास्तेषां द्वैधा[५] विभक्तो यज्ञ आहुतय एव देवानां दक्षिणा मनुष्यदेवानां ब्राह्मणानाꣳ शुश्रूषामनूचानाꣳ[६] स आहुतिभिरेव देवान्प्रीणाति दक्षिणाभिर्मनुष्यदेवान्ब्राह्मणाञ्छुश्रूषो[७]ऽनूचानाꣳस्त एनमुभये देवाः प्रीताः सुधायां दधति यथो वै रेतो योनौ

१. षुण्वन्ति तं घ्न H.

२. See Notes.

३. कामं TE, P1, P2, H.

४. मनुष्य B.

५. द्वेधा TE, B.

६. See Notes.

७. न्ब्राह्मणानाञ्छुश्रूषो P2; see Notes.

BRĀHMAṆA II

1. In that they perform (elaborately) the sacrifice,they kill it. In that they press (ritually prepare the juice) the King (the Soma plant), they kill it. In that they quieten and immolate the (sacrificial) animal, they kill it. With mortar and pestle and with a pair of mill-stones they kill the *haviryajña* (the sacrificial food offerings). The sacrifice having been killed thus became incapable of producing the desired result. The gods made it capable with fees (ritual gifts to priests). As they invigorated (the sacrifice) with these, these (fees) came to be known as *Dakṣiṇā* (invigorating means). Therefore, indeed, must one give the fees. Whatever (part) of this destroyed sacrifice flags, that very thing of the sacrifice does one invigorate by means of the sacrificial fees that one gives. Then the sacrifice becomes verily rich (prospers).

2. One should give six of them (fees/cows). Indeed six are the seasons of the year; the year is the sacrifice, (it is) Prajāpati. As much as is the sacrifice, as much as is its measure, by so much (many) fees only does he (the sacrificer) thereby invigorates it.

3. Or, one may give twelve; indeed twelve are the months of the year. The year is the sacrifice, Prajāpati. As much as is the sacrifice, as much as is its measure, by so much only does he thereby invigorate it.

4. Or, one may give twenty-four. Indeed twenty-four are the half-months of the year. The year is the sacrifice, Prajāpati.As much as is the sacrifice, as much as is its measure, by so much only does he thereby invigorate it. These have been indicated (advised). One may give more according to his faith.

5. Verily the gods are of two kinds. The Gods indeed are of a different (one) kind of gods.Then theseBrāhmins who have studied the*Vedas* and teach (them) are the humar gods. Their sacrifice (also) is divided into two kinds: the very oblations (form the sacrifice) for the gods, for the human gods viz., theBrāhmins who have studied the Vedas and teach them, it is the sacrificial fee. He (the sacrificer) propitiates the gods only by the oblations and (propitiates) the human gods. the Brāhmins who have studied theVedasand teach them, with sacrificial fees. Those two (kinds of) gods, being pleased, place this (sacrificer) in nectar (a state of bliss). As one would deposit semen into the genitals (of a woman), in the

दध्यादेवमेतदृत्विजः स्वर्गे लोके यजमानं दधति तेभ्य एतद्ददाति ये मेदꣳ संप्रापिपन्नितीति[८] नु दक्षिणानाम् ॥ ५ ॥

अथ देवाश्च ह वा असुराश्चोभये प्राजापत्या अस्पर्धन्त ते होभयेऽनात्मान आसुर्मर्त्या ह्यासुर्[९]नात्मा हि स यो मर्त्यस्तेषु हाग्निरेवामृतमास तमुभय उपाजीवꣳस्तेषाꣳ ह स्म यं घ्नन्ति तद्ध स्मैव स भवति ततो ह देवास्तनीयाꣳस इव परिशिशिषिरे ते हार्चन्तः श्राम्यन्तः कथꣳ सपत्नानसुरानभिभवेमेति ते हैतदेवाग्न्याधेयं ददृशुः ॥ ६ ॥

ते होचुर्हन्तेदममृतमन्तरात्मन्याधायेत्यमृता भूत्वा स्तर्यास्तर्यान्त्सपत्नान्मर्त्यानसुरानभिभविष्याम इति ॥ ७ ॥

ते[१०] होचुरुभयेषु वै नोऽयमग्निरिति हन्तासुरेभ्यः प्रतिप्रब्रवामेति ते हासुरानेत्योचुरा वै वयमग्निं धास्यामहेऽथैनं यूयं किं करिष्यथेति ते हासुरा असूयन्त इवोचुरथैनं वयं न्येव धास्यामह इत्यत्र तृणानि दहात्र दारूणि दहात्र माꣳसं पचात्रौदनं पचेति सोऽयमग्निर्येनेदं मनुष्या भुञ्जते यदिदमिमाः[११] प्रजा उपजीवन्ति ॥ ८ ॥

अथैनं देवा अन्तरात्मन्याधायामृता भूत्वास्तर्या[१२]स्तर्यान्त्सपत्नान्मर्त्यानसुरानभ्यभवꣳस्तस्मै कमग्नी आदधीत नामृतत्वस्याशास्त्य[१३]स्तर्यो हैव भवति न हैनं तुस्तूर्षमाणश्च न स्तृणुते तस्माद्यदाहिताग्निश्चानाहिताग्निश्च स्पर्धेते[१४] आहिताग्निरेवाभिभवत्यस्तर्यो हि स भवति ॥ ९ ॥

८. सं प्रापि TE, सं प्रापिपन्नितीति

९. ह्यासुर TE, H.

१०. ते Ca.

११. यमिदमिमाः M, V1, Ca; see Notes.

१२. स्तर्या स्तर्या सप M, My, Ca.

१३. शास्त्य Ca.

१४. स्पर्धते TE.

same manner, these priests place the sacrificer in heaven. The sacrificer presents this (fee) to them (priests), thinking, "These are those who have made me reach this (heaven)". This is indeed, concerning sacrificial fees.

6. The Devas and Asuras, both of them sprung from Prajāpati, contended (with each other). Both of them were without 'Ātman' (eternal soul). Indeed they were mortals. Verily he who is mortal has no (abiding) soul. Among them only Agni was immortal. Both of them (Devas and Asuras) lived by resorting to him (Agni). Whom (soever) among them they killed; he remained so (slain). Then the gods remained (were left over) thinner (in number or strength). They worshipped and tired themselves (in austerities), thinking, "How can we overcome our rivals the Asuras?" They indeed discovered this very *'Agnyādheya'* (installation of Agni).

7. They said, "Ah! installing this immortal thing (Agni) within ourselves and thereby becoming immortal and invincible, we shall overcome the Asuras, our mortal conquerable rivals.

8. They said, "Verily this Agni is in both of us. Well, let us speak to the Asuras in a contrary way." They went to the Asuras and said, "Verily we are going to set up Agni (ceremoniously). What are you going to do with him (Agni)?" The Asuras spoke, as it were, maliciously "Then we shall surely lay it down," saying, 'Burn the (blades of) grass here'; 'burn the logs of wood here;' 'cook meat here' and 'cook rice here'. This (what the Asuras laid down) was the fire with which men eat and resorting to which these creatures live.

9. Then, the gods, installing this (Agni) within themselves and becoming immortal and invincible, overcame their rivals, the conquerable mortal Asuras. For that (which) there are two fires, shall one set up? There is no hope of (attaining) immortality. (But) he (the sacrificer) indeed becomes unconquerable. One who wishes to conquer him does not conquer him at all. Therefore, when one who has set up his fires and one who has not set up his fires contend (with each other), only the one who has set up his fires overcomes (the other). For he, indeed, becomes invincible

तं यत्रादो मन्थन्ति तदेनं जातमभिप्राणिति प्राणो वा अग्निर्जातमेवैनं तज्जनयत्यथोद[१५]निति तदेनमन्तरात्मन्याधत्तेऽथेतरमुज्वल[१६]यन्तीह यक्ष्य इह साधु करिष्यामीति ॥ १० ॥

तद्धैकेषामाग इव भवत्यन्वगन्निति तदु नाद्रियेत न वा अस्यैषोऽनुगच्छति योऽस्यान्तरात्म[१७]न्याहितो भवत्यनो[१८] व्ययासीद्रथो व्ययासीत् ॥ ११ ॥

अन्तरागादिति हैकेषामाग इव भवति तदू नो एवाद्रियेत न वा अस्यैतमनो वि[१९]याति न रथो वियाति नान्तरेणैति कश्चन योऽस्यान्तरात्मन्याहितो भवति ॥ १२ ॥

ते वा एते प्राणा एवाग्नयः प्राणोदानावेवाहवनीयश्च गार्हपत्यश्च व्यानोऽन्वाहार्यपचनस्तस्य वा एतस्याग्न्याधेयस्य सत्यमेवोपचारः ॥ १३ ॥

स यथा समिद्धमग्निं घृतेनाभिषिञ्चेत्तस्य वै भूयो भूयस्तेजो भवति स श्वः[२०] श्वः श्रेयान्भवत्येवꣳ हैव कीर्त्या यशसा श्रिया श्वः[२१] श्वः श्रेयान्भवति योऽग्नी आधाय सत्यं वदति ॥ १४ ॥

अथ यथा समिद्धमग्निमुदकेनाभिषिञ्चेत्तस्य वै कनीयः कनीयस्तेजो भवति स श्वः श्वः[२२] पापीयान्भवत्येवꣳ हैव कीर्त्या यशसा श्रिया श्वः श्वः पापीयान्भवति योऽग्नी आधाय मृषा वदत्यरुणꣳ हौपवेशिं ज्ञातय ऊचुः स्थविरो वा अस्यग्नी आधत्स्वेति ॥ १५ ॥

स होवाच तन्मैतद्ब्रूथ वाचंयम एवैधीति मा ब्रूथेति नह्यग्नी आधाय मृषा वदेन्नो वाचा वदतोऽमृषोद्यमस्ति तस्मादु सत्यमेव वि[२३]वदिषेत् ॥ १६ ॥ इति द्वितीयं ब्राह्मणम् ॥

१५. दनिति TE, H.

१६. ज्वलयतीह Ca.

१७. रात्मनाहितो P1, P2.

१८. भवत्यतो P1, P2.

१९. वीयति Ca, Co.

२०. श्वः श्वः TE; श्वश्वः H; श्वःश्व, B.

२१. श्वः श्वः TE; श्वश्वः H; श्वःश्व, B.

२२. श्वः श्वः TE; श्वश्वः H; श्वःश्व, B.

२३. विवदिषेत् B, V2.

10. Then, where they churn that (produce that fire by churning), then he (the sacrificer) breathes upon this (fire) that has been born. Indeed Agni is breath. It produces (enlivens) this one that has been born. Then he inhales the breath up. By that he installs this (fire) within himself. Then he makes the other one blaze up, thinking, "Here shall I put the oblation"."Here shall I perform the sacrifice" and "Here shall I do it properly (I shall do the right thing here)".

11. To some, this appears to be a fault, that it (the fire) might go out. One need not mind it. The fire that has been installed in his own self, that does not go out. "The cart passed; the chariot passed (in between me and the fire)."

12. "It passed in between" --such, indeed, is a sense of fault (wrong) for some. That too one need not mind at all. The cart does not pass through this (inner fire) of this (sacrificer), nor does a chariot pass nor does any one come in between the fire that has been established within himself.

13. These breaths themselves are the fires. The *Prāṇa* (exhaled breath the vital breath) and *Udāna* (the inhaled/up-drawn) breaths verily are the *Āhavanīya* and *Gārhapatya* (fires). The *Vyāna* (pervasive breathing is the *Anvāhāryapacana* (the fire for cooking subsequent offerings). For this consecrated fire, worship consists, verily in (speaking the) truth.

14. Just as one may sprinkle the kindled fire with *ghee* and its lustre becomes more and more and it (the fire) becomes greater day by day, in a very similar manner does a person who, having installed the fire,speaks the truth; becomes greater day by day with renown, glory and splendour (wealth).

15. Now, Just as (if) one sprinkles fire with water, its lustre becomes less and less and day by day it becomes weaker (more pitiable), verily like this, he who having installed the fire speaks untruth becomes weaker (more pitiable) by (in the matter of) renown, glory and splendour. The relatives told Aruṇa Aupaveśi, thus, "You are, indeed, old; set up the two fires".

16. He said, "Do not tell me this. Do not say, "Be one with a vow of silence (one with complete and habitual restraint on speech)" for one should, indeed, not speak untruth after having installed the two fires. For one who speaks, there is no non-speaking of untruth. Therefore, indeed, one must wish (strive) to speak only the truth.

(Second Brāhmaṇa Ends)

तृतीयं ब्राह्मणम्

वरुणो हैनद्राज्यकाम आदधे स राज्यमगच्छत्तस्माद्यश्चैतद्वेद यश्च न[1] वरुणो राजेत्येवाचक्षते सोमो यशस्कामः स यशोऽभवत्तस्माद्ये च सोमे लभन्ते ये च न लभन्त उभय एवैनदागच्छन्ति यश एवैतद्द्रष्टुमागच्छन्ति यशो ह भवति राज्यं गच्छति य एनदेवं विद्वानाधत्ते[2] ॥ १ ॥

अग्ना उ ह वै देवाः सर्वाणि रूपाणि संनिदधिरे यानि च ग्राम्याणि यानि चारण्यानि विजयं वोपपरैष्यन्तः कामचारस्य वा कामायायं नो गोपिष्ठो गोपायत्विति वा तान्ह्यग्निर्नि[3]चकमे तान्त्संगृह्यर्तून्प्रविवेश पुनरेम इति देवा एतदग्निं तिरोभूतं तेषाꣳ हेयसेवास[4] किमिह कार्यं केह प्रज्ञेति ॥ २ ॥

ततो हैतत्त्वष्टा पुनराधेयं ददर्श तदादधे योऽग्नेः[5] प्रियं धामोपजगाम तस्मा एतान्यग्निरुभयानि रूपाणि प्रतिनिःससर्ज यानि च ग्राम्याणि यानि चारण्यानि तस्माद्वा आहुस्त्वाष्ट्राणि रूपाणीति त्वष्टुर्ह वै सर्वꣳ रूपमुप तु हैवान्याः प्रजा यावच्छो यावच्छस्तिष्ठन्ते[6] ॥ ३ ॥

तस्मै कं पुनराधेयमादधीत तथा हैवाग्नेः प्रियं धामोपगच्छति तस्मा एतान्यग्निरुभयानि रूपाणि प्रति निःसृजति यानि च ग्राम्याणि यानि चारण्यानि तस्मिन्नेतान्युभयानि रूपाणि दृश्यन्ते परमता वै सा स्पृहयँन्ति[7] हास्मै तथा पुष्यति लोक्यमु वा अप्याग्नेयोऽयं यज्ञो ज्योतिरग्निः पाप्मनो दग्धा सोऽस्य पाप्मानं दहति स ज्योतिरेवेह श्रिया यशसा भवति ज्योतिरमुत्र पुण्यलोकत्वा[8] ॥ ४ ॥

१. नो H.

२. नाधत्ते V2.

३. तान्हाग्नि Ca.

४. ह+इयसा+इव (इयसा= Lacitude or shirking)

५. सोऽग्निः TE.

६. स्तिष्ठन्ते P1, P2, H.

७. स्पृहयन्ति Ca., P2.

८. पुण्य Ca.

BRĀHAMAṆA III

1. Varuṇa indeed, established this (fire) being desirous of sovereignty. He attained sovereignty. Therefore, he who knows this and he who does not, all say, "Varuṇa is the King". Soma was desirous of glory. (He established this fire). He became glorious. Therefore those who acquire (in the matter of) Soma and those who don't, both of them acquire this (glory) verily. People do come to see the glorious. He who, knowing this is so, sets up (the fires), indeed, becomes glorious and attains sovereignty.

2. The Gods deposited, once, all forms --(things and forms),those that were rural and those that were of the forest (domestic and wild), either because they (the gods) were going out to achieve victory (in battle against the enemies) or with a desire for free activity or with the thought, "This (Agni) is the best protector and may he protect us". Agni, indeed, coveted them much. Gathering them (the forms) he entered the seasons. The gods thought, "Let us go back" and came to (the place of) Agni who had disappeared.

What is to be done here? What knowledge is there about this?

3. Then, indeed, did Tvaṣṭā see (intuitively discovered) this, 'Re-installation' (re-installed fire). He established it and he reached Agni's favourite abode. Agni gave out to him both these forms, the domestic and the wild. Therefore they say, verily, "The forms are of Tvaṣṭā". For all form belongs to Tvaṣṭṛ. All other creatures (too) as much as they experience it.

4. So one should set up a re-installed fire for him (Tvaṣṭṛ)? Thus, indeed, one reaches the favourite abode of Agni. To him, Agni re-delivers both these forms that are domestic and that are wild. In it (the fire) are seen both these forms. That is indeed the supreme state. They (people) like him. So does he flourish. (His position) is also noticeable, indeed.

This sacrifice belongs to Agni. Agni is the light (flame), the burner of evil. He destroys the evil of this person (sacrificer). He (the sacrificer) becomes the very light with splendour and glory here (in this world) and the light in the yonder world (heaven), the state of a world of merit (the auspicious world).

स वै वर्षास्वेवादधीत वर्षा वै सर्व ऋतवो वर्षा हि वै सर्वऋतवोऽथादो वर्षमकुर्मादो वर्षमकुर्मेति वर्षाभिरेव संवत्सरान्त्संपश्यन्ति वर्षा हि वै सर्वऋतवोऽथ वर्षा एव सर्वेषामृतूनाꣳ रूपम् ॥ ५ ॥

भवति वै तद्वर्षासु यत्राहुर्ग्रीष्म एवाद्येति भवति तद्यत्राहुः शिशिर एवाद्येति वर्षादिदु वर्षेष्वथैतत्परोक्षमिव रूपं यदेव पुरस्ताद्वाति तद्वसन्तस्य रूपं यत्स्तनयति तद्ग्रीष्मस्य यद्वर्षति तद्वर्षाणां यद्विद्योतते तच्छरदो यद्वृष्टोद्गृह्णाति तद्धेमन्तस्य वर्षाः सर्वऋतव ऋतून्प्राविशदृतुभ्य[9] एवैनमेतन्निर्मिमीते ॥ ६ ॥

आदित्यो वाव सर्वऋतवः स यदैवोदेत्यथ वसन्तो यदा संगवोऽथ ग्रीष्मो यदा मध्यन्दिनोऽथ वर्षा यदा न्यह्णोऽपराह्णोऽथ शरद्यदास्त[10]मेत्यथ हेमन्तः ॥ ७ ॥

स यत्र मध्यन्दिनः स्यात्तर्ह्येवादधीत तर्हि वा एषोऽस्य लोकस्य नेदिष्ठो भवति[11] नेदिष्ठादेवैनमेतन्मध्यान्निर्मिमीते छायो[12] वा अयं पाप्मा मनुष्यमनुषक्तश्चरति सोऽत्र कनिष्ठो भवत्यधस्पदमिव ह्यसीति कनिष्ठमेवैतत्सन्तं पाप्मानमवबाधते ॥ ८ ॥

स वै कुशैरुद्धरति दारुभिर्वा अग्र उद्धरति दारुभिरग्रे दारुभिरपरं जामि कुर्यात्समदं कुर्यादापो वै वर्षा आपः कुशा वर्षा ऋतून्प्राविशदद्भिरेवैनमेतदद्भ्यो निर्मिमीते[13] ॥ ९ ॥

सोऽर्कपलाशाभ्यां व्रीहिमयमपूपं कृत्वा यत्र गार्हपत्यमाधास्यन्भवति तन्निदधाति तद्गार्हपत्यमभ्यादधाति ॥ १० ॥

अर्कपलाशाभ्याम्वेव यवमयमपूपं कृत्वा यत्राहवनीयमाधास्यन्भवति तन्निदधाति तदाहवनीयमभ्यादधाति पूर्वाभ्यामेवैनमेतदग्निभ्यामन्तर्दधाति ॥ ११ ॥

९. दृतुभ्य TE.

१०. द्यदास्त H; द्यदास्त V2.

११. भवति Ca., M,T.

१२. छायो TE, L; त्सायो M.

१३. मीते Ca., M,T,Ca.

5. He may set up (the fire - a second time)only in the rainy season. Indeed the rainy season (itself) is all the seasons. Verily is the rainy season all the seasons. Hence, they consider (count) the years only with the rainy season, saying "We did (this) for a year (in that year) ","We did this that year," for the rainy season is all the seasons. And therefore the rainy season itself is the form of all the seasons.

6. Indeed, it happens in the rainy season when they say, "Today is verily summer!" It happens in the rainy season when they say, "Today is verily winter!" From the rain (it goes) into the years, indeed. And besides, this is, as it were, (the year's) invisible form. What blows in the east, that itself is the form of spring; what thunders is of summer, what rains is of the rainy season, what flashes (lightning) is of autumn and what, having rained sucks it up is of the season of snow. The rainy season is all the seasons. He (Agni) entered the seasons. From the seasons themselves does he produce this (fire).

7. Indeed, the Sun is all the seasons. When it rises, even then is it spring; when it is the time for being gathered together (for milking) it is summer; when it is mid-day it is the rainy season; when the day declines, i.e.when it is afternoon, it is autumn. When he sets, then it is the season of snow (winter).

8. When it is mid-day, then only should one establish (the fire). Then, indeed, does this (Sun) remain closest to this world (earth). He produces this (fire) from the nearest centre of this (world). This evil, indeed, moves about clinging to a man as his shadow. That (evil) becomes smallest here (at mid-day). (Thinking thus), "You are as if under (my) foot", he afflicts (and drives away) that evil even when it remains smallest.

9. Verily he takes it (fire) up by means of sacrificial grass. Or he takes it out with (pieces of) wood, the first time. (Should he take the fire) first with (pieces of) wood and the second time (too) with (pieces of) wood, he would be committing repetition and he would be doing it with arrogance. Waters are the rainy season. Waters are the (blades of) sacred grass and the rainy season. He (Agni) entered the seasons. Therefore he produces this (fire) with waters themselves from waters.

10. Having prepared a cake of rice with two leaves of the *arka* plant, he places it at the spot where he is going to establish the *Gārhapatya.* And then he lays down the *Gārhapatya* there.

11. Having prepared a cake of barley with two leaves of the *arka* plant, he puts it at the place where he is going to establish the *Āhavanīya.* And then he lays down the *Āhavanīya* there. He covers this verily with the first two fires.

तदु नाद्रियेत रात्रिभिर्वाव सोऽन्त्तर्हितो[१४]ऽथैतमाग्नेयं पञ्चकपालं पुरोळाशं निर्वपति तस्य पञ्चपदाः पङ्क्त्यो याज्यानुवाक्या भवन्ति पञ्चर्तव ऋतून्प्राविशदृतुभ्य एवैनमेतन्निर्मिमीते ॥ १२ ॥

आग्नेयः सर्वो भवति तथा ह्यग्नेः प्रियं धाम त्वष्टोपागच्छदुपांश्वेनेन चरन्ति यद्वै ज्ञातिभ्यो वा सखिभ्यो वा निष्केवल्यं[१५] करिष्यन्[१६]भवति तिर इव वै तेन बोभुवत्तिर इव स्विद्वा एतद्यदुपांशु वैश्वदेवोऽन्यो यज्ञोऽथैष निष्केवल्यं[१७] एवाग्नेय उत्तममनुयाजमुच्चैर्यजति कृतकर्मेव हि तर्हि भवति सर्वो हि कृतमनुबुध्यते ॥ १३ ॥

स यत्राध्वर्युरतिक्रम्याश्राव्याह समिधो यजेत्याग्नेयमेव तद्रूपं परोक्षमिव त्वग्नीन्यजेति हैव तंत्र[१८] ब्रूयात् ॥ १४ ॥

स यजत्यग्न आज्यस्य व्यन्तुं[१९] वौषळित्यग्निमाज्यस्य वेतु वौषळित्यग्निनाज्यस्य व्यन्तु वौषळित्यग्निराज्यस्य वेतु वौषळिति ॥ १५ ॥

अथ स्वाहाग्निं स्वाहाग्निं पवमानमिति यद्यग्नये पवमानाय ध्रियेरन्त्स्वाहाग्निमिन्दुमन्तमिति यद्यग्नय इन्दुमते ध्रियेरन्त्स्वाहाग्नीनाज्यपाञ्जुषाणा अग्नय आज्यपा[२०] आज्यस्य व्यन्तु वौषळित्येवमेतान्प्रयाजान्त्सर्वानाग्नेयान्करोति ॥ १६ ॥

अथाहाग्नयेऽनुब्रूहीत्याग्नेयमाज्यभाग[२१]ं सोऽन्वाहाग्निं स्तोमेन बोधय समिधानो अमर्त्यम् । हव्या देवेषु नो दधदिति स्वपितीव स्विद्वा एतद्यदुद्वासितो भवति बोधयत्येवैनमेतत्समुद्दीपयति जुषाणो अग्निराज्यस्य वेत्विति यजति ॥ १७ ॥

१४. सोऽन्त्तर्हितो TE, Co, Ca.

१५. Should have been निष्कैवल्यं.

१६. करिष्य TE.

१७. Should have been निष्कैवल्यं.

१८. तत्र TE.

१९. See Notes.

२०. आज्यपा Ca. P1, H.

२१. त्याग्नेय TE.

12. One need not favour that (practice), for it becomes covered indeed by the nights. Then he offers this oblation *(puroḍāśa)* cooked in five potsherds and dedicated to Agni. For it, the offering *mantras* and (connected) subsequent utterances *(Yājyās* and *anuvākyās)* are in *Paṅkti* (metre) with five *pādas* (feet); for, the seasons are five. He (Agni) entered the seasons. He (the sacrificer) thus produces this (fire) from the very seasons.

13. The whole (sacrifice) belongs to Agni. That way, indeed, Tvaṣṭṛ reached the favourite abode of Agni. They perform it with this (formula), in a low voice, what one is going to do purely for his relatives or friends, he is verily secretive with it. This (which is uttered in) –a low voice is indeed like a secret.

The other sacrifice belongs to all the gods. But this that belongs to Agni is special. The last 'subsequent offering' he (the sacrificer) offers in a loud voice. Then, indeed, he becomes, as it were, one who has done his work. Every one understands that it has been done (completed).

14. When the Adhvaryu, having stepped beyond and having called (drawn attention) says, "Worship (offer) (pronounce the offering prayer for) *'Samidhs'*, it is, indeed, the form of Agni and it appears to be indirect. There one should say (directly) only "Worship the Agnis".

15. Then he recites (in worship) "Oh! Agni! May they *(Samidhs)* well reach (accept) the *ghee* ". "*Vauṣaṭ* ". May he accept the fire of the *ghee*". *vauṣaṭ*". May they accept the *ghee* through Agni". "*Vauṣaṭ* ". or "May Agni accept the *ghee*". "*Vauṣaṭ*".

16. Then he says, *"Svāhāgnim"*. *"Svāhāgnim Pavamānam"*. If they decide on (offering it to) *Agni Pavamāna*. If they decide on (offering it to) *Agni-Indumat* -(he says) "*Svāhāgnim indumantam*". He (the sacrificer) makes all these principal sacrificial ceremonies dedicated to Agni, (uttering) "*Svāhāgnīm-ajyapām*" *(Svāhā;* the fires that consume *ghee*) "May the Agnis, drinkers of *ghee,* coming together (being pleased), accept the *ghee*", *"Vauṣaṭ"*.

17. Then he says, "Pronounce the inviting prayer for Agni ", with regard to Agni's portion of *ghee*. He (the Hotṛ) recites (following this instruction), "Wake up Agni" with praise, enkindling him the immortal, so that he takes our offerings to the gods". Indeed, having been removed, he (Agni) appears to sleep. He wakes him thus and makes him blaze up. He makes the offering, saying "May Agni be pleased and may he accept the *ghee*".

अथाहाग्नये पवमानायानुब्रूहीति यद्यग्नये पवमानाय ध्रियेरन्त्सोऽन्वाहाग्न आयूꣳषि पवस आसुवोर्जमिषं च नः । आरे बाधस्व दुच्छुनामिति तथा[२२]हाग्नेयो भवति सोमो वै पवमानो नो सौम्यादाज्यभागाद्यन्ति जुषाणो अग्निः पवमान आज्यस्य वेत्विति यजति ॥ १८ ॥

अथाहाग्नय इन्दुमतेऽनुब्रूहीति यद्यग्नय इन्दुमते ध्रियेरन्त्सोऽन्वाहेह्यूषु ब्रवाणि तेऽग्न इत्थेतरा गिरः । एभिर्वर्धास इन्दुभिरिति तथाहाग्नेयो[२३] भवति सोमो वा इन्दुर्नो सौम्यादाज्य-भागाद्यन्ति जुषाणो अग्निरिन्दुमानाज्यस्य वेत्विति यजति ॥ १९ ॥

अथाहाग्नयेऽनुब्रूहीत्यग्निं यजेत्यग्नये स्विष्टकृतेऽनुब्रूह्यग्निꣳ स्विष्टकृतं यजेति[२४] ॥ २० ॥

स यत्राध्वर्युरतिक्रम्याश्राव्याह देवान्यजेत्यग्नीन्यजेति हैव तत्र ब्रूयात् ॥ २१ ॥

स यजत्यग्नेर्वसुवने वसुधेयस्य[२५] वेतु वौषळिति अग्ना उ वसुवने वसुधेयस्य वेतु वौषळिति देवो अग्निः स्विष्टकृदिति स्वयमाग्नेयस्तृतीयोऽनुयाजः ॥ २२ ॥

ता वा एताः · षड्विभक्तयश्चतस्रः प्रयाजेषु द्वे अनुयाजेषु षड्वा ऋतव ऋतून्प्राविश-दृतुभ्य एवैनमेतन्निर्मिमीते तासाꣳ षण्णां विभक्तीनां द्वादश वा त्रयोदश वाक्षराणि द्वादश वा वै त्रयोदश वा संवत्सरस्य मासाः संवत्सर ऋतून्प्राविशदृतुभ्य एवैनमेतन्निर्मिमीते न द्वे[२६] चन सह करोति जामि हि कुर्याद्यद्द्वे[२७] चित्सह कुर्याद्वेतु व्यन्त्विति प्रयाजानाꣳ रूपं वसुवने वसुधेयस्य वेत्वि[२८]त्यनुयाजानाꣳ हिरण्यं दक्षिणाग्नेयोऽयं यज्ञोऽग्नेर्हि रेतो हिरण्यम-

२२. तथा V2, Ca.

२३. तथा हाग्नियो TE; तथाहाग्नेयो Ca.

२४. कृतं यजेते वषट्कृते जुहोति; Excess in M only.

२५. वसुधेय TE.

२६. द्वै P1, P2, TE.

२७. द्यद्वे TE, P1, P2.

२८. वेत्वेत्यनु P1, P2.

18. Then he says, if they decide on (offering to) *Agni-Pavamāna,* "Make the call for *Agni-Pavamāna*". Then he(Hotṛ) says,"Oh Agni! you breath (blow) life. Please produce for us food and strength. Drive far away misfortune". Thus indeed, it becomes of Agni. Soma indeed is the *Pavamāna* (the purifier). (The Soma elements) do not go away from the *ghee* portion belonging to Soma. "May *Agni-Pavamāna* being pleased, accept the *ghee!*" So he recites (on making the offering).

19. If they decide on (offering to) *'Agni-Indumat'* he says, "Make the call for *'Agni-Indumat'*". He(Hotā) says, following this, "Come here, Oh Agni! I shall gladly say these and other words (of praise). May you grow with these drops." Then, indeed does it become of (dedicated to) Agni. Soma, indeed, is Indu (the drop). They (the Soma elements) do not go away from the portion of *ghee* belonging to Soma. He recites, in worship, "May *Agni-Indumat* (possessor of drops), being pleased, accept the *ghee*".

20. Then he says, "Make the call for Agni".
"Worship (recite the offering prayers to) Agni".
"Make the call for *Agni Sviṣṭakṛt.*(who makes the offerings well offered)".
"Recite the offering prayers to *Agni Sviṣṭakṛt*".

21. Where the Adhvaryu (priest) over-stepping (these) and calling attention says "Worship(recite the prayers) for the gods," there he should verily say (recite the prayers for) "worship Agnis".

22. He recites "May it *(Barhis)* accept (the offering) for Agni re-acquisition of abundant wealth"."*Vauṣaṭ*". "The divine *Agni Sviṣṭakṛt*". This third subsequent offering by itself belongs to Agni.

23. These are indeed the six case-forms. Four (are used) in primary offerings and two in after-offerings. Verily six are the seasons. He (Agni) entered the seasons. He, thus, produces him (Agni) only from the seasons. Of the six case-forms, there are twelve or thirteen syllables. Indeed twelve or thirteen are the months of the year. The year entered the seasons. He (Agni) entered the year, the seasons. He verily produces him (Agni) from the seasons. He does not put two together. Should he perform two together, he would be doing a fault. The form of (usage of) primary offerings is "May it accept". "May they accept". The form of (expression) after-offerings is "May it accept for abundant acquisition of riches" Gold is the sacrificial fee. This sacrifice verily belongs to Agni. Indeed gold is the seed of Agni. Or it (the sacrificial fee) is an ox. Verily

नड्वान्वानड्वान्हि वहसाग्नेयोऽग्न्यवदग्र्धमिव[२९] ह्यनळुहो वहो भवति देवानाꣳ हव्यवाह-नोऽग्निर्वहत्येष मनुष्येभ्यः ॥ २३ ॥ इति तृतीयं ब्राह्मणम् ॥

चतुर्थं ब्राह्मणम्

प्रजापतिर्ह वा इदमेक एवास स हेक्षां चक्रे कथं नु प्रजायेयेति सोऽश्राम्यत्स तपोऽतप्यत सोऽग्निमेव मुखाज्जनयां चक्रे तस्माद्वा अग्निरन्नादो मुखाद्धि जातो मुखेन ह्यन्नमद्यते ॥ १ ॥

स वा एषोऽग्रे देवतानामजायत तस्मादग्निर्नामाग्निर्ह[१] वै नामैतद्यदग्निरित्याहुः स उ जातः पूर्वः प्रेयाय तद्वैवास्य द्वितीयमग्निर्त्वं[२] पूर्वꣳ हि यन्तमाहुरग्र एतीति ॥ २ ॥

तस्माद्ध प्रजापतिर्बिभयांचकारान्नादं वा इममजीजन आत्मनो नो वा इहान्यदन्नमस्ति यं वा अयं नाद्यादिति काल्वालीकृतो हेयं तर्हि पृथिव्यास तद्धैवास्य[३] मनस्यासाथैनमग्नि-र्व्यात्तेनोपपर्यावर्त तस्य भीतस्य स्वो महिमापचक्राम वाग्वै स्वो महिमा वाग्घैवास्मादप-चक्राम[४] स आत्मन्येवाहुतिमियेष स इत्युदमृष्ट तस्मादिदं चालोमकमिदं च तत्रो एव विवेद घृताहुतिं वा पय आहुतिं वोभयं त्वेव तत्पयः ॥ ३ ॥

सा हास्मै न छदयांचकार केशमिश्रेव हास तामोषं[५] धयेति व्यौक्षत्तत ओषधयः संबभूवुस्तस्मादोषधयो नाम स द्वितीयमुदमृष्ट तत्रो एव विवेद घृताहुतिं वा पय आहुतिं वोभयं त्वेव तत्पयः ॥ ४ ॥

२९. दग्धमिव TE.

१. दग्निर्नामाग्निर्ह V1.

२. मग्नित्वं My, P1, P2, H.

३. तद्धैवास K.

४. तस्मादपक्राम P1.

५. तामोषधयेति TE; तामोषं Co; see Notes.

the ox is related to Agni, by its shoulder. The shoulder of the ox looks as if it is burnt by fire. Agni is the carrier of the oblations to the gods. This ox carries (burdens) for the sake of men.

(Third Brāhmaṇa Ends)

BRĀHMAṆA IV

1. Prajāpati alone existed here. He saw (thought),"How can I be born (become abundant progeny)?"He toiled. He performed penance. He produced Agni, indeed, from his mouth. Therefore, it is that Agni is a consumer of food. For, he was born from the mouth. Indeed, it is by the mouth that food is eaten.

2. This (Agni) was born before the gods. Therefore he is known as Agri. It is indeed Agri which they say 'Agni'. Being born, he went at first (ahead). That indeed is his second 'ahead-ness/firstness'. They say (of) one who goes at first (before others) 'he goes ahead'.

3. Of him, indeed, was Prajāpati afraid. "I have created this (fire) as a food-consumer. There is no food here, except myself, which he will not eat". Then this earth was as if rendered bald. This was verily (disturbing) in his mind. Then Agni turned towards him with an open mouth. As he (Prajāpati) was frightened, his greatness departed away (from him). His own greatness was, indeed, 'speech'. It was verily speech that went out of him. He wished for an offering in his own self. He thus rubbed (his hands).Therefore this (palm) is hairless and so is this (other palm) too. There he obtained (knew/considered)a *ghee*-offering or a milk-offering. Indeed both are milk.

4. It was not pleasing to him. It was as though mixed with hair. He poured it away saying, "*Oṣamdhaya*" "Drink it hot". From that were born the plants. Hence they are known as '*Oṣadhayaḥ*'. He rubbed his hands a second time. Then he obtained (found) a *ghee*-offering or a milk-offering. Both indeed are milk.

साहास्मै छदयां चकार स ह प्रजापतिर्व्यचिकित्सज्जुहवानी[6] मा हौषा[7]मिति तꣳ स्वो महिमाभ्युवाद जुहुधीति स विदां चकार स्वो वै मा महिमाह जुहुधीत्याहेति स स्वाहेत्येव जुहवां चकार तत एवासा उदियाय योऽसौ तपति ततोऽयं प्रबभूव योऽयं पवते ततोऽग्निः शान्तः पराङ्[8]पर्यावव्रतैष उ एव स्वाहाकारस्य बन्धुस्तस्मादप्येतर्हि स्वाहेत्येवं[9] जुह्वति ॥ ५ ॥

स एवꣳ हुत्वा प्रजापतिः प्र चाजायताग्नेश्च मृत्योरत्स्यत आत्मानमत्रायतैवꣳ ह वाव प्रजायत एवमग्नेर्मृत्योरत्स्यत आत्मानं त्रायते य एवमेतद्वेद ॥ ६ ॥

तं यत्रां[10]दोऽभ्यादधति यथा मातुर्वोपस्थात्पितुर्वा संभवेदेवꣳ हैव संभवति शरीरꣳ हैवास्य दहति तस्मादाहुर्नानाहिताग्निः संभवतीति स यत्र हुत्वोपामृष्ट ततो विकंकतः संबभूव स वा एष वृक्षो यज्ञियो यज्ञपा[11]त्रियोह्येतद्वेव विचिकित्सायाः जन्म यः प्रजापतिर्व्यचिकित्सत्स वै स श्रेयस्य[12]ध्रियत यः प्र चाजायताग्नेश्च मृत्योरत्स्यत आत्मानमत्रायत श्रेयसि ह वाव ध्रियते विचिकित्सन्य एवमेतद्वेद ॥ ७ ॥

ते वा एते वीरा देवानामजायन्तायमग्निर्योऽयं पवते सूर्य आ ह वा अस्य वीरो जायते य एतान्वीरान्देवानां वेद ॥ ८ ॥

ते होचुरस्मान्प्रजापतिः पिताजीजनते[13]ति हन्त वयं तज्जनयामहै यदस्मानन्वसदिति ते ह गायत्रेण तुष्टुविरेऽपहिंकारेण परिवृ[14]त्य ते यत्पर्यवृण्वन्त्सोऽयꣳ समुद्र इयमेव पृथिव्यास्तावस्ते ह प्राञ्च उच्चक्रमुः पुनरेम इत्येद्गां जाताꣳ सा हैनानुदीक्ष्य हिंचकार ते विदांचक्रुरेष

६. See Notes on I-1-1-2; जुहवानी ३ in Mss.

७. See Notes on I-1-1-2; हौषा ३ in Mss.

८. परावव्रतैष Ca., M.L.T.

९. स्वाहेत्येव Ca.

१०. तं यत्रा TE, V1, Ca.

११. पात्र्यो Ca.

१२. श्रेयस्य V1.

१३. जीजनदिति V1.

१४. परिवत्य Ca.

5. It was pleasing to him. Prajāpati then doubted, "Shall I offer?" "Shall I not offer?" His greatness addressed him, "Offer." He realized that his own greatness had indeed said, "Offer". He offered (the oblation) saying only "*Svāhā*." From it verily arose the yonder one (Sun) who burns. Then arose this one that blows (the wind). Thereupon Agni becoming calm turned away. This is indeed the significance of *svāhākāra*. Therefore, too, even now they offer the oblations only uttering "*Svāhā*".

6. That Prajāpati, having thus made the offering came to be born (again) (produced progeny) and saved himself from Agni, death, who would have devoured him. Thus indeed one who knows this to be so is born and thus verily saves himself from Agni, the devouring death.

7. Where they place him therefrom (from the fire) would he come into being just as one would be born out of the genitals of the father and of the mother. It (the fire) burns up only his body. Therefore they say, "One who has not performed *Agnihotra* does not come into being". Where he (Prajāpati) rubbed (his hands) after making the offering, from there a *vikaṅkata* (tree) sprung forth. This is the very tree that is suitable for sacrifice and for sacrificial vessels. Indeed this is the origin of doubt. Prajāpati who doubted remained steadfast in well-being. He (Prajāpati) who was born saves himself from Agni, the devouring death. He who after doubting knows this to be so is maintained verily in 'good' (welfare).

8. These are the heroes who were born among gods; this fire, this one (wind) that blows and the Sun. Indeed to him, who knows these to be heroes among gods, a (virile) son is born.

9. They said, "Prajāpati, our father, produced us". "Ha! let us produce that which will take after us". They verily praised (with *mantras*) in *Gāyatrī* metre, changing it , to be without the sound 'Him' . What surrounded, that was this ocean. This very earth was the ground where the praise was sung. Then went forth eastward, saying, "Let us come again". They came upon a cow that had just been born. Looking at them she uttered the sound 'Him' . They realized ' This ' indeed is the sound 'Him' of the *Sāman* (musical rendering of *Ṛks*). Thereafter the *Sāman* chants came to be with the sound 'Him' . Before then

वाव साम्नो हिंकार इति ततो हार्वाक्सहिंकाराणि सामान्यपहिंकाराणि हैव ततः पुरा[१५] बभूवुस्तस्माद्धै गौरुपजीवनीया साम्नो हि हिंकारं बिभर्त्युपजीवनीयो ह वाव भवति य एतꣳ साम्नो हिंकारं वेद ॥ ९ ॥

ते होचुर्भद्रं वा इदम्[१६]जीजनामहि य इमामजीजनामहीत्यन्नꣳ ह्यजनयन्त न ह्यृतेग्वन्नमस्ति यज्ञꣳ ह्यजनयन्त न ह्यृते गुर्यज्ञस्तायते तद्धैतदेव यज्ञस्य नाम यदेतासां तस्माद्भद्रं पुण्यमिति[१७] परिहरेदुपनामुको हैनं यज्ञो[१८] भवति बह्व्यो हास्यैता भवन्ति य एवं विद्वान्भद्रं पुण्यमिति परिहरति ॥ १० ॥

ताꣳ हाग्निरभिदध्यौ मिथुन्येनाꣳ स्यामिति ताꣳ संबभूव तस्याꣳ रेतः प्रसिषेच तत्पयोऽग्नेर्हि वा एतद्रेतस्तस्मादेता आमाः सत्यः शृतं दुहते तस्मान्नानारूपाः सत्यः सदृशमेव दुहतेऽग्नि[१९]संकाशमग्नेर्हि रेतस्तस्मात्प्रथमदुग्धमुष्णमिव भवत्यग्नेरेतसꣳ हि ॥ ११ ॥

ते होचुर्जुहवामहा इदं प्रेदं जनयामहा इति स होवाचाग्निर्मह्यमेव प्रथमाय जुहुतेति मह्यमिति योऽयं पवते मह्यमितिं सूर्यस्ते होचुरसंपादयन्तः प्रजापतिं पितरं प्रत्ययामेति यस्मै स आह तस्मै प्रथमाय जुहवामेति ॥ १२ ॥

स होवाच प्रजापतिरग्नय एव प्रथमाय जुहुतेति स स्वꣳ रेतोऽनुष्ठ्या प्रजनयिष्यत इति सूर्याय प्रातरित्यथ यदेव हूयमानस्य व्यश्नुषे तत्तवेतीममुवाच योऽयं पवते तदप्येतर्हि तथैव जुह्वत्यग्नय एव सायꣳ सूर्याय प्रातरथ यदेव हूयमानस्य व्यश्नुते तदेतस्य य एष पवते त एवं जुह्वतो देवा इमां प्रजातिं प्राजायन्त येयमेषां प्रजातिरिमां जितिमजयन्येयमेषां जितिरिमां विजितिं व्यजयन्ताग्निरेवेमं लोकमजयद्योऽयं पवते सोऽन्तरिक्षं दिवमेव सूर्यः

१५. पुरा Ca.
१६. इमम M.
१७. पुण्यमित TE.
१८. यज्ञं P1.
१९. तेऽग्नि TE.

they had indeed been without the sound "Him". Therefore indeed is the cow to be depended upon for living. She verily bears the sound 'Him' of the *Sāman*. He who knows this (to be) the sound 'Him' of the *Sāmans* verily becomes one who is to be resorted to for living (who becomes the support of life).

10. They said, "We who have produced this thing (cow) have indeed produced an auspicious thing". They verily produced food. Indeed there is no food without the cow. They indeed created the sacrifice. For indeed the sacrifice is not performed without the cow. Therefore this (cow) is verily the name of the sacrifice. This which is (the name) of these (cows). Therefore one should avoid (disrespect or harm to) it (the sacrifice, the cow), thinking, "(This is) auspicious". "(This is) meritorious." The sacrifice inclines towards (favours) him, indeed and these (cows) surely become many, for him who avoids (them) (disrespecting or harming them) thinking, "(This is) auspicious". (This is) meritorious".

11. Verily Agni coveted her (the cow) (and thought), "May I pair with her". He united with her. He deposited his semen in her. That is the milk. Indeed it (the milk) is the semen of Agni. Therefore these cows, being raw (not hot) yield (milk) what is cooked (warm). Therefore, being of different forms, (yet) they yield similarly (the same form of milk). It (the milk) shines like fire. Indeed it is the seed of Agni. Therefore what is first milked appears to be hot. For it is Agni's seed.

12. They (the men) said, "Let us offer this oblation (milk), let us produce this well". He, Agni said, "Offer (oblations) to me, verily who am the first ", "To me" (said) this (god) who blows (the wind). The Sun said, "To me". Not making it up (not coming to an understanding), they said, "Let us go to our father, Prajāpati. Let us offer milk to him, the first, to whom he (Prajāpati) says (we should offer)".

13. He, Prajāpati, verily said, "Offer (oblations/milk) only to Agni the first". "He will employ his seed and will produce (will be reproduced)". "At dawn (offer) to the Sun". "What (part) of (the oblation) that is offered, you consume; that (will be) yours." So he (Prajāpati) told this (god) who blows (wind) . They offer (the oblations/milk) even now the same way, only to Agni in the evening, (only) to the Sun in the morning. And whatever (portion) of the oblation is

स य एवं विद्वान्[२०]जुहोत्येताꣳ हैव प्रजातिं प्रजायत एतां जितिं जयत्येतेषाꣳ सलोको भवति ॥ १३ ॥ इति चतुर्थं ब्राह्मणम् ॥

इति एकपात्काण्डे द्वितीयोऽध्यायः

२०. विद्वा Ca.

offered he appropriates. That belongs to this one (wind) who blows. Those gods, offering (oblations) like this, came to be born in this form of birth that is theirs; they attained this victory which is theirs. They won this great victory. It was verily Agni who conquered this world; this one (wind) who blows (conquered) the mid region and the Sun (conquered) verily the sky. He who, offers (oblations), understanding this, is indeed born in this very form of birth (as of the three gods), wins this victory (as of the three gods) and becomes one (residing) in the same world (as the three gods).

(Fourth Brāhmaṇa Ends)

(Chapter Two ends)

तृतीयोऽध्यायः

प्रथमं ब्राह्मणम्

सूर्यो ह वा अग्निहोत्रꣳ स यदेतस्या आहुतेरग्र उदैत्तस्माद्ध सूर्य ए[1]वाग्निहोत्रं तद्यदस्त-
मिते जुह्वति य इदं तस्मिन्निह सति जुहवामेत्यथ यत्पुरोदेतोर्जुह्वति प्रातर्य इदं तस्मिन्निह
सति जुहवामेति स वा एषोऽस्तं यन्नग्निमेव योनिं गर्भो भूत्वा प्रविशति तं गर्भं
भवन्तमिमाः सर्वाः प्रजा अनु गर्भो भवन्तीळिता इव हि शेरतेऽसंजानाना अथ यद्रात्रिस्तिर
एव तत्कुरुते तिर इव हि गर्भः ॥ १ ॥

स यत्सायं जुहोति गर्भमेवैनं तत्सन्तमभिकरोति गर्भाꣳ सन्तमभिजुहोति तस्मादन-
श्नन्तो गर्भा जीवन्त्यथ यत्प्रातर्जुहोति[2] प्रैवैनं तज्जनयति स एष तेजो भूत्वा विभ्रा[3]ꣳशमान
उदयते शश्वद्ध नोदियाद्यदस्मिन्नेतामाहुतिं न जुहुयुः स यथाहिस्त्वचो निर्मुच्येतैवꣳ रात्रेः
सर्वस्मात्पाप्मनो निर्मुच्योदयते यथा ह वा अहिस्त्वचो निर्मुच्येतैवꣳ सर्वस्मात्पाप्मनो
निर्मुच्यते य एवमेतद्वेद तं जायमानमिमाः सर्वाः प्रजा अनु प्रजायन्ते विसृज्यन्ते हि
यथार्थान्[4] ॥ २ ॥

तदाहुः पुरास्तमेतोरुद्धरेदित्येते वाव रश्मयो विश्वेदेवा अथ यत्परं भाति प्रजापतिर्वैव
स इन्द्रो वा ते हैतेऽस्तं यन्तोऽग्निहोत्रमेव जुह्वतो गृहानभ्यागच्छन्ति ते[5]ऽस्याहवनीयमेव
प्रविशन्ति स यथा श्रेयसेऽभ्यागमिष्यत आवसथमुपकल्पयेदेवमेतत्ते यस्योद्धृतमा-
ग[6]च्छन्ति तस्य प्रविशन्त्यथ यस्यानुद्धृतमप ह तस्मात्प्रयन्ति तस्मै वै व्यृ[7]ध्यते यस्मादेवा

१. एवा Ca.

२. र्जुहोति TE.

३. विभ्लाश M.

४ यथार्थानाम् Ca. and all Mss except V1 and B; see Notes.

५. तस्याह P.

६. मागच्छ TE, B.

७. व्युध्यते TE, K.

Chapter Three

BRĀHMAṆA I

1. The Sun is indeed *Agnihotra*. It is because he rose ahead of this offering that the Sun is himself *Agrihotra* (= *Agnihotra*). That they offer (oblation) after sunset, thinking, "Let us offer while he (the Sun) is here ", and that they offer before sunrise in the morning, thinking, "Let us offer while he is here" (is because of this?) He (this Sun), as he sets, verily enters Agni, the source (genetals) becoming an embryo. Following him who becomes an embryo all these creatures became embryos. Indeed they lie down as if coaxed and unaware (of anything). That the night verily covers (conceals) that is because the embryo is, as it were, indeed covered.

2. That he, (the sacrificer) offers (oblation) in the evening, he does it for the sake of this (Sun) who is an embryo (in the womb); he offers it for the sake of what is an embryo. Therefore, the embryos here live (survive) without eating food. What he offers in the morning, that produces (regenerates) this (Sun) well. He (the Sun) becoming a light, rises shining brilliantly. If they do not offer this oblation, surely he would not rise. Just as a snake is freed from its slough, in the same manner does he (the Sun) rise freeing himself from all evil of the night. He who knows this to be so, will be freed from all evil. All creatures are born after him (the Sun) who is born; they are set free indeed according to their purposes.

3. About this, they say, "One should take out the (*Āhavanīya* from *Gārhapatya*) before the setting (of the Sun). These rays are verily all the gods. What shines afterwards (high up)– that indeed is Prajāpati or Indra. All those gods, setting (disappearing) come only to the residence of the person who performs *Agnihotra*. They enter verily his *Āhavanīya*. This is just as one would prepare a residing place, for his (own) welfare, for a (revered) guest who is to arrive. They enter his (residence) whose *(Āhavanīya)* has been taken out. They go away from him whose *(Āhavanīya)* has not been taken out. From whom the Gods go away,

अप प्रयन्ति तामनु व्यृद्धिं यश्चैतद्वेद यश्च नानुद्धृतमस्याभ्यस्तमगादिति सर्व एव निन्दति ॥ ३ ॥

स यत्सायं जुहोत्यग्नावेवैभ्यस्तत्प्रविष्टेभ्यो जुहोत्यथ यत्प्रातर्जुहोत्यप्रेतेभ्य एवैभ्यस्तज्जुहोति तस्माद्वयं मन्यामह उदितहोमिनो व्यवच्छिन्नमग्निहोत्रमिति होवाचासुरिर्यथा शून्यमावसथमाहरेदेवमेतदिति ॥ ४ ॥

द्वयमु वा इदं न तृतीयमस्ति मूलि चैवामूलं च तदुभयं देवानाꣳ सन्मनुष्या उपजीवन्ति मूलिन्य इमा ओषधयोऽमूलाः पशवस्त इमेऽमूलाः पशवो मूलिनीरोषधीर्जग्ध्वापः पीत्वा तस्यैष उभयस्य रसः संभवति ॥ ५ ॥

स यत्सायं जुहोत्यस्य रसस्य जीवनस्य देवेभ्यो जुहवामेति यदेषामिदꣳ सदुपजीवाम इति स यत्ततो रात्र्याश्नाति हुतोच्छिष्टमेव तन्निरवत्तबल्यश्नाति हुतोच्छिष्टस्योह्यशिताग्निहोत्रं जुह्वदथ यत्प्रातर्जुहोत्यस्य रसस्य जीवनस्य देवेभ्यो जुहवामेति यदेषामिदꣳ सदुपजीवाम इति स यत्ततोऽह्नाश्नाति हुतोच्छिष्टमेव तन्निरवत्तबल्यश्नाति हुतोच्छिष्टस्योह्यशिताग्निहोत्रं जुह्वदथ यत्प्रातर्जुहोत्यस्य रसस्य जीवनस्य देवेभ्यो जुहवामेति यदेषामिदꣳ सदुपजीवाम इति स यत्ततोऽह्नाश्नाति हुतोच्छिष्टमेव तन्निरवत्तबल्यश्नाति हुतोच्छिष्टस्योह्यशिताग्निहोत्रं जुह्वत्[८] ॥ ६ ॥

तद्वै समेवान्ये यज्ञास्तिष्ठन्तेऽग्निहोत्रमेव न संतिष्ठतेऽपि वै द्वादशसंवत्सरमन्तवदेवाथैतत्सायꣳ हुत्वा वेद होष्याम्येव[९] प्रातरिति प्रातर्हुत्वा वेद होष्याम्येव सायमित्येतस्यानुपस्थितिमन्वनुपस्थिता इमाः प्रजाः प्रजायन्तेऽनुपस्थितो ह वै श्रिया प्रजया प्रजायते य एवमेतद्वेद तद्दुग्ध्वाधिश्रयति शृतꣳ हि देवानाम् ॥ ७ ॥

तदाहुर्यदोद[१०]न्तमिव स्यादथ जुहुयात्तर्हि ह्येतच्छृतं भवतीति तदु तथा न कुर्यादुपहैनत्स दहेद्यस्तथा कुर्यादप्रजनिष्णु वै रेत उपदग्धं तस्मादधिश्रित्यैव जुहुयादग्नेरु वा एतद्रेतस्तेनो

८. जुह्वत् TE.

९. होष्यामेव TE.

१०. See Notes.

to him occurs ruin (adversity /decline). Following that decline, every one censures that non-taking out (of the *Āhavanīya*) of one who knows this and who does not, has gone towards (caused) the setting (of the Sun).

4. "What he offers in the evening into Agni, he offers verily to these (gods) who have entered into it. And what he offers in the morning, he verily offers it to these (gods) who have not yet departed. Therefore, we think that the *Agnihotra* of one who offers (oblation) after sunrise is broken (cut off)"–so said Āsuri, "Just as one might take (food) to an empty house".

5. This (world of food) is twofold– there is no third (variety)–viz., what has root and what is rootless. Men live by resorting to both which belong to the gods. These plants have roots. These animals (cattle) have no roots. These rootless animals eat the rooted plants and drink water; (therefrom) then arises this juice of both (milk).

6. He offers (oblation) in the evening thinking, "Let us offer to the gods this life-giving juice and let us live upon this (good thing) that belongs to these (gods)". What he eats, there, from that night; he eats verily the left over from what has been offered and portions of which have been distributed (to beings). The person who performs *Agnihotra* is indeed the eater of the left over from what has been offered (to the gods). And he offers in the morning thinking, "Let us offer to the gods this juice that gives life and let us subsist on this that belongs to these (gods)". What he then eats during day time from that, he eats verily the left over from what has been offered and portions of which have been distributed (to beings). For, the performer of *Agnihotra* is indeed the eater of the left over from what has been offered (to the gods).

7. It is sure that other sacrifices come to an end; only *Agnihotra* does not come to an end. Even the twelve-year thing (ritual) (sacrifice) has an end. But he (the sacrificer) performing *Agnihotra* having offered (oblation in *Agnihotra*) in the evening knows (thinks),"I am surely going to offer in the morning". Having offered in the morning he knows "I am surely going to offer in the evening". Following this endlessness, these creatures are born endlessly. He who knows this to be so is born endlessly with prosperity and progeny. Milking that (milk) he (the sacrificer) heats it on the fire. For cooked food (is meant) for gods.

8. About this they say, "When it rises to the brim (on boiling), then one may offer it. Then it becomes cooked, indeed". One need not do it so. For this will scorch him,who may do so. Verily the seed that is burnt becomes incapable of reproduction. Therefore one should offer (the milk) only warming it up. This

वा एतच्छृतं यदग्ने रेतस्तस्मादधिश्रित्यैव जुहुयादथ [11]यद्वैनदग्नावधिश्रयन्ति तेनो एव शृतं तस्मादधिश्रित्यैव जुहुयात् ॥ ८ ॥

तदवज्योतयति शृतं वेदानीत्यपः प्रत्यानयत्यग्निरेतसं वा एतच्छान्तिरापः शान्तय एव तस्माद्यद्येनमासक्तिपानं क्षीरमभ्याभवेदुदस्तोकमाश्चोतयेत्येव ब्रूयाच्छान्तये पयसश्चैव सर्वत्वायेदꣳ हि यदा वर्षत्यथौषधयो जायन्त ओषधीर्जग्ध्वापः पीत्वा तस्यैष उभयस्य रसः संभवति तस्मादुदस्तोकं प्रत्यानयति ॥ ९ ॥

उद्वास्य चतुरुन्नयति चतुर्धा विहितꣳ हीदं पयः समिधमादायोदाद्रवति समिद्धहोमाय सोऽनुपसाद्य पूर्वामाहुतिं जुहोति यद्धोपसाद्य जुहुयाद्यथा यस्मा [12]आहरिष्यन्त्स्यात्ततो [13]न्वन्तरेण निदध्यादेवꣳ ह तदथ यदनुपसाद्य जुहोति यथा यस्मा [14]आहरिष्यन्त्स्यात्तस्मा आहृत्यैवोपनिदध्यादेवं तदुपसाद्योत्तरां नानावीर्ये एवैने एतत्करोति [15]मनश्चैव वाक्चैते आहुती मनश्चैवैत[16]द्वाचं च व्यावर्तयति तस्मान्मनश्च वाक्च समानमेव सन्नानेव ॥ १० ॥

स वै द्विर्जुहोति द्विरुपमृष्टे द्विः प्राश्नाति चतुरुन्नयति तद्दश दशाक्षरा वै विराड्विराळु वै यज्ञो विराजमेवैतद्यज्ञमभिसंपादयति ॥ ११ ॥

स यदग्नौ जुहोति तद्देवेषु जुहोति तस्माद्देवाः सन्ति यदुपमृष्टे तदोषधिषु च पितृषु च जुहोति तस्मादोषधयश्च पितरश्च सन्ति यत्प्राश्नाति तन्मनुष्येषु [17]जुह्वति तस्मान्मनुष्याः सन्ति मनुष्याननु पशवो देवाननु वयाꣳस्योषधयो वनस्पतयो यदिदं किंचान्यदेवम्विमाः प्रजा [18]यज्ञ आभजति या इमा अपराभूताः ॥ १२ ॥

११. यद्वै TE.

१२. आहरि TE, B,K.

१३. त्वन्तरेण Ca., see Notes.

१४. आहरि TE, B,K.

१५. मनश्च ह वै M; मनश्च वै Ca.

१६. श्चैवत K.

१७. जुहोति M., Ca.

१८. यश V1; see Notes.

(milk) is indeed the seed of Agni. Therefore, this seed of Agni is warm (warmed by Agni himself). Therefore one should offer it only after warming it up (on fire). Or since they put it over the fire, thereby itself it becomes cooked. Therefore one should offer it only after warming it up (over the fire).

9. He illumines it thinking, "Let me know if it has been heated". He pours water (into the milk). This (milk) is indeed the seed Waters are (represent) calmness (pacification).(This pouring of water into the boiling milk) is for pacification (making the milk calm down). Therefore, if milk, the much desired drink, should come to this person, then he should say verily, "Sprinkle a little water". This is indeed, for the calming down of the (hot) milk and for its fullness. When it rains here, then the plants spring up. (On the cattle) having eaten the plants and having drunk water, this (milk), the juice of both of these (plants and cattle)is produced. Therefore one adds a little water (into the milk).

10. Removing (the milk from the fire), he (the sacrificer) ladles out four times, for this milk has been produced in four ways (by the four teats of the udder). He then takes a kindling stick *(Samidh)* and rushes (to the *Āhavanīya*) for making the offering in the kindled (fire). He makes the first offering without placing down (the wooden spoon). Should he offer (the oblation) after placing it down,it would be just as if one taking food for somebody places it down in the middle (before reaching him). Then, that he offers without placing it down is just as if one taking food for somebody places it down only after taking it to him. After placing it down (he offers) the second offering. This makes these two (offerings) to be of different (kinds of) vigour. These, two offerings are mind and speech. This (offering one oblation without placing the spoon down and the other oblation after placing it down) seperates the mind and the speech. Therefore, the mind and the speech, being verily alike, appear as if they are different.

11. He offers twice, wipes twice, drinks (of the milk) twice and ladles out four times. This makes ten. Indeed *Virāṭ* (metre) has ten syllables (per foot). The sacrifice is verily *Virāṭ* (shining much).This (ten-fold action) brings about this bright sacrifice.

12. That he offers into the fire (means) he offers to the gods. Therefore the gods are (present at the sacrifice). What he wipes that he offers to the plants and manes. Therefore the plants and manes are (present). What he drinks (after offering) that he offers to the men. Therefore men are (present). The animals are behind men. Behind gods are the birds, plants and trees and whatever else there is. Thus he apportions shares to these creatures which are not discarded.

तदुहोवाच याज्ञवल्क्यो न यज्ञो मन्तवै[19] अग्निहोत्रं पाकयज्ञ इवैवेतीदं हि यदन्यस्मि-
न्यज्ञे स्रुच्यवद्यन्ति सर्वमेव तज्जुह्वत्यथैतद्धुत्वोत्सृप्याचामति निर्लेढि तदस्य पाकयज्ञस्ये-
वेति तद्वस्य तत्पशव्यमेव रूपं पशव्यो हि पाकयज्ञः ॥ १३ ॥

सा वा एषैकैवाग्र आहुतिर्यां प्रजापतिरजुहोदथ यथेमे पश्चाद्ध्रियन्तायमग्निर्योऽयं
पवते सूर्य एवमेषा द्वितीया हूयते तद्यामग्रे जुहोति सा तस्यै देवतायै यस्या अग्निहोत्रमथ
[20]यां द्वितीयां स्विष्टकृद्भाजनमेव सा तस्मात्तामुत्तरतो जुहोत्येषा हि तस्य देवस्य दिङ्मिथुनायो
वा एषा प्रजननार्यै[21] द्वितीया हूयते ॥ १४ ॥

ते वा एते आहुती भूतं च भविष्यच्च जातं च जनिष्यमाणं चागतं चाशा चाद्य च श्वश्च
तद्वा एतद्द्वयमेवानु ॥ १५ ॥

आत्मा वाव भूतोऽद्धा वै तद्यद्भूतमद्धो तद्यदात्मा प्रजैव भविष्यदनद्धा वै तद्यद्भवि-
ष्यदनद्धो तद्यत्प्रजा ॥ १६ ॥

आत्मा वाव जातोऽद्धा वै तद्यज्जातमद्धो तद्यदात्मा प्रजैव जनिष्यमाणानद्धा वै
तद्यज्जनिष्यमाणमनद्धो तद्यत्प्रजा[22] ॥ १७ ॥

आत्मा वा आगतोऽद्धा वै तद्यदागतमद्धो तद्यदात्मा [23]प्रजैवाशानद्धा वै तद्यदाशानद्धो
तद्यत्प्रजा ॥ १८ ॥

आत्मा वा अद्याद्धा वै तद्यदद्याद्धो तद्यदात्मा प्रजैव श्वोऽनद्धा वै तद्यच्छ्वोऽनद्धो
तद्यत्प्रजा ॥ १९ ॥

तां तां मन्त्रेण प्रथमामाहुतिं जुहोति स आत्मानमभि हूयते[24]ऽद्धा वै तद्यन्मन्त्रोऽद्धो
तद्यदात्मा तूष्णीमुत्तरां सा प्रजामभि हूयतेऽनद्धा वै तद्यत्तूष्णीमनद्धो तद्यत्प्रजा ॥ २० ॥

१९. मन्तवा TE.

२०. यां TE.

२१. प्रजननाय TE; V1. P1. Ca.

२२. तद्यत्प्रजा V1.

२३. प्रजै My, V1. TE.

२४. हूयते TE, V1. P. Ca.

13. On this Yājñavalkya said, "*Agnihotra* should not be thought of as a sacrifice (with offering of *havis* or burnt offerings) but this is verily a *Pākayajña* (domestic sacrifice)". In the other sacrifice (of *havis*), they ladle out into the offering spoon and they offer the entire thing. And here (in *Agnihotra*), stepping aside he (the sacrificer) makes *ācamana* (ceremonial intake of a little water); he (completely) licks off (the milk). This is only (a characteristic) of a *Pākayajña*. This is the very animal form of this *(Agnihotra)*. Indeed, the *Pākayajña* pertains to (the welfare of) beasts (cattle).

14. This is, indeed, the only first offering which Prajāpati offered. Then just as these (gods) later maintained–viz., Agni, this one (Wind) that blows and the Sun, so is this second (offering) offered. Therefore that which one offers first is for that divinity to whom *Agnihotra* belongs. The second one which (one offers), that is indeed what reaches *Sviṣṭakṛt* (Agni who makes all the offerings heretofore offered good). Therefore he (the sacrificer) offers it on the northern side. For this is the direction of that god. This second offering is made for pairing and for production, indeed.

15. These two offerings are verily the past and the future; the one (already) born and the one which is going to be born; what has (already) come and the hope (of what is to come): today and tomorrow; (all) this is indeed a pair, in accordance.

16. Verily the past is the self *(Ātman)*. For what has (already) been is certain. Indeed, the self is certain. The progeny is the future. Verily, what is going to be is uncertain. Indeed, progeny is uncertain.

17. The self has (already)been born. What has been born is, indeed, certain. Certain, verily, is the self. It is only progeny that is going to be born. What is going to be born is, indeed, uncertain. Therefore progeny is uncertain.

18. The self, indeed, has already come. Certain, verily, is what has come. Therefore the self is certain. Progeny only is the hope. 'Hope', indeed, is uncertain. Therefore progeny is verily uncertain.

19. 'To-day', indeed, is the self. What is today is verily certain. Certain, indeed, is the self. Only progeny is 'tomorrow'.'What is to-morrow' is indeed uncertain. Therefore progeny is verily uncertain.

20. Each first offering he offers with a *mantra* (sacred chant). That *(mantra)* is chanted towards (for the sake of) the self. True is the sacred chant. The self also, indeed, is true. (He offers) the second (offering) silently. It is offered towards (for the sake of) progeny. What is silently (done) is, indeed, uncertain. Therefore progeny is verily uncertain.

स जुहोत्यग्निर्ज्योतिर्ज्योतिरग्निः स्वाहेति सायꣳ सूर्यो ज्योतिर्ज्योतिः सूर्यः स्वाहेति प्रातस्तद्धैतत्सत्सत्येनैव हूयत इदꣳ हि यदा सूर्योऽस्तमेत्यथाग्निरेव ज्योतिर्भवति यदो वै सूर्य उदेत्यथ सूर्य एव ज्योतिर्भवति तदु ह वै देवान्गच्छति यत्सत्येन जुह्वति ॥ २१ ॥

तदुहोवाच दक्ष आरुणये ब्रह्मवर्चसकामस्यैनेन जुहुयादित्यग्निर्वर्चो ज्योतिर्वर्चः सूर्यो वर्चो ज्योतिर्वर्चो ब्रह्मवर्चसी हैव भवति यस्यैवं जुह्वतीत्यस्त्युवेवं[२५] प्रजननस्यैवं[२६] रूपमग्नि-ज्योतिर्ज्योतिरग्निः स्वाहेति तदिदं ज्योती रेत उभयतो देवतया परिगृह्णात्युभयतः परिगृहीतꣳ हि रेतः प्रजायत इत्युभयत एवैतत्परिगृह्य प्रजनयति सूर्यो ज्योतिर्ज्योतिः सूर्यः स्वाहेति तदिदं ज्योती रेत उभयतो देवतया परिगृह्णात्युभयतः परिगृहीतꣳ हि रेतः प्रजायत इत्युभयत एवैतत्परिगृह्य प्रजनयति ॥ २२ ॥

तदु होवाच जीवलश्चैलकिर्गर्भानेवारुणिः करोति न तु प्रजनयतीति स ह स एवमेव सायꣳ होतव्यं मेनेऽथ प्रातर्ज्योतिः सूर्यः सूर्यो ज्योतिः स्वाहेति तदिदं ज्योती रेतो बहिर्धा करोतीति होवाच बहिर्धा हि रेतः प्रजातं भवतीति ॥ २३ ॥

तदाहुरग्निमेवैते सायꣳ सूर्ये जुह्वति सूर्यं प्रातरग्नावितीदꣳ हि यदा सूर्योऽस्तमेत्यथाग्नि-रेव ज्योतिर्भवति[२७] यदो वै सूर्य उदेत्यथ सूर्य एव ज्योतिर्भवति तत्तदुदितहोमिनामेव नास्यैषा परिचक्षा तस्यै त्वेव देवतायै नाद्धा जुह्वति यस्या अग्निहोत्रम् ॥ २४ ॥

अग्निर्ज्योतिर्ज्योतिरग्निः स्वाहेति नाग्नये स्वाहेत्यग्निः स्वाहेत्येव सूर्यो ज्योतिर्ज्योतिः सूर्यः स्वाहेति न सूर्याय स्वाहेति सूर्यः स्वाहेत्येव तस्मादनेनैव जुहुयात् ॥ २५ ॥

सजूर्देवेन सवित्रेति सवितृमत्प्रसवाय सजू रात्र्येन्द्रवत्येति रात्र्या मिथुनीकरोतीन्द्रो यज्ञस्य देवता सेन्द्रं करोति जुषाणो अग्निर्वेतु स्वाहेति प्रत्यक्षं तस्यै देवतायै जुहोति यस्या अग्निहोत्रम् ॥ २६ ॥

२५. तीत्यस्तु वेव TE, V1, My, P; तीत्यस्तु एव M.

२६. प्रजननस्येव Ca.

२७. र्भवतीति TE.

21. He offers in the evening (chanting),"Agni is the light; the light is Agni, *Svāhā*" and in the morning, "The Sun is the light; the light is the Sun, *Svāhā*". This is verily offered with truth. It is indeed this : when the Sun sets, then it is only Agni that becomes the 'light'. And when the Sun rises, then, verily, the Sun becomes the 'light'. What they offer with truth–that indeed reaches the gods.

22. Regarding this, Dakṣa said to Āruṇi, " One who desires *'Brahmavarcasa'* (spiritual lustre) should offer with this *(mantra)*,: "Agni is the lustre; the light is the lustre". Sūrya is the lustre; the light is the lustre. He, for whom they offer thus, verily becomes one possessing *'Brahmavarcasa'*. There is a form as of procreation in (the other *mantra*). "Agni is the light; the light is *Agni-Svāhā*". This light, the seed, one encloses on both sides, with the deity. The seed that is verily enclosed on both sides germinates. Therefore, enclosing it verily on both sides, he causes it to be born. "Sūrya is the light; the light is *Sūrya Svāhā*". This light, which is the seed, one encloses on both sides with the deity. Verily, the seed, enclosed on both sides, germinates. Therefore, enclosing it, verily on both sides, he causes it to be born.

23. Regarding this, Jīvala Cailaki said, "Āruṇi only brings about conception but does not cause birth". He indeed thought that it should be so offered only in the evening and then, in the morning (it should be offered) with (the chant), "The light is the Sun; the Sun is the light,*Svāhā*". Then he places this light, the seed, outside. So he said, indeed, "The seed is verily born outside (as an off-spring)".

24. Then, they say, "These (performers of *Agnihotra*) offer verily Agni into Sūrya in the evening and Sūrya into Agni in the morning". This is, indeed, when the Sun sets and then Agni himself becomes the light. But when the Sun rises, the Sun himself becomes the light. All that is only for those who offer after sun-rise. This does not amount to a rejection of this. (This is no fault committed by the sacrificers). Only they do not offer directly to the deity itself to whom *Agnihotra* belongs.

25. It is, "Agni is the light; the light is Agni,*'svāhā*" and not "*svāhā* to Agni". It is only "*Agniḥ svāhā*." It is "Sūrya is the light; the light is Sūrya-*svāhā*"and not "*svāhā* to Sūrya". It is only *'Sūryaḥ svāhā'*. Therefore one should offer only with this (chant).

26. (He chants,"Along with the divine Savitṛ" for the production (of the sacrifice) possessed of Savitṛ. (Chanting),"Along with the night united with Indra" he couples it with the night. Indra is the deity of the sacrifice. He (the sacrificer) makes it (the sacrifice) possessed of Indra. (Chanting),"May Agni, being pleased, accept." *'Svāhā'* he directly offers to that deity to whom *Agnihotra* belongs.

सजूर्देवेन सवित्रेत्येव प्रातः सवितृमत्प्रसवाय सजूरुषसेन्द्रवत्येति वा सजूरह्नेन्द्रवत्येति वोषसा वा मिथुनीकरोतीन्द्रो यज्ञस्य देवता सेन्द्रं करोति जुषाणः सूर्यो वेतु स्वाहेति प्रत्यक्षं तस्यै देवतायै जुहोति यस्या अग्निहोत्रम् ॥ २७ ॥

ते होचुः को न इदं जुहुयादिति ब्राह्मण इति ब्राह्मणेदं नो जुहुधीति किं मम ततः स्यादित्यग्निहोत्रोच्छिष्टमिति तद्धैतदग्निहोत्रोच्छिष्टं यत्स्रुचि परिशिष्यतेऽथ यत्स्थाल्यां यथा कौष्ठा[२८]द्वा परीणहो वा निर्मिमीतैवं तत्तस्मात्तद्य एव कश्च पिबेन्न त्वब्राह्मणोऽग्नौ ह्येनदधिश्रयन्ति ॥ २८ ॥ इति प्रथमं ब्राह्मणम् ॥

द्वितीयं ब्राह्मणम्

तदुहोवाच कहोळः[१] कौषीतकिरनयोर्वा एष द्यावापृथिव्यो रस इत्यस्य रसस्य देवेभ्यो हुत्वाथाश्नानीति[२] तस्माद्वा आग्रयणेन यजेतेत्यथ होवाच याज्ञवल्क्यः ॥ १ ॥

देवाश्च ह वा असुराश्चोभये प्राजापत्या अस्पर्धन्त ततो हासुराः कृत्ययेव त्वद्विषेणेव त्वदिमा उभयीरोषधीः प्रलिलिपुर्याश्च पशव उपजीवन्ति याश्च मनुष्या उतेत्थंचिद्देवानभिभवेमेति ततो न पशव आलिशन्त न मनुष्या आश्नꣳस्ता एता उभय्यः प्रजा अनशनेन नोत्पराबभूवुः ॥ २ ॥

तदु वै देवा अस्पृण्वतानशनेन वा इमाः प्रजाः पराभवन्तीति हन्तासामोषधीनां कृत्यां त्वद्विषं[३] त्वदपहनामेति केनेति यज्ञेनेति होचुर्यज्ञेन ह स्म वैतद्देवाः कल्पयन्ते यदेषां कल्प्यं[४]मासर्षयश्च ॥ ३ ॥

२८. कौष्ठाद्वा C,B, P1, P2, H.

१. कफोलः TE. Co.

२. श्नातीति V1, P1, P2; see Notes.

३. द्विषं K;B; Ca.

४. क्लृप्य M; कल्प Co.

27. (Chanting) only,"Along with the divine Savitṛ" in the morning for the production (of the sacrifice) possessed of Savitṛ and (chanting) either "Along with the dawn united with Indra" or "Along with the day united with Indra" he couples it with either dawn or the day. Indra is the deity of the sacrifice. He makes it (the sacrifice) possessed of Indra (chanting),"May Sūrya being pleased accept, *Svāhā*" he offers directly to that deity to whom *Agnihotra* belongs.

28. They said, "Who will offer this to us?" "Brāhmaṇa" (the Brahmin), "oh Brahmin offer this to us". (The Brahmin asked),"What will accrue to me from that?" They (the gods) replied,"The residue of the *Agnihotra* ". Indeed this is the residue of the *Agnihotra*-what remains left over in the ladle and also in the pot. It is like what one builds up (garners) from the store-room or from a confined place. Therefore any one may drink it but not one who is not a Brāhmin. For, they cook it indeed, on the (sacrificial) fire.

(First Brāhmaṇa Ends)

BRĀHMAṆA II

1. Said, Kahola Kauṣītaki, "This is the essence of these heaven and earth. Therefore one eats of it after offering this essence to the gods". "Therefore one should perform the *Āgrayaṇā* (offering of the first fruits). And Yājñavalkya said.

2. "Gods and Asuras, both sprung from Prajāpati contended. Then the Asuras smeared with (destructive) magic, with poison these plants of both-the plants on which animals subsist and those on which men too (subsist), thinking, "Thus indeed shall we overcome the Devas". Therefore, the animals did not move out (to graze) and men did not eat. These creatures of both kinds (men and cattle) did not overcome (hunger), for want of food.

3. Then the gods heard that these creatures were suffering (perishing) verily for want of food. (They said to each other),"Ah! let us remove that magic and that poison of these plants". "By what means?" "By means of sacrifice". Indeed, by means of sacrifice the gods accomplished what was to be accomplished by them (so did) the Ṛṣis too.

ते होचुः कस्य न इदं भविष्यतीति ते ह मम ममेति न संपादयांचक्रुस्ते होचुरसंपादयन्तो हन्तास्मिन्नाजिमजामहा[५] इति स य उज्जेष्यति तस्य न इदं भविष्यतीति तथेति तस्मिन्नाजिमाजन्त ॥ ४ ॥

तद्धेन्द्राग्नी उज्जिग्यतुस्तस्मादेतदैन्द्राग्नं यदाग्रयणमिन्द्राग्नी ह्यस्य भागधेयमुदजयतां तस्मादेष ऐन्द्राग्नो द्वादशकपालः पुरोळाशो भवति ॥ ५ ॥

तौ ह यत्रेन्द्राग्नी उज्जिगिवाꣳसौ तस्थतुस्तद्ध विश्वेदेवा अन्वाजग्मुः क्षत्रं वा इन्द्राग्नी विशो विश्वेदेवा यत्र वै क्षत्रमुज्जयत्यन्वाभक्ता वै तत्र विट् तदेतद्विश्वान्देवानन्वाभजन्त्स एष वैश्वदेवश्चरुर्भवति ॥ ६ ॥

स पुराणानाꣳ स्यात्क्षत्रं वा इन्द्राग्नी विशो विश्वेदेवा नेत्क्षत्रं विशाभ्यारोहयाणीत्यथो अपि नवानामेव स्याद्यद्वा इतरः पुरोळाशश्चरुरितरस्तेनैवानभ्यारूळ्हं तस्मादपि नवानामेव स्यात् ॥ ७ ॥

त उ होचुर्विश्वेदेवा अनयोर्वा अयं द्यावापृथिव्यो रस ऐवेमे[६] अस्मिन्भजामेति तथेति तत आभ्यामेतं भागमकल्पयन्त्स एष द्यावापृथिव्य एककपालः स यदेककपालो भवतीयं वै पृथिवी कपालꣳ[७] सेयमेकेवैव तस्मादेककपालो भवति ॥ ८ ॥

तदाहुर्नैककपालः स्यादस्मिन्परिचक्षेतीदं नु यस्यै कस्यै च देवतायै हविर्गृह्णन्ति सर्वत्रैव स्विष्टकृदन्वाभक्तः सर्वमेतं जुह्वति सा न्वेव परिचक्षार्थो पर्याभवति ॥ ९ ॥

तदाहुः पर्याभूद्वा अयं मोहिष्यतीदꣳ राष्ट्रमिति नास्य सा परिचक्षाहवनीयो वा आहुतीनां प्रतिष्ठा स यदाहवनीयं प्राप्यापि दशकृत्वः पुनः पुनः पर्यावर्तेत कस्तेनार्थोऽन्यस्तु यदाह किं तं[९]त्संधर्युपेयात्तस्माद्वाज्यस्यैव यजेदेष वै प्रत्यक्षं द्यावापृथिव्यो रसो यदाज्यं तत्प्रत्यक्षमेवैने एतेन रसेन मेधेन प्रीणाति ॥ १० ॥

५. See Notes.

६. रस एवेमे Ca, V1, P1, (रसः-आ-एव-इमे).

७. कपालꣳ TE.

८. परिचक्षाथो M; परिचक्षोतो Caland; चक्षातो L; see Notes.

९. किन्तच्छन्तर्यु M. see Notes.

4. They said, "To which of us shall this accrue?" They did not agree (each one claiming). "To me ", "To me ". Not agreeing, they said, "Let us run a race. Whoever wins, to him shall this be". Saying "So be it", they ran the race.

5. Indra and Agni won it. Therefore this *Āgrayaṇa* (first offering) is dedicated to Indra and Agni (together). Indeed, Indra and Agni won the share of it. Therefore there is (offered), in these (rituals) a sacrificial offering *(puroḍāśa)* on twelve potsherds.

6. Where those two, (Indra and Agni), remained victorious, there all the gods followed. For, Indra and Agni are Kṣatra (warriors) and the 'All-gods' are the Viṭs (the common subjects). Where the Kṣatra conquers, there the Viś is given a subsequent share. Hence they gave this subsequent share to the Viśvedevas. That is this oblation (of boiled rice or barley) to Viśvedevas.

7. It (the offering to Viśvedevas) should be (made) of old (grains). For Indra and Agni are Kṣatra and the 'All-gods' are Viś (the common subjects), (old grains should be used for preparing the offering to Viśvedevas) lest he (sacrificer) should think, "I shall elevate the Viś with Kṣatra "(i.e. elevate the Viś to the level of Kṣatra). Nevertheless, it should be only (made) of new (grains). Or, even by the fact that one is *Puroḍāśa* (a cake) and the other *caru* (a pap), (the Kṣatra) is not mounted (by the Viś) . Therefore, too, it should be only of new (grains).

8. They, the Viśvedevas, said, "This is indeed the essence of these two, heaven and earth. Let us take them in (for a share) in this". "Yes". Then they assigned this share to them. This (offering) on one potsherd is dedicated to Heaven and Earth (together). That it is (offered on) one potsherd is because this earth is a bowl (vessel) and it is only one indeed. Therefore is (the offering to heaven and earth) on one potsherd.

9. About this they (some) say, "It should not be one of one potsherd. There is a flaw (censure) in it". It is this, when they take out sacrificial food for any deity, in all places (Agni) *Sviṣṭakṛt* is given a share. (But) here they offer the entire thing (to heaven and earth). That is indeed the flaw and moreover it (the offering) turns round.

10. Therefore, they say, "This (offering) has verily turned round. This kingdom will fall into confusion". "That is not a flaw of this (sacrificer). Indeed the *Āhavanīya* is the firm basis of oblations. If it (the offering), after reaching the *Āhavanīya* should turn, again and again, ten times, what of it?" Then some-body else says,"What will one have in that combination? Therefore one should offer only *ghee*. Indeed this *ghee* is the visible essence of Heaven and Earth. Therefore he verily pleases these two, directly with this sap offering.

त एतेनेष्ट्वा देवा आसामोषधीनां कृत्यां त्वद्विषं त्वदं[10]पाघ्नꣳस्तत आलिशन्त पशव आश्नन्मनुष्या अथ यदेष एतेन यजते नाहैवैतंस्य कृत्ययेव त्वद्विषेणेव त्वदोषधयः प्रलिप्ता भवन्तीति देवा अकुर्वन्निति त्वेवैष एतत्करोति यमु चैव देवा यज्ञे भागमकल्पयꣳस्तमु चैवैभ्य एष एतत्करोतीमा उ चैवैतदुभयो[11]रोषधीरनमीवा अकिल्बिषाः कुरुते ता अनमीवा अकिल्बिषा उपजीवन्ति तस्य प्रथमजो गौर्दक्षिणाग्र्यमिव हीदमित्येतत्तस्य कर्म य ईजानो वा स्याद्दर्शपूर्णमासाभ्यां वा यजेताथ योऽनीजानोऽन्वाहार्यपचन एवौदनं चातुष्प्राश्यं पचेत्तं ब्राह्मणेभ्य उपनिदध्यात् ॥ ११ ॥

द्वया वै देवा देवा अहैवान्यद्देवा अथेमे मनुष्यदेवा य इमे ब्राह्मणाः शुश्रुवाꣳसोऽनूचा-नास्तदेवास्य यथा हुतमेवं भवति तत्र यच्छक्नुयात्तद्द्यादग्निहोत्र उ हैके जुह्वति तदु तथा न कुर्यात्समदꣳ ह स करोत्यन्यद्ध्येवाग्रयणमन्यं[12]दग्निहोत्रम् ॥ १२ ॥ इति द्वितीयं ब्राह्मणम् ॥

तृतीयं ब्राह्मणम्

प्रजापतिꣳ ह वै भूतान्युपसेदुः प्रजा वै भूतानि विधेहि नो यथा जीवामेति तं देवा यज्ञोपवीतिनो दक्षिणं जान्वाच्योपसेदुस्तान्होवाच यज्ञो वोऽन्नमित्यूर्ग्वोऽमृतं वः सूर्यो वो ज्योतिरिति ॥ १ ॥

अथ हैनं पितरः प्राचीनाववीतिनः सव्यं जान्वाच्योपसेदुस्तान्होवाच मासि मासि वोऽन्नमिति स्वधा वो मनोजवो वश्चन्द्रमा वो ज्योतिरिति ॥ २ ॥

अथ हैनं मनुष्याः प्रावृता एवोपस्थं कृत्वोपसेदुस्तान्होवाच सायंप्रातर्वोऽन्नमिति प्रजा वो मृत्युर्वोऽग्निर्वो ज्योतिरिति ॥ ३ ॥

१०. तदपा P1.

११. दुभयीरो P1, H.

१२. मन्यदग्नि TE.

11. Performing sacrifice with this, those gods removed the magic and poison of these plants. Then the animals (cattle) went out (to graze) and men ate. That one performs that sacrifice (with this offering), is verily for the reason that his plants here should not become smeared with magic and with poison at all and that the gods did so (performed this offering), and whatever share the gods assigned in the sacrifice (to themselves), that very thing he prepares for them. He renders these plants of both (men and animals) free from disease and free from fault (evil). (These creatures) subsist on those diseaseless and faultless (plants). His (the priest's) sacrificial fee is first-born calf. This is indeed the foremost (best) as it were. This is the ritual of that person who performs a sacrifice or performs the New Moon and Full Moon offerings. But one who does not perform a sacrifice should cook rice-food on *Anvāhāryapacana* (the southern fire on which subsequent offerings are cooked), enough for four persons to eat and place it before the Brāhmins (priests).

12. Indeed, there are two kinds of gods. The very gods are of a separate kind of gods. Then there are these human gods viz., the Brāhmins who have studied the Vedas and teach them. That (feeding of the four priests) verily is like the offering (made in Agni). He should give (as fee) in that (ritual) as much as he can afford. Some offer in *Agnihotra* (milk from new cow). One should not do so at all. For, thereby he makes it çonflicting (between two deities of the two offerings). Indeed, different is *Āgrayaṇa* (the offering of first produce) and different is *Agnihotra.*

(Second Brāhmaṇa Ends)

BRĀHMAṆA III

1. The living beings approached Prajāpati. The beings are indeed creatures. (They said), "Please ordain to us as to how we may live". Then the gods approached him, wearing the sacirificial thread (in the normal way) and bending the right knee. (He) told them, "The sacrifice is verily your food, immortality (nectar) your strength and the 'Sun' your light".

2. Thereafter the manes approached him, with the sacred thread on the right shoulder and under the left arm and bending the left knee. He told them, "Your food (will be) (once) every month, *Svadhā* (will be your carrier) with the speed of your mind and the moon your light."

3. Then the human beings approached him covered (with dress) and bending their bodies. He told them, "Your food (will be) in the evening and in the morning, progeny your death and fire your light."

अथ हैनं पशव उपसेदुस्तेभ्यो ह स्व एषं[13] चकार यदि यूयं काले यद्यकाले लभाध्वै[14] तर्ह्येवाश्नाथेति तस्मात्पशवो यदि काले यद्यकाले लभन्ते तर्ह्येवाश्नन्ति स्व एषो ह्येभ्यः कृतः ॥ ४ ॥

अथ हैनꣳ शश्वदप्यसुरा उपसेदुस्तेभ्यो ह तमश्च मायां च प्रददावस्ति ह्येवासुरमायेतीव पराभूतास्त्वेव ताः प्रजास्ता इमाः प्रजास्तथोपजीवन्ति यथाभ्यः प्रजापतिर्व्यदधात् ॥ ५ ॥

तन्न देवा अतिक्रामन्ति न पितरो न पशवो मनुष्या एवातिक्रामन्ति तस्मान्मनुष्याणां यो मेद्यत्यशुभे मेद्यति वि हि हूर्छति नह्ययनाय चन भवत्य[15]नृतꣳ हि कृत्वा मेद्यति तस्मादु सायंप्रातराश्येव स्यात्स य एवं विद्वान्त्सायंप्रातराशी भवति सर्वꣳ हैवायुरेति यदु ह किं च वाचा वदति तथा हैव तद्भवति देवसत्यꣳ हि गोपायति ॥ ६ ॥

तद्धैतत्तेजो नाम ब्राह्मणं योऽस्य शक्नोति व्रतं चरितुꣳ स मासि मासि पितृभ्यो ददद्यदहरेष पुरस्ताच्चन्द्रमा नोदेति तदहर्ददात्येष वै सोमो राजा[16] देवानामन्नं यच्चन्द्रमाः स एताꣳरात्रिं क्षीयते तत्क्षीणे देवानामन्ने पितृभ्यो ददाति तथैभ्योऽसमदं करोति ॥ ७ ॥

सोऽपराह्णे ददाति पूर्वाह्णो वै देवानां मध्यन्दिनो मनुष्याणामपराह्णः पितॄणां तस्मादपराह्णे ददाति ॥ ८ ॥

अथ[17] खलु प्राचीनाववीती भूत्वा जघनेन गार्हपत्यं दक्षिणासीनः सव्यं जान्वाच्य तूष्णीमेवैतं चरुं गृह्णाति स तत एवोपोत्थायोत्तरेणान्वाहार्यपचनं दक्षिणा तिष्ठन्नवहन्ति स सकृदेव फलीकरोति सकृद्ध्येव पराञ्चः पितरः स यदेतां दिशꣳ सचन्त एषा हि पितॄणां दिक् श्रपयित्वैतं[18] चरुमधिश्रित आज्यं प्रत्यानयत्यग्नौ वै देवेभ्यो जुह्वत्युद्धृत्य मनुष्येभ्य उपनिदधत्यथैवं पितॄणां तस्मादधिश्रित आज्यं प्रत्यानयति ॥ ९ ॥

१३. स्वैषं चकार L.
१४. See Notes.
१५. भवत्यनृ Ca.
१६. राजाराजा देवा TE.
१७. अथ यत्खलु TE.
१८. त्वैनं P1, P2.

4. Then the beasts approached him. To them he granted their wish (saying), "Whenever you get (any food) in time or untimely, then verily may you eat". Therefore whenever they get (any food) in proper time or out of time, then indeed do they eat. For, it was their wish that had been granted.

5. And then the Asuras, too, approached him again and again. To them he gave darkness and illusion. There is certainly what is called *Āsuramāyā* (demonic illusion). Those creatures have really perished. These creatures so subsist as Prajāpati has ordained for them.

6. That (the decree of Prajāpati) the gods do not transgress, nor do the manes, nor the animals. Only men violate (it). Therefore whoever, among men, grows fat, he grows fat in unrighteousness; he indeed cheats. He cannot move about. For he grows fat, doing falsehood. Therefore one should eat only in the evening and morning, He who knowing this eats (only) in the evening and morning, attains full (span of) life; whatever he speaks, it verily becomes so (true). For he keeps the truth of gods.

7. This is indeed Brahmanic lustre. He who can keep his (Prajāpati's) rule, offers (food) to the manes every month. He gives it on that day when the moon does not rise in the east (i.e. on the New Moon day). This moon is indeed King Soma, the food of the gods. This night (of the New Moon day) he declines. When that food of gods is exhausted, he (the sacrificer) offers (food) to the manes. Thus he brings about absence of discord between them (gods and manes

8. He gives (food to the manes) in the afternoon. For the forenoon is of the gods and mid-day of men and the afternoon of the manes. Therefore does he give in the afternoon.

9. Then, wearing the sacred thread over his right shoulder and under his left arm, being seated behind the *Gārhapatya* and facing south, bending his left knee, he silently takes out the *caru* (vessel with paddy for preparing the offering). Then getting up and standing to the north of *Dakṣiṇāgni* over which subsequent offerings are cooked and facing south he pounds it (the paddy for *caru*). Only once does he winnow it (to remove the chaff). For, once only (once for all) the fathers have passed away. That he takes to the southern quarter (is because) this is the quarter of the manes. Putting the *caru* on fire, he adds *ghee* when it is cooked. Verily they offer to the gods into Agni; for men they take it off (the fire) and place it down. And for the manes (the pitṛs) (it is) this same way (as for men). Therefore he adds *ghee* after cooking it (while it is still on the fire).

उद्वास्याग्नौ द्वे आहुती जुहोति देवान्वा एष उपावर्तते य आहिताग्निर्दर्शपूर्णमासाभ्यां यजतेऽथेदं पितृभ्यो दास्यन्भवति स यानेव देवानुपावृत्तो भवति तेभ्य एवैतन्निह्नुते[१९] स देवैरतिसृष्टः पितृभ्यो ददाति स वा अग्नये चैव सोमाय च जुहोति स यदग्नये जुहोति सर्वत्र ह्येवाग्निरन्वाभक्तोऽथ यत्सोमाय पितृदेवत्यो हि सोमः ॥ १० ॥

स जुहोत्यग्नये कव्यवाहनाय स्वाहा सोमाय पितृमते स्वाहेत्यभ्याधाय मेक्षणं जघनेनान्वाहार्यपचनꣳ सकृदेव स्फ्येनोल्लिखति तद्वेदिभाजनꣳ सकृदुल्लिखति सकृद्ध्येव पराञ्चः पितरः ॥ ११ ॥

अथोल्मुकं दक्षिणतो निदधाति यद्ध वा अनिधायोल्मुकं पितृभ्यो ददत्यसुररक्षसानि हैषां तद्विमथ्नते स यदुल्मुकं निदधात्यसुररक्षसानामेवापहतये ॥ १२ ॥

स निदधाति ये रूपाणि प्रतिमुञ्चमाना असुराः सन्तः स्वधया चरन्ति परापुरो निपुरो ये भरन्त्यग्निष्टाँल्लोकात्प्रणुदात्यस्मादिति[२०] ॥ १३ ॥

अथावनेजयत्यसाववनेनिक्ष्वेति यजमानस्य पितरमसाववनेनिक्ष्वेति यजमानस्य पितामहमसाववनेनिक्ष्वेति यजमानस्य प्रपितामहं यथाशिष्यतोऽवनेजयेदेवमेतदथोपमूले दितानि सकृदाच्छिन्नानि भवन्त्यग्रमिव वै देवानां मध्यमिव मनुष्याणां मूलमिव पितृणां तस्मादुपमूले दितानि भवन्ति सकृदाच्छिन्नानि भवन्ति सकृद्ध्येव पराञ्चः पितरः ॥ १४ ॥

तानि दक्षिणास्तीर्त्वा तेषु ददाति स इति ददातीति वै देवेभ्यो जुह्वतीति मनुष्येभ्य उद्धरन्त्यथैवं पितृणां तस्मादिति ददाति ॥ १५ ॥

स ददात्यसावेतत्त इति यजमानस्य पित्रे ये च त्वाम[२१]न्वञ्च इति वा हैक आहुर्याꣳश्च त्वम[२२]न्वङ्ङसीति वा तदु तथा न ब्रूयात्स्वयꣳह्येव तेषाꣳ सह येषाꣳ सहासावेतत्त इत्येव

१९. एवैतं निह्नुते TE, My, Ca, Po.

२०. स्मादिति Ca.

२१. त्वाम Ca.

२२. त्वम Ca.

10. After removing it (from the fire) he offers two offerings in the fire. For this *Āhitāgani* (one who has set up his fires) who makes the New Moon and the Full moon offerings returns to the gods. Then he has to offer this to the manes. He keeps this away from those gods to whom he has returned. Being permitted by the gods, he gives (the offering) to the manes. He offers to Agni and to Soma. He offers to Agni for Agni has a share in everything (offeing). And then (He offers) to Soma for Soma is the deity of the manes.

11. He offers, chanting, "To Agni the conveyer of oblation to the departed ancestors,*Svāhā*". "To Soma associated with the *pitṛs* (manes),*Svāhā*". Placing the lid of the vessel down, he makes a furrow with the wooden sword behind the fire (west of the fire) only once. That is a representation of the altar. He makes a furrow once. For the fathers have passed away once only.

12. Then he places a fire-brand at the south. For when they offer (food) to the manes without placing the fire brand, Asuras and Rākṣasas indeed disturb that (food) of these (manes). That he places the firebrand is for driving away the Asuras and Rākṣasas.

13. He places (the fire brand) (chanting), "The Asuras who, assuming (many) forms move about at their will and who bear huge bodies or small bodies—may Agni drive them away from this world".

14. Then he causes the (deceased) father of the sacrificer to wash his hands saying, "(Uttering the name of the father)(in the vocative)—wash (your hands)", the (deceased) grandfather of the sacrificer, "(Uttering the name of the grandfather in the vocative) wash (your hands)", and the (deceased) great grandfather of the sacrificer "(Uttering his name in the vocative) wash (your hands)". This is just as one would make those who are about to eat, wash (their hands) . They (the stalks of sacred grass) are cut near the root, cut once (only) (at one stroke). Indeed the top (top portion of the sacred grass) belongs to the gods, the middle to the men and the bottom to the manes. Therefore they are cut near the root. They are cut (only) once; for, the fathers have passed away (only) once.

15. Spreading them (their tops pointing) southward, he gives (food to the *pitṛs*) on them. He gives thus because they offer (oblation) to the gods (in fire). For men, they take it out (and serve) and for *pitṛs* (they give) thus (on sacred grass). Therefore he gives thus.

16. He presents (the food) to the father of the sacrificer, saying, "(Name of the father in vocative), this is for you". Some say (in addition), "And those who come following you", and "Those after whom you come".One should not say it so. For, he himself is with them with whom he is. So he should present (the food)

यजमानस्य पित्रेऽसावेतत्त इति यजमानस्य पितामहायासावेतत्त इति यजमानस्य प्रपिताम-हायेतः पराङ्ददाति सकृद्ध्येव पराञ्चः पितरः ॥ १६ ॥

अथाहात्र पितरो मादयध्वं यथाभागमावृषायध्वमित्यत्र पितरो यथाभागमश्नीतेत्येवै-तदाहाथ पराङ् पर्यावर्तते तिर इव वै पितरस्तिर इवैतद्भवति ॥ १७ ॥

तदाहुरा तमितोरासीत तावान्ह्यसुरिति तदु मुहूर्तमेवासित्वोपपर्यावर्तेताथाहामीमदन्त पितरो यथाभागमावृषायिषतेत्याशिषुः पितरो यथाभागमित्येवैतदाह ॥ १८ ॥

अथावनेजयत्यसाववनेनिक्ष्वेति यजमानस्य पितरमसाववनेनिक्ष्वेति यजमानस्य पितामहमसाववनेनिक्ष्वेति यजमानस्य प्रपितामह यथो[२३] जक्षुषोऽवनेजयेदेवमे-तत् ॥ १९ ॥

अथ नीविमुद्वृह्य[२४] नमस्करोति पितृदेवत्या वै नीविर्यज्ञ उ वै नमो यज्ञियानेवैतत्पितॄन्क-रोति षट्कृत्वो नमस्करोति षड्वा[२५] ऋतव ऋतवो वै पितर ऋतुष्वेवैतद्यज्ञं प्रतिष्ठापयति गृहान्नः पितरो दत्तेत्याहैषो हैतस्याशीः कर्मणो गृहाणामु ह वै पितर ईशते तस्मादाह गृहान्नः पितरो दत्तेत्यथोखामवजिघ्रति स यजमानभागः पुनः पिण्डान्त्समवदधत्यग्नौ सकृदाच्छि-न्नान्यभ्यादधति पुनरुल्मुकमप्यर्जति ॥ २० ॥ इति तृतीयं ब्राह्मणम् ॥

चतुर्थं ब्राह्मणम्

प्रजापतिर्ह वा एतेन यज्ञेनेजे प्रजाकामो बहुः प्रजया पशुभिः स्यां प्रजायेय श्रियं गच्छेयं यशः स्यामन्नादः स्यामिति स वै दक्षो नाम तद्यदेनेन सोऽयजत तस्माद्दाक्षायणयज्ञ इत्याख्यायत उत हैके वसिष्ठयज्ञ इत्याचक्षते स उ वा एकेन नाम्ना वसिष्ठस्तमेव

२३. यथा TE, V1.

२४. मुद्वृज्य Co.

२५. षड्ऋतव TE.

to the sacrificer's father, saying only "(name in the vocative),This is for you ",and to the sacrificer's grandfather saying, "(name in the vocative),This is for you ", and to the sacrificer's great grandfather saying, "(name in the vocative),This is for you ". Thus he presents (the food in a sequence) (moving) away from the present. For the fathers have passed away only once.

17. Then he says, "Oh! fathers! regale yourselves here. Act like bulls, according to your share". In that he says (means), Oh! fathers, eat each one his share". Then he turns away (his face in the opposite direction, away from the food offered). For, the fathers are hidden (from view).This (offering) becomes, as it were, concealed (when he turns his face away).

18. They (some) say with regard to that, "He should remain (so turning away, holding his breath) till fainting. For, thus far is his vital strength". But then, he may turn round, after remaining (thus) for a very short time only. Then he says, "The fathers have regaled themselves; they have acted like bulls according to their share". He says (means) verily this, "The fathers have eaten according to their share".

19. Then he makes the father of the sacrificer wash (his hands) saying, "(name in the vocative), Wash (your hands)", the grandfather of the sacrificer saying, "(name in vocative), Wash (your hands)", and the sacrificer's great grandfather saying "(name in the vocative),Wash(your hands) ".This is just as one would make those who have eaten wash (their hands).

20. Then, loosening the tuck (of his garment) at the navel, he prostrates (in obeisance). For, the tuck at the navel is sacred to the *pitṛs*. Indeed, obeisance is sacrifice. (By this) he makes these fathers worthy of worship (sacrifice). He performs obeisance six times. The seasons are six. Indeed the manes are the seasons. He establishes this sacrifice in the very seasons. He says, "Oh fathers! give us homes". This is indeed the blessing (he seeks) of this (ritual). The fathers, verily, have power over the houses. Therefore, he says, "Oh fathers! give us houses". Then he smells at the pot. That is the share of the sacrificer. They again put the rice-balls together. The once-cut (stalks of sacrificial grass) they put into the fire. He moves the fire brand, too, back (to the fire).

(Third Brāhmaṇa Ends)

BRĀHMAṆA IV

1. Prajāpati desirous of progeny, sacrificed with this (form of) sacrifice, thinking, "May I become prolific with progeny and cattle; may I be born well (may I produce); may I attain prosperity; may I become glorious; may I be the consumer of (fine) food". He was indeed Dakṣa. In that he sacrificed with this

तदन्वा[1]चक्षते स एतेन यज्ञेनेष्ट्वा येयं प्रजापतेः प्रजातिर्या श्रीस्तद्बभूवैवꣳ ह वाव प्रजायत एवꣳ श्रियं गच्छति य एनेनैवं विद्वान्यजते ॥ १ ॥

तेनो ह वै तत ईजे प्रतिदर्शः श्वैक्नः[2] स एतं प्रत्यासुस्तेषाꣳ ह विवाचनमिवास विवाचनमिव ह वै भवति य एवं विद्वानेतेन यज्ञेन यजते तमु[3] ह सुप्ला सार्ञ्जयो ब्रह्मचर्यमाजगाम तस्माद्धैतं च यज्ञमनूच्यान्यं च पुनः सृञ्जयानाजगाम ते ह सृञ्जया विदांचक्रुर्यज्ञं वै नोऽनूच्यागमदिति ते होचुः स ह वै नो देवैरागमदिति यो नो यज्ञमनूच्यागमदिति तद्वाव सहदेवः सार्ञ्जयोऽपि निवचनमिवास्त्यन्यद्वै सुप्ला नाम दध इति स एतेन यज्ञेनेष्ट्वा यैषा सृञ्जयानां प्रजातिर्या श्रीस्तद्बभूवैवꣳ ह वाव प्रजायत एवꣳ श्रियं गच्छति य एनेनैवं[4] विद्वान्यजते ॥ २ ॥

तेनो ह वै तत ईजे देवभागः श्रौतर्षः स उभयेषां कुरुसृञ्जयानां पुरोहित आस परमता वै सा ययान्वेकस्य[5] राष्ट्रस्य पुरोहितोऽसत्सेन्न[6] परमताथ किं यो द्वयोः परमतामिव ह वै गच्छति य एवं विद्वानेतेन यज्ञेन यजते ॥ ३ ॥

तेनो ह वै तत ईजे दक्षः पार्वतिः स ह राज्यमिव प्राप त इमे दाक्षायणा एदा[7]नमेव राज्यमिव ह वै प्राप्नोति य एवं विद्वानेतेन यज्ञेन यजते तस्माद्वा एतेन यज्ञेन यजेत तदंन्वहमेकैकः पुरोळाशो भवति तथा हास्यानुपबाधासप[8]त्ना श्रीर्भवति स द्वे पौर्णमास्यौ यजते द्वे अमावास्ये द्वन्द्वं वै मिथुनं मिथुनमेवैतत्प्रजननं क्रियते ॥ ४ ॥

१. तमेतदन्वाचक्षते Ca.

२. स्वैक्नः M; श्वैक्कः Po; श्वैक्नः My.

३. तमू Ca.

४. एतेनैवं as alternate reading in TE.

५. ययन्वे TE, Ca, Po; ययंन्वे VI, य इण्वेक M; see Notes; यो न्वेकस्य Ca.

६. ऽसत्सेन्न TE, H,B; see Notes. ऽसत्सेन्नु Ca.

७. See Notes.

८. सपत्ना Ca.

(form of) sacrifice, it is thereby called *Dākṣāyaṇa* sacrifice. And some moreover say, "(This is) Vasiṣṭha sacrifice". He (Dakṣa) was, indeed, (known) by one name, 'Vasiṣṭha' (the wealthiest). They call it verily after him. On his sacrificing with this sacrifice, there came to be this which is the progeny of Prajāpati and what prosperity (there is). He who knowing thus sacrifices, with this *(Dākṣāyaṇa* sacrifice), multiplies (in progeny) like this and attains similar prosperity.

2. Then Pratidarśa Śvaikaṇa indeed sacrificed with that (sacrifice). To those who looked up to him, he was like an authority [(authoritative) explanation]. He who, knowing thus, sacrifices with this (sacrifice) indeed becomes an authority as it were. Suplā Sārñjaya came to him, verily, for disciplined Vedic study. Having studied from him this sacrifice and another too, he came back to the Sṛñjaya country. They, the Sṛñjayas knew, "He has come after studying the sacrifice for our sake". They said, "He who has come after studying the sacrifice has verily, come to us with the gods ". Therefore (he came to be known as) Sahadeva Sārñjaya. There is also the saying, "Suplā has taken another name!" On his sacrificing with this sacrifice, there came to be this progeny which is of the Sṛñjayas and what prosperity (there is). He who, knowing it to be thus, sacrifices with this sacrifice, produces (progeny) in this very manner and attains prosperity like this, indeed.

3. Then Devabhāga, Śrautarṣa sacrificed verily with that sacrifice. He was the *Purohita* (an honoured family priest) of both the Kurus and Sṛñjayas. That indeed is a supreme (superior) position that one is the *Purohita* of one kingdom. What then is the superiority (of one) who (is the *Purohita*) of two (kingdoms)? He who knowing thus, sacrifices with this sacrifice surely attains superiority.

4. Then, Dakṣa Pārvati verily sacrificed with that sacrifice. He acquired sovereignity (a kingdom). These descendants of Dakṣa, even now have acquired royal status. He who, knowing thus, sacrifices with this sacrifice, surely attains royal status. Therefore indeed one should sacrifice with this sacrifice. In it, there is (to be offered) one *Puroḍāśa* (cake) every day. Thus (thereby) his prosperity becomes free from disturbance and without a rival (to share it). He performs the sacrifice (on) two Full Moon days and two New Moon days. Indeed a pair is a group of two. Verily this, a productive pair is made.

5. On the first day of Full Moon he sacrifices with a *Puroḍāśa* (cake offering) consecrated to Agni and Soma (together). They are two deities. A group of two is a pair indeed. Verily this, a productive pair is made. Then at dawn (the next day) there is a *Puroḍāśa* consecrated to Agni. There is *Sānnāyya* (offering)

स पूर्वेद्युः पौर्णमास्या अग्नीषोमीयेण पुरोळाशेन यजते[9] ते द्वे देवते द्वन्द्वं वै मिथुनं मिथुनमेवैतत्प्रजननं क्रियतेऽथ प्रातराग्नेयः पुरोळाशो भवत्यैन्द्रꣳ सान्नाय्यं ते द्वे देवते द्वन्द्वं वै मिथुनं मिथुनमेवैतत्प्रजननं क्रियते ॥ ५ ॥

अथ पूर्वेद्युरमावास्याया ऐन्द्राग्नेन पुरोळाशेन यजते[10] ते द्वे देवते द्वन्द्वं वै मिथुनं मिथुनमेवैतत्प्रजननं क्रियतेऽथ प्रातराग्नेयः पुरोळाशो भवति मैत्रावरुणी पयस्या नेद्यज्ञादयानीत्येवाग्नेयः पुरोळाशो मित्रावरुणावेव द्वे देवते द्वन्द्वं वै मिथुनं मिथुनमेवैतत्प्रजननं क्रियते एतद्धास्य तद्रूपं येन बहुर्भवति येन प्रजायते ॥ ६ ॥

अथ यद्वेव पूर्वेद्युः पौर्णमास्या अग्नीषोमीयेण पुरोळाशेन यजते यमेवाद उपवसथेऽग्नीषोमीयं पशुमालभते स एवास्य सोऽथ प्रातराग्नेयः पुरोळाशो भवत्यैन्द्रꣳ सान्नाय्यं प्रातःसवनमेवास्याग्नेयः पुरोळाशो गायत्रꣳ हि प्रातःसवनं गायत्रमग्नेश्छन्दो माध्यन्दिनमेवास्य सवनमैन्द्रꣳ सान्नाय्यमैन्द्रꣳ हि माध्यन्दिनꣳ सवनम् ॥ ७ ॥

अथ पूर्वेद्युरमावास्याया ऐन्द्राग्नेन पुरोळाशेन यजते[11] तृतीयसवनमेवास्य स वैश्वदेवꣳ हि तृतीय[12]सवनꣳ सर्वा हि देवता इन्द्राग्नी अथ प्रातराग्नेयः पुरोळाशो भवति मैत्रावरुणी पयस्या नेद्यज्ञादयानीत्येवाग्नेयः पुरोळाशोऽथ यामेवामूमनूबन्ध्यां वशामालभते सैवास्य मैत्रावरुणी पयस्यैतदु पौर्णमासेन चेष्ट्वामावास्येन च यावतीꣳ सौम्येनाध्वरेण जितिं जयति तावतीं जयति तन्महायज्ञो भवति ॥ ८ ॥

अथ यद्वेव पूर्वेद्युः पौर्णमास्या अग्नीषोमीयेण पुरोळाशेन यजत एतेन वा इन्द्रो वृत्रमहन्नेतेनो एव व्यजयत येयमस्य विजितिस्तथो वा एष एतेन पाप्मानं द्विषन्तं भ्रातृव्यꣳ हन्ति तथो एव विजयतेऽथ प्रातरामावास्यꣳ सान्नाय्यं वा आमावास्यं दूरे तद्यदमावास्येत्येनमेतद्वृत्रं जघ्निवाꣳसं क्षिप्रमेतेन रसेनाप्रीणन्क्षिप्रꣳ ह वै पाप्मानमपहते य एवं

९. यजते Ca.

१०. यजते Ca.

११. यजते Ca.

१२. सवनꣳ TE.

(a mixture of sour milk and fresh milk) consecrated for Indra. They are two deities. Indeed a group of two is a pair. Verily thus.a productive pair is made.

6. And on the first day of New Moon, he sacrifices with a *Puroḍāśa* consecrated to Indra and Agni (together). They are two deities. A group of two is indeed a pair. Verily thus,a productive pair is made. Then at dawn (of the morrow) there is one *Puroḍāśa* consecrated for Agni. (There is an offering of) curds dedicated to Mitra and Varuṇa (together). The *Puroḍāśa* (sacrificial cake) for Agni is for the very reason that if (it is) not (offered), (Agni would say), "Let me go away from (this) sacrifice". Mitra and Varuṇa themselves are the two deities. Indeed a group of two is a pair. Verily this, a productive pair is formed. This indeed is that form of this (sacrifice), by means of which he becomes many (multiplies) and by which he is born (is reproduced)

7. And, when, verily, on the first (previous) day of Full Moon, he sacrifices with a *Puroḍāśa* sanctified for Agni and Soma (together) that indeed is for this sacrificial animal dedicated to Agni and Soma, which he slaughters (for the sacrifice) on the day of fasting (and preparation). Then, in the morning, there is (an offering of) a *Puroḍāśa* dedicated to Agni. The *Sānnāyya* (offering of a mixture of sour milk and fresh milk) is dedicated to Indra. The *Puroḍāśa* for Agni is in itself his morning libation. The (*mantra* for offering) morning libation is *Gāyatra (in Gāyạtrī mantra)*;*Gāyatra* is Agni's metre. The *sānnāyya* for Indra is itself his mid-day libation. Indeed the mid-day libation belongs to Indra.

8. On the first day (previous day) of New Moon, he sacrifices with (the offering of) a *Puroḍāśa* consecrated to Indra and Agni (together). That is indeed his third (evening) libation. Verily the third libation is what has the Viśvedevas as its deity. For, Indra and Agni are (they constitute) all the gods. Then on the (next) morning, there is (the offering of) a *Puroḍāśa* dedicated to Agni. (There is an offering of) curd sanctified for Mitra and Varuṇa (together). The *Puroḍāśa* for Agni is for the very reason that if not; (Agni would say) "Let me go out of (this) sacrifice". That very barren cow, the *anubandhyā* (that should be subsequently tethered,i.e. offered) which he slaughters (for the sacrifice) is to him the curds (offering) sanctified for Mitra and Varuṇa (together). Thus preforming the Full Moon and New Moon offerings, one wins as much gain as one wins by means of a Soma sacrifice. That becomes a great sacrifice (or, by that he becomes one who has performed a great sacrifice).

9. And what he sacrifices with a *Puroḍāśa* dedicated to Agni and Soma (together) on the first (previous)day of Full Moon, with this indeed did Indra kill Vṛtra and with this only did he attain this victory which is his. In that very same manner does this (sacrificer) kill his evil hateful enemy and similarly becomes victorious. And now about the offering on the morning of the New Moon day; the oblation for New Moon day is indeed *Sānnāyya*(mixture of sour milk and fresh milk). *Amāvāsya* is indeed far away (from the FullMoon).Thus he who knowing thus, makes an offering of *sānnāyya* on Full Moon day, quickly

विद्वान्पौर्णमास्याꣳ सन्नयत्यथ यद्वेव पौर्णमास्याꣳ सन्नयत्येष वै सोमो राजा देवानामन्नं यच्चन्द्रमास्तमेतत्पूर्वेद्युः पौर्णमास्या देवा अभिषुण्वन्ति प्रातर्भक्षयिष्यन्तस्तमेतद्भक्षयन्ति यदपक्षीयते स यत्पूर्वेद्युः पौर्णमास्या अग्नीषोमीयेण पुरोळाशेन यजतेऽभिषुणोत्येवैनं तत्तस्मिन्नभिषुत एतꣳ रसं दधाति तं तीव्रीकरोति स्वदयति[१३] ह देवेभ्यो हव्यꣳ स्वदते हास्य देवेभ्यो हव्यं य एवं विद्वान्पौर्णमास्याꣳ सन्नयति ॥ ९ ॥

अथ पूर्वेद्युरमावास्याया ऐन्द्राग्नेन पुरोळाशेन यजते दर्शपूर्णमासयोर्वै देवते स्त इन्द्राग्नी एव प्रत्यक्षꣳ हास्य दर्शपूर्णमासाविष्टौ भवतो य एवं विद्वान्यजते[१४]ऽथ प्रातराग्नेयः पुरोळाशो भवति मैत्रावरुणी पयस्या नेद्यज्ञादयानीत्येवाग्नेयः पुरोळाशोऽथैतावेवार्धमासौ मित्रावरुणौ य एवापक्षीयते स मित्रो य आपूर्यते स वरुणः ॥ १० ॥

तवेताꣳ रात्रिमुभौ सह समागच्छतस्तावेतदुभौ सह[१५] सन्तौ प्रीणाति सर्वꣳ ह वा अस्य प्रीतꣳ सर्वमाप्तꣳ सर्वं जितं भवति य एवं विद्वान्यजते ॥ ११ ॥

तदेताꣳ रात्रिं मित्रो वरुणे रेतः सिञ्चति तेन रेतसैतत्प्रजायते यदापूर्यतेऽथ यदेषात्र पयस्यावक्लृप्तमावास्यावै सान्नाय्यभाजना तत्पौर्णमास्याꣳ सन्नयति स यत्सन्नयेत्पौर्णमास्याꣳसन्नयेदमावास्यायां जामि कुर्यात्समदं कुर्यादेतद्वैवैनमेष एतदद्भ्यश्चौषधिभ्यश्च संभृत्याहुतिभ्यो जनयति मिथुनादिद्वा एनं जनयति योषा पयस्या रेतो वाजिनं तद्वा अनुष्ठ्या यन्मिथुनात्प्रजायते ॥ १२ ॥

अथ वाजिभ्यो वाजिनं जुहोत्यृतवो वै वाजिनो रेतो वाजिनमृतुष्वेवैतद्रेतः सिञ्चति तदृतवो रेतः सिक्तमिमाः प्रजाः प्रजनयन्ति तत्पश्चा यज्ञस्य जुहोति पश्चाद्वै परीत्य योषां वृषाधिद्रवति तस्याꣳ रेतः सिञ्चति तस्मात्पश्चा यज्ञस्य जुहोत्यग्ने[१६] वीहीति तत्स्विष्टकृद्भाजनं तदु प्राङेव जुहोति ॥ १३ ॥

१३. स्वदयतीह Ks, H; स्वदयति वा M; See Notes.

१४. विद्वान्यजते Ca, TE gives both the readings.

१५. सह Ca.

१६. त्यग्नये TE; see Notes.

destroys evil, well propitiating him quickly by means of this juice; him who had killed Vṛtra by means of this offering . And then that he (the sacrificer) makes an offering of *Sānnāyya* (means this). This moon is himself the King Soma, the food of the gods. On the first (previous) day of Full Moon the gods ceremoniously extract him (the juice of Soma), (so that) they would be consuming it in the (next) morning. Then they eat him up, wherefore he decreases. As he sacrifices with the *Puroḍāśa* consecrated for Agni and Soma (together) on the first (previous) day of Full Moon, in that he (the sacrificer) verily extracts him (Soma) thus and when that has been extracted he adds this juice (essence), makes it strong and (also) makes the oblation to be offered palatable to the gods. Whoever, knowing thus makes the *Sānnāyya* offering during Full Moon, his oblation indeed is sweet (palatable) to the gods.

10. And now, the first (previous) day of New Moon he sacrifices with the *Puroḍāśa* dedicated to Indra and Agni (together). Indeed Indra and Agni are the deities of the New Moon and Full Moon days. Verily, directly are the New Moon and Full Moon worshipped (with sacrifice) (thus) by him who, knowing thus, sacrifices. Then, in the (next) morning there is (offered) a *Puroḍāśa* sanctified for Agni and curds dedicated to Mitra and Varuṇa (together) for, if not (Agni would say), "Let me go away from the sacrifice". Therefore, indeed, there is (offered) the *Puroḍāśa* to Agni. And these two half months (half moons) are Mitra and Varuṇa. That which wanes is verily Mitra and that which fills up (waxes) is Varuṇa.

11. This night (of New Moon), the two come together. He (the sacrificer) thus propitiates these two who are then together. To him who, knowing thus, preforms the sacrifice, everything is pleasing, everything is accomplished and everything is won.

12. Then during this night Mitra deposits his (virility) seed in Varuṇa. By that seed springs up this which fills up (waxes). Now (regarding) this (offering of) curds that is most appropriately designed; indeed the New Moon day is the worthy recipient for *Sānnāyya*. He (the sacrificer) leads (mixes and offers) during the Full Moon (too). Should he make the *Sānnāyya* during the Full Moon and make the *Sānnāyya* during New Moon, he would be doing a repetition and would create a conflict. This (sacrificer), collecting him (Soma) verily from these waters and plants, causes him (the moon-Soma) to be born from the oblations. Indeed, he produces this (Soma-moon) from the pair. The 'Curds' is female; the whey (produced by mixing lime juice with milk) is the seed. Therefore that is to be performed by which, it (the moon) is born from the pair.

13. He then offers the whey to the (divine) horses. Indeed the seasons are the horses; the whey is the seed (semen). He (the sacrificer) deposits this seed verily

अथ दिशो व्याघारयति दिशः प्रदिश आदिशो विदिश उद्दिशो दिग्भ्यः स्वाहेति पञ्च
दिशः पञ्चर्तव ऋतूनेवैतद्दिग्भिर्मिथुनान्करोति [१७]पञ्चो एव भक्षयन्ति होता चाध्वर्युश्च ब्रह्मा
चाग्नीच्च यजमान ऋतूनामेवैतद्रूपं कृत्वर्तुष्वेव रेतः प्रतिष्ठापयन्ति प्रथमो यजमानो भक्षयति
प्रथमो रेतः परिगृह्णा[१८]नीत्यथोत्तमो मय्युत्तमꣳ रेतः प्रतितिष्ठादित्युपहूत उपह्वयस्वेति सोममे-
वैतत्कृत्वा भक्षयन्ति ॥ १४ ॥ इति चतुर्थं ब्राह्मणम्

॥इति तृतीयोऽध्यायः॥

१७. पञ्च एव P1, P2, H; see Notes.

१८. गृह्णामीत्य TE, T.

into the seasons. Then the seasons bring forth the seed that had been deposited as (in the form of) these creatures. Therefore does he offer it behind the sacrifice. Verily the male runs towards the female covering her from behind. He deposits his semen into her. Therefore does he (the sacrificer) offer behind (in the fire of) the sacrifice saying, "Go verily in front". That is the receptacle of '*Sviṣṭakṛt*' (Agni who renders all offerings already made properly offered) Therefore he verily offers that in the east.

14. He then sprinkles the quarters (with the whey),—(1) the quarters, (2) the fore-quarters, (3) the by-quarters, (4) the intermediate quarters, (5) the upper-quarters, uttering "To the quarters *Svāhā* !" The quarters are five. The seasons are five. He thus makes the seasons themselves become pairs with the quarters. Five only indeed eat (the residual whey)—(1) the Hotṛ, and (2) the Adhvaryu,(3) the Brahmā and (4) the Agnidh and (5) the sacrificer. Making this verily the form of the seasons, they establish the seed in the seasons themselves. The sacrificer, the first person, eats (first), thinking, "May I, the first person receive the seed (first)" and then the last (best), thinking, "May the best (last) seed stay firmly in me!" "Being invited, you please invite!"—thus saying and having verily rendered this (whey) as Soma itself, they (other four) eat (it).

(Fourth Brāhmaṇa Ends)

(Chapter Three ends)

चतुर्थोऽध्यायः

प्रथमं ब्राह्मणम्

अग्नौ ह वै देवाः सर्वान्पशून्त्सन्निदधिरे ये च ग्राम्या ये चारण्या विजयं वोपपरेष्यन्तः[1] कामचारस्य वा कामायायं नो गोपिष्ठो गोपायत्विति तान्हाग्निर्निचकमे तान्त्संगृह्य रात्रिं प्रविवेश पुनरेम इति देवा एदग्निं[2] तिरोभूतं ते ह विदांचक्रुरिह वै प्राविशद्रात्रिं वै प्राविक्षदिति तमेतत्प्रत्यायत्याꣳ रात्रा उपातिष्ठन्त देहि नः पशून्पुनर्नो देहि पशूनिति तेभ्यो ह पुनर्ददौ ॥ १ ॥

तस्मै कमग्नी उपतिष्ठेताग्नी वै दातारौ तावेवैतत्पशून्याचते यदुपतिष्ठते तस्मात्सायमुपतिष्ठेत सायꣳ हि देवा उपातिष्ठन्त दत्तो हास्मै पशून्य एवं विद्वानुपतिष्ठते ॥ २ ॥

अथ यस्मान्नोपतिष्ठेत सह वा इदमग्र आसुर्देवाश्च मनुष्याश्च तद्ध स्म यन्मनुष्याणां न भवति तद्ध स्म देवान्याचन्त इदं वै नो नास्तीदं नोऽस्त्विति ते देवास्तस्या याच्ञ्याया द्वेषेण तिर आसुस्तस्मान्नोपतिष्ठेत नेद्धिनसानि नेद्द्वेष्योऽसानीति[3] ॥ ३ ॥

अथ यस्मादुपैव तिष्ठेत् यज्ञो वै देवानामाशीर्यजमानस्य स एष यज्ञो देवानां यदाहुतिरथैषाशीर्यजमानस्य यदुपतिष्ठते स यदेवास्यात्र तदेवैतदात्मनि कुरुते तस्मादुपैव तिष्ठेत ॥ ४ ॥

अथ यस्मान्नोपतिष्ठेत यो वै ब्राह्मणं वा राजन्यं वा शꣳसमानोऽनुचरति गृहान्मे करिष्यतीति यो वै तत्र तं वाचा वा कर्मणा वा रिराधयिषति तस्मै वै स देयं मन्यतेऽथ य एनमाह कस्मै नु मम त्वमर्थायासि यो मे न ददासीतीश्वरो वै स तं द्वेष्टोँ[4]स्तस्मान्नोपतिष्ठेत नेद्धिनसानि नेद्द्वेष्योऽसानीत्येतत्त्विद्वा एनमेष याचते यदिन्द्धे यज्जुहोति ॥ ५ ॥

अथ यस्मादुपैव तिष्ठेतोत वै याचँल्लभत एव दातारमुतो भर्ता नानुबुध्यते यदा वै भार्यो भर्तारमाह बिभृहि मेत्यथ वै स तं बिभर्ति वा भार्यं वा मन्यते तस्मादुपैव तिष्ठेतेदं नु[5] समस्तं

१. परेष्यन्त Ca.

२. एतदग्निं see Notes.

३. ऽसानीति TE, M,K.

४. See Notes.

५. तु H.

Chapter Four

BRĀHMAṆA I

1. The gods deposited all animals, those that were rustic (domestic) and those that were wild, into Agni, because they were going out to achieve victory or because of a desire for moving about (freely) as they wished or with a thought, "This (Agni) is the best protector (and) let him protect (these animals of) ours". Agni coveted them very much and gathering them together he entered the night. The gods (said), "Let us get back" and verily (came) to Agni who was concealed. They came to know, "(Agni) has entered here; indeed he has entered the night ". When the night returned, they waited upon him saying, "Please give our animals back, please give us our animals". He gave (the animals) back to them.

2. For that one should worship the two fires. Indeed the two fires are the bestowers. He (the sacrificer) thus verily supplicates only them for cattle, wherefore he worships them. Therefore he should worship them in the evening. For the gods waited upon (Agni) in the evening. To him who, knowing thus, worships (the two Agnis), they give (cattle).

3. Now (this is the reason) why he should not approach (them) (with *mantras*). Indeed men and gods were here together in the beginning. Whatever there is not for men, that verily they asked of the gods, "This indeed we do not have. Let this be for us". Those gods, out of dislike for that request disappeared. Therefore one should not approach (the gods); (he should think), "If not (i.e. if I request them) I shall hurt (them) and if not (if I request them) I shall become one to be hated".

4. Now (here is the reason) why one should verily worship (them): Indeed the sacrifice belongs to the gods and the prayer for the blessing is the sacrificer's. The oblation is (in itself) this sacrifice belonging to the gods, that he worships is (in itself) the prayer for blessing of the sacrificer. What indeed is there for him here, that very thing he takes to himself. Therefore one must verily worship (approach the gods).

5. And now (is the reason) why one should not approach (with worship for a blessing); whoever follows a Brāhmin or a Kṣatriya (Rājanya; a crowned monarch) praising him, thinking, "This man will give me homes", he (the Brāhmin or Kṣatriya) thinks that it should be given to him who tries to please him with word or action. But whoever says to him, "Of what use are you to me? You who do not give me (anything). That master hates him (the suppliant). Therefore one should not approach (the Agnis with a request), thinking, "If not I may hurt; if not I may become hateful". Thus really does this (sacrificer) request this (Agni) in that he kindles (the fire) and in that he makes offerings (in it). (So he should not request again).

यस्मादुपैव तिष्ठेत प्रजापतिर्वा एष एतद्भूत्वा यावदेनमनु यावत ईष्टे तस्य सर्वस्य रेतः सिञ्चति यदग्निहोत्रं जुहोति तदुपतिष्ठमानो भूमानमनु विकरोति भूमानमनु प्रजनयति तस्मादुपैव तिष्ठेत ॥ ६ ॥

स वा उपवत्या प्रथमयोपतिष्ठत इयं वा उप सा वा इयं द्वयेनोप यद्वै किं च जायतेऽस्यामेव तदुपजायते यदु किं च न्यृच्छत्यस्यामेव तदुपकीर्यते तदिदमह्ना रात्र्या भूयो भूय एव भवति भूम्नैवैतदक्षय्येण[६] प्रतिपद्यते ॥ ७ ॥

स आहोपप्रयन्तो अध्वरमिति यज्ञो वा अध्वर उपप्रयन्तो यज्ञमित्येवैतदाह मन्त्रं वोचेमाग्नय इति मन्त्रँ ह्यस्मै वक्ष्यन्भवत्यारे अस्मे च शृण्वत इति यद्यप्यस्मद्दूरमस्यथ न इदमेव शृण्वित्थमेवेदमस्त्विँ[७]त्येवैतदाह ॥ ८ ॥

अथाग्निर्मूर्धा दिवः ककुत्पतिः पृथिव्या अयम्। अपाँ रेताँसि जिन्वतीति यथा याचन्क[८]ल्याणं वदेदामुष्यायणो वै त्वमस्यलं वै त्वमेतस्मा असीति प्रमुमोदयिषन्नुपस्तुयादेवम्वेवैषा ॥ ९ ॥

अथैन्द्राग्न्यैष वा इन्द्रो य एष तपति स वा एषोऽस्तं यन्नग्नि[९]मेव प्रविशति तस्मादैन्द्राग्न्योभा वामिन्द्राग्नी आहुवध्या उभा राधसः सह मादयध्यै[१०]। उभा दातारा इषाँ रयीणामुभा वाजस्य सातये हुवे वामित्युभौ मे दातारौ सह सन्तौ दत्तमित्येवैतदाह ॥ १० ॥

अथायन्ते योनिर्ऋत्वियो यतो जातो अरोचथाः। तं जानन्नग्न आरोहाथ नो वर्धया रयिमिति पुष्टं वै रयिः स्वन्त इदं यदस्माकं पुष्टं तन्नो भूयो भूय एव कुरु तन्नो वर्धयेत्येवैतदाह ॥ ११ ॥

६. दक्षीयेण Ca

७. मस्तीत्ये TE.

८. वाचं कल्याणं P1, P2, B,H.

९. नयन्नग्नि TE, V1, B.

१०. मादयध्वै Ca. has no basis in the Saṁhitā text.

6. And now (is the reason) why one should verily approach (with a request): he who asks verily finds a bestower. Also,the master does not know (the wants of the dependant). Only when the dependant says to the master, "Please support me" then does he (the master) supports him or does he consider him worthy of support. Therefore one must approach (the two fires with a prayer). This is the whole (argument) wherefore one must verily approach (the fires with worship and request). Indeed this (Agni), being Prajāpati (or Prajāpati becoming this,(Agni) thus,deposits the seed of everything, all that is about him and all that he rules over, in that one who performs the *Agnihotra*. Performing that (worship) *(Agnihotra)* one imitates abundance and produces abundance continuously. Therefore one must verily worship.

7. He prays with a first (prayer) that contains (the word) *'upa'*. Indeed this (earth) is *'upa'*. This *upa* is with two (meanings). Whatever is born, that surely is born upon this (earth). Whatever perishes, that is scattered upon this earth only. This verily becomes more and more, by day and by night. Thus, he (the sacrificer) takes up with this imperishable abundance.

8. He says,"Approaching verily the *Adhvara*–" Indeed, the sacrificer is *Adhvara*. Saying, "Approaching the *Adhvara*–" he says (means) this only,viz., "Let us utter the chant (of prayer) to Agni ",for, he is going to utter the chant *(mantra)*,"Who hears us also from afar". He verily says (means) this, "Though you are far away from us, please do hear this (prayer) of ours. Let this be verily thus".

9. And then, (he prays), "This Agni (is) the head, the shoulder of the sky, the lord of the earth. He pleases (excites) the seeds of waters". Just as one who supplicates will speak auspiciously (thus), "You are verily the descendant of such and such a (great) person! Indeed you are capable of this (achievement)", and will praise (the donor) wishing to make him happy; so indeed is this (*Ṛk* of praise).

10. Then (is chanted) this of Indra and Agni; this one (Sun) who burns is verily Indra. This is the one who, setting, enters Agni indeed. Therefore is (the chant) to Indra and Agni—"I invoke you both Indra and Agni! Both of you together do I delight with pleasing service. Both of you are bestowers of strength and wealth. I invoke you two for acquisition of food". He verily says (means) this only,viz., "You two, the bestowers, remaining together give to me".

11. Then (he chants), "This is thy seasonal source (womb), born from which you shone forth. Knowing that, Oh! Agni! climb up (grow) and increase our wealth". Indeed wealth is nourishment. He verily says (means) this: "This our nourishment is your own. Please make it more and more (abundant) to us. Please increase that (nourishment) of ours".

अयमिह प्रथमो धायी धातृभिर्होता यजिष्ठो अध्वरेष्वीड्यः। यमप्नवानो भृगवो विरुरुचुर्वनेषु चित्रं विभ्वं विशे विश इति यथा याचन्कल्याणं वदेदामुष्यायणो वै त्वमस्यलं वै त्वमेतस्मा असीति प्रमुमोदयिषन्नुपस्तुयादेवम्वेवैषाथो यथैवैष तथैनमाह विभूर्ह्येष विशे विशे। अस्य पत्नामनु द्युतꣳ शुक्रं दुदुह्रे अह्रयः। पयः सहस्रसामृषिमित्येषा वै परमा सनिर्यत्सहस्रसनिस्तस्या एवैतदवरुद्धये तस्मादाह पयः सहस्रसामृषिमिति ॥ १२ ॥

तद्वा एतत्समाहार्यꣳ षळृचं तस्योपवती प्रथमा प्रत्नवत्युत्तमावोचाम तद्यस्मादुपवत्यसौ वाव प्रत्नं यावन्तो ह्येव स नाग्रे देवास्तावन्त एवाप्येतर्ह्येते उ वा अन्तरेण सर्वे कामास्ताभ्यामेवैतन्निवेदयति ते हास्मै संजानाने सर्वान्कामान्त्सन्नमतः ॥ १३ ॥

त्रिः प्रथमां जपति त्रिरुत्तमां त्रिवृत्प्रायणा हि यज्ञास्त्रिवृदुदयना यदु ह वा अग्निहोत्रं जुह्वद्वाचा वा कर्मणा वानृतं वा वदत्यनृतं वाव[११] करोत्यात्मनो हैव तदायुषो वा वर्चसो वा प्रजाया वावद्यति ॥ १४ ॥

स उपतिष्ठते तनूपा अग्नेऽसि तन्वं मे पाह्यायुर्दा अग्नेऽस्यायुर्मे देहि। वर्चोदा अग्नेऽसि वर्चो मे देहि। अग्ने यन्मे तन्वा ऊनं तन्मा आपृणेति यदेवेह वाचा वा कर्मणा वायुषो वा वर्चसो वा प्रजाया वावादाम तन्नः पुनराप्यायतामित्येवैतदाह तथा हास्य तत्पुनराप्यायते ॥ १५ ॥

इन्धनास्त्वा शतꣳ हिमा द्युमन्तꣳ समिधीमहीति शतं वर्षाणि जीव्यासमित्येवैतदाह यदाह शतꣳ हिमा इति द्युमन्तꣳ समिधीमहीति महान्तꣳ समिधीमहीत्येवैतदाह वयस्वन्तो वयस्कृतꣳ सहस्वन्तः सहस्कृतमिति वयस्वन्तो वयं भूयास्म वयस्कृत्त्वमसीत्येवैतदाह सहस्वन्तो वयं भूयास्म सहस्कृत्त्वमसीत्यग्ने सपत्नदम्भनमदब्धासो अदाभ्यमिति सपत्नाꣳस्त्वया पापीयसः करवामेत्येवैतदाह[१२] ॥ १६ ॥

चित्रावसो स्वस्ति ते पारमशीयेति त्रिर्जपति रात्रिर्ह वै चित्रावसुरेषा हीमानि चित्राणि संगृह्येव वसति तस्मान्नक्तं नारकाच्चित्रं ददृशे तस्या ह स्मैवमृषयः पुरा स्वस्ति पारꣳ

११. वाव Ca, Pl, B; वा करोति Ca.
१२. करवामे TE.

12. This one was the first here; he was upheld by the upholders: he is the (greatest) offerer (of oblations) (the Hotṛ priest), the best sacrificer, worthy of praise at the sacrifices. (He is the one) whom Apnavāna and the Bhṛgus (the Bhṛgus–who acquired him) made bright, the colourful one in the forests, the one who pervades in every home". Just as one making a request would speak auspiciously (thus), "You indeed are the descendant of such and such a (great) person! You surely are capable of this (achievement)" and desiring to make (the donor) happy,will praise him, so indeed is this. As he (Agni) really is, so does he (the sacrificer) speak of him (thus). " This (Agni) is pervading in house after house. In accordance with his old splendour, unflinching have milked the white milk of the accessible one who makes it a thousandfold". This is verily the supreme gift–this which is a thousandfold gift. This (praise) is indeed for keeping up that very thing (gift). Therefore does he say,"The milk, (from) the wise (sage) (the accessible one) who gives a thousandfold".

13. This is that collection containing six *Ṛks* of that (collection), the first *(Ṛk)* has the word *'upa'*, the last has the word *'Pratna'* . We recited that because she (the earth) has the word *'upa'* (upon) (and) the yonder (sky) is indeed old (contains the word *'Pratna'*). As many gods as there were, of old in the beginning, so many are there even now. In between (the sky and the earth, the gods of old and the gods now) are all the wishes (of the sacrificer). He conveys (respectfully) this only to those two. They indeed in accord, bring to him (the fulfilment of) all the wishes.

14. He mutters the first *(Ṛk)* thrice and the last one (too) thrice. Indeed sacrifices have threefold beginning and threefold conclusion. Performing the *Agnihotra,* whatever one speaks falsely by word or does falsely in action, by that he verily cuts off his own body, life span, splendour or progeny.

15. He (worships) utters the *mantras,* "Oh Agni! You are the protector of the body; please protect my body. Oh Agni! you are the bestower of life-span. Please give me (long) life. Oh Agni! you are the giver of splendour. Please give me splendour. Oh Agni! what is deficient in my body, please fill it up". He verily, in this says (means), "Whatever we cut off here of (our) life, splendour or progeny by our expression or action, may that be made up again for us". That way his (deficiency) is made up again.

16. (He prays), "Kindling you the brilliant one, may we (continue to) kindle (the fire) a hundred winters (snowy seasons). What he says, viz., "A hundred winters",–he verily says (means),"May I live a hundred years". (Saying),"May we kindle the brilliant one", he verily says (means),"May we kindle the great one", "(We) having vigour (enkindle) (you) the maker (giver) of vigour. (We) (having strength) (enkindle) you the maker (giver) of strength"–(by this) he only says (means) this,viz., "May we be possessors of vigour! you are the maker (giver) of vigour ", and "May we be possessors of strength! you are the maker (giver) of

समश्नुवते तथैनात्रात्र्या न नाष्ट्रा विवेद तथो वा अस्या एष एतत्स्वस्ति[१३] पारꣳ समश्नुते तथैनꣳ रात्र्या न नाष्ट्रा विन्दति तस्मादाह चित्रावसो स्वस्ति ते पारमाशीयेत्येतावत्तिष्ठन् जपत्यथोपविशति ॥ १७ ॥

स जपति संत्वमग्ने सूर्यस्य वर्चसागथा इति यदेनꣳ सूर्यः प्रविशति समृषीणाꣳ स्तुतेनेति यदेनमुपतिष्ठते सं प्रियेण धाम्नेत्याहुत्यैतदाहाहुतिर्हि वा अस्य प्रियं धाम समहमायुषा संवर्चसा संप्रजया सꣳरायस्पोषेण ग्मिषीयेति यथा त्वमेतेन समगथा एवमहमायुषा वर्चसा प्रजया संगच्छमानो भूयासमित्येवैतदाह सꣳरायस्पोषेण ग्मिषीयेति भूमा वै रायस्पोषो भूम्नेत्येवैतदाह ॥ १८ ॥

अथ गामुपपरैत्यन्धस्थान्धो वो भक्षीय सहःस्थ महो वो भक्षीयेति यानि वो महाꣳसि यानि वो वीर्याणि तानि वो भक्षीयेत्येवैतदाहोर्जःस्थोर्जं वो भक्षीयेति रसःस्थ रसं वो भक्षीयेत्येवैतदाह रायस्पोषः स्थ रायस्पोषं वो भक्षीयेति भूमा स्थ भूमानं वो भक्षीयेत्येवैतदाह ॥ १९ ॥

रेवती रमध्वमिति पशवो वै रेवन्तस्तस्मादाह रेवती रमध्वमित्यस्मिन्योना अस्मिन्गोष्ठेऽस्मिन्क्षयेऽस्मिँल्लोके। इहैव स्तेतो मापगातेत्यहं वः प्रियो भूयासमित्येवैतदाह ॥ २० ॥

अथ गामभिमृशति सꣳहितासि विश्वरूपीति सꣳहिता ह्येषा सर्वैः कामैर्विश्वरूपीति[१४] विश्वरूपा हि पशव ऊर्जमाविश गौपत्येनेति रसेनेति तदाह यदाहोर्जेति गौपत्येनेति भूम्नेत्येवैतदाह ॥ २१ ॥

अथ गार्हपत्यमुपपरैत्युपत्वाग्ने दिवे दिवे दोषावस्तर्धिया वयम्। नमो भरन्त एमसीति नम एवास्मा एतया करोति राजन्तमध्वराणां गोपामृतस्य दीदिविम्। वर्धमानꣳ स्वे दम इति स्वं त इदं यदस्माकं पुष्टं तन्नो भूयो भूय एव कुरु तन्नो वर्धयेत्येवैतदाह स नः पितेव सूनवेऽग्ने सूपायनो भव। सचस्वा नः स्वस्तय इति यथा पिता पुत्राय सूपचर एवं नः

१३. त्वास्ति ते पारꣳ H.

१४. विंश्व TE.

strength". And ahead (when he says),"(You) the uninjurable injurer of enemies, (we) the uninjured (enkindle)". He says, (means) verily this,viz. "May we, with you, make our enemies more miserable".

17. He mutters thrice,"Oh you, the one of colourful wealth! May it be well (auspicious) for you! May I reach the other shore (end). (Oh one of variegated riches! May I reach safely your other shore!) Indeed the night is the possessor of brilliant (coloured) wealth. For this one (the night) remains as though having gathered these things of various colours (the stars). Therefore, at night one does not see clearly from afar. (With) her (help) indeed, the sages formerly safely reached the shore (of the night). Therefore, the destructive one (Rākṣasa)did not find them by night. In that manner indeed, this person (the sacrificer) safely reaches this shore of this (night) and similarly the destructive one (the Rākṣasa) does not find him by night. Therefore does he say, "Oh one with wealth of bright colours! May I safely reach your shore!" So much he mutters standing. Thereafter he sits down.

18. He mutters, "Oh Agni! you have been united with the splendour of the Sun", for, the Sun enters this (Agni) along with the praise of the Ṛṣis (the sages); wherefore he (the sacrificer) worships him with (at) his pleasing abode with this offering. He says, "Indeed, it is this offering that is his (Agni's) favourite abode. May I well be united with (long) life, with splendour, with progeny and with rich wealth ". "Just as you are united with this (your favourite abode). So may I be united with (long) life, splendour and progeny. This (is) what he verily says (means). (He says), "May I be united with rich wealth". Indeed rich wealth (nourishment of wealth) is 'Abundance'. He verily says (means) this "With abundance".

19. He then approaches the cow, (saying), "You are food! May I eat your food! You are wealth! May I enjoy your wealth!" He verily says (means) this, "Whatever your riches are, whatever your virilities are, them may I enjoy!" He says (means) verily "You are 'strength'! May I enjoy your strength!" "You are the essence! May I enjoy your essence!" He verily says (means) this, "You are the nourishment of wealth! May I enjoy your rich wealth!" "You are abundance! May I enjoy your abundance!"

20. (He says), "Oh rich ones! engage in sport". Indeed cattle are rich. Therefore does he say, "Oh rich ones! revel in this sex, in this cowshed, in this residence, in this world". He verily says (means) this, "Remain there itself; don't go away from here. Thus may I become dear to you"!

21. Then he touches the cow (saying), "You are greatly favourable, having all forms". Indeed is this (cow) very benign and has all forms, with (fulfilment of) all wishes. Indeed cattle have all forms. (He says), "Enter me (come to me) with strength and with possession of cows". When he says, "With strength", he says

सूपचर एधीत्येवैतदाह यथा स तं न[१५] केनचन हिनस्त्येवं त्वा मा केनचन हिंसिष्मेत्यग्ने त्वं नो अन्तम उत त्राता शिवो भवा वरूथ्यः । वसुरग्निर्वसुश्रवा अच्छा नक्षिद्युमत्तमं रयिं दाः । । तं त्वा शोचिष्ठ दीदिवः सुम्नाय नूनमीमहे सखिभ्यः । स नो बोधि श्रुधी हवमुरुष्याणो अघायतः समस्मादिति ॥ २२ ॥

यदाहवनीयमुपतिष्ठते पशूंस्तद्याचते तस्मात्तमुच्चावचैश्छन्दोभिरुपतिष्ठत उच्चावा[१६]चा हि पशवो यद्गार्हपत्यं पुरुषांस्तच्च[१७] गायत्रेण तृचेन पूर्वेणोपतिष्ठते गायत्रमग्नेश्छन्दः स्वेनैवैनं तच्छन्दसोपतिष्ठतेऽथ द्विपदाभिः पु[१८]रुषछन्दसं वै द्विपदा द्विपाद्ध्ययं पुरुषः पुरुषान्वा एतद्याचते पशुमान्ह पुरुषवान्भवति य एवं विद्वानुपतिष्ठते ॥ २३ ॥

अथ गामुपपरैतीळ एह्यदित एहि काम्य एहीतीळा हि गौरदितिर्हि गौः काम्या हि गौः कामो ह्यासु मनुष्याणां प्रविष्टो मयि वः कामधरणमित्यहं वः प्रियो भूयासमित्येवैतदाह ॥ २४ ॥

अथान्तराहवनीयं च गार्हपत्यं च तिष्ठन्प्राङ् तिष्ठन्नाहवनीयमीक्षमाणो जपति सोमानं स्वरणं कृणुहि ब्रह्मणस्पते । कक्षीवन्तं य औशिजः । यो रेवान्यो अमीवहा वसुवित्पुष्टिवर्धनः । स नः सिषक्तु यस्तुरः । मा नः शंसो अररुषो धूर्तिः प्रणङ्मर्त्यस्य । रक्षाणो ब्रह्मणस्पत इति ॥ २५ ॥

यदाहवनीयमुपतिष्ठते दिवं तदुपतिष्ठते यद्गार्हपत्यं पृथि[१९]वीं तदथैतदन्तरिक्षमुपतिष्ठते तस्माद्ब्राह्मणस्पत्येन तृचेनोपतिष्ठत एषा हि दिग्ब्रह्मणस्पतेरेतां हि दिशमुपतिष्ठते महि त्रीणामवोऽस्तु द्युक्षं मित्रस्यार्यम्णः । दुराधर्षं वरुणस्य । न हि तेषाममा चन नाध्वसु वारणेषु । ईशे रिपुरघशंसः । ते हि पुत्रासो अदितेः प्र जीवसे मर्त्याय । ज्योतिर्यच्छन्त्य-

१५. तत्र TE.

१६. वचा TE, V2, W.

१७. स्तत्स Ca, V1.

१८. पुरुष Ca.

१९. पृथिवी TE.

(means), "With essence". (By saying),"With possession of cows", he verily says (means) this, "With abundance".

22. Then he goes near the *Gārhapatya* (chanting), "Oh Agni! we approach you every day, at dusk and dawn, conveying our obeisance with our thought". By this *(Ṛk)* he verily performs obeisance to this (Agni). (He chants), "(We approach you) Who are the shining protector of sacrifices and the effulgent (protector) of the Sacred Law *(Ṛta)* and who thrives in your own home".He (in this) verily says (means) this, "What is our nourishment, this is your own thing. Make it more and more for us! That of ours please increase". (He chants), "Oh Agni! be of good (easy) access to us, like a father to his son. Take us (on) for the sake of well-being "."Just as a father is easy for a son to serve (to move near), thus you please be easy for us to serve (approach)–this is just what he says (means), (as also) "Just as he (the son) does not in any way hurt him (the father), in the same way, may we not hurt you in any way". (He further chants), "Oh Agni! you please be proximate to us, (be) our protector, (be) auspicious, you—the head of a host (of gods)! (you who provide security)!" Agni is the wealth, (Agni has) wealthy fame. (Agni is famed for wealth). Come towards us, you the bestower of most glowing wealth!" Oh most bright one! Oh resplendent one! We come to you for happiness for (our) friends. Please understand us, listen to our call (prayer). Please be desirous of saving us from all evil-doers".

23. That he worships the *Āhavanīya,* (means) that he prays (in that) for (obtaining) cattle. Therefore he worships it *(Āhavanīya)* with metres, lofty and short. Indeed cattle are (of sizes) great and small. (That he worships) *Gārhapatya* (means that he prays for obtaining) men. Therefore he worships (the *Gārhapatya)* first with a triad of *Ṛks* in *Gāyatri* metre.*Gāyatra* is the metre of Agni. He (the sacrificer) therefore, worships this (Agni) with its own metre. Then (he worships *Gārhapatya)* with *Ṛks* with two feet (*pādas*). Indeed the *dvipadā* (*Ṛk* with two feet) is man's metre. Verily this, the man is a biped. Indeed with this he (the sacrificer) prays for (obtaining) men. He who knowing thus, worships becomes verily one possessed of cattle and possessed of men.

24. Then he goes very near the cow (chanting),"Oh Iḍā! come here". "Oh Aditi! Come here!" "Oh covetable one! Come here". Indeed the cow is Iḍā; indeed the cow is Aditi; indeed covetable is the cow! verily desire for them (cows) entered men as,"In me is the bearing of desire for you (I desire for you)". He verily says (means) this, "May I become dear to you".

25. Then standing between *Āhavanīya* and *Gārhapatya* and facing east, looking at the *Āhavanīya,* he (the sacrificer) mutters, "Oh lord of *Brahman* (Veda)! Make the offerer of Soma sweet-voiced—(the offerer) Kakṣīvant who is the son of Uśij, who is the possessor of wealth, who destroys woe, who finds wealth and who increases nourishment, may he the fleet one, get attached to us. Let not the curse of the evil-doer (enemy) and the hurt of (caused by) man reach us. Oh Lord of Veda! Protect us".

जस्त्रमितीमे वा अध्वनो वारणाय इमेऽन्तरा द्यावापृथिव्यौ तानेवैतदुपतिष्ठते तथा हैनमेतेष्वध्वसु वारणेषु न नाष्ट्रा रक्षाꣳसि विन्दन्ति ॥ २६ ॥

अथैन्ध्रेन्द्रो[२०] यज्ञस्य देवता सेन्द्रमेवैतदग्न्युपस्थानं करोति कदाचन स्तरीरसि नेन्द्र सश्चसि दाशुष इति कदा चन यजमानाय द्रुह्यसीत्येवैतदाहोपोपेन्नु मघवन्भूय इन्नु ते दानं देवस्य पृच्यत इत्युपोपेन्नु यं न[२१] इदं पुष्टं तन्नो भूयो भूय एव कुरु तं[२२] नो वर्धयेत्येवैतदाह ॥ २७ ॥

अथ सावित्र्या सविता वै देवानां प्रसविता तथो हास्मा एते सवितृप्रसूताः सर्वे कामाः समृध्यन्ते तत्सवितुर्वरेण्यं भर्गो देवस्य धीमहि । धियो यो नः प्रचोदयादिति ॥ २८ ॥

अथाग्नेय्या तदग्न य एवोत्तमं गुप्तये परिधत्ते परि ते दूळभो रथोऽस्माँ[२३]ꣳ अश्नोतु विश्वतः । येन रक्षसि दाशुष इति यजमाना वै दाश्वाꣳसो यस्तेऽनाधृष्यतमो रथो येन यजमानान्गोपायसि तेन नः सर्वतो गोपायेत्येवैतदाह ॥ २९ ॥

अथ पुत्रस्य नाम गृह्णातीदं मे कर्मेदं वीर्यं पुत्रोऽनुसन्तनोत्विति तथा हास्यैतत्कर्मैतद्वीर्यं पुत्रोऽनुसन्तनोति यदि पुत्रो न स्यादप्यात्मन एव गृह्णीयात् ॥ ३० ॥ इति प्रथमं ब्राह्मणम् ॥

द्वितीयं ब्राह्मणम्

स वा अग्निहोत्रꣳ हुत्वा सायमुपतिष्ठते भूर्भुवः स्वरिति तद्वाचꣳ सत्येन समर्धयति तया समृद्धयाशिष आशास्ते सुप्रजाः प्रजया भूयासमिति तत्प्रजामाशास्ते सुवीरो वीरैरिति तद्वीरानाशास्ते सुपोषः पोषैरिति तत्पुष्टिं भूमानमाशास्ते यद्वा अदोऽपि दीर्घमग्न्युपस्थान-

२०. अथै ह्येन्द्रो TE.
२१. यन्न Ca.
२२. तन्नो Ca., B, K.
२३. See Notes on pluta.

26. That he worships the *Āhavanīya* (amounts to this) that he worships the sky; (that he worships) the *Gārhapatya* (means that he worships) the earth. Then does he worship this mid region (ether). Therefore he worships (it) with a triad of *Ṛks* that praises Brahmaṇaspati (the lord of Vedas) (the lord of expression). Indeed this (mid region, the ether) is the direction of Brahmaṇaspati. Indeed he worships this direction (thus), "May the great heavenly and unassailable protection of the three, viz., Mitra, Aryaman and Varuṇa be (with us)! The enemy who speaks ill (curses) indeed does not have power over them (who are thus protected), at home or on the roads that might prevent (one's movement). For, verily, those sons of Aditi constantly provide light for the man to live". These indeed are the obstacles of the paths, these that are in between heaven and earth. He verily worships them thus. Therefore, indeed, the destructive demons (Rākṣasas) do not find him out in these paths that would (otherwise) be beset with obstacles.

27. Then (he worships) with a prayer dedicated to Indra. Indra is the deity of the sacrifice. He (the sacrificer) makes this worship of Agni verily to be (connected) with Indra. (He says) "Oh Indra! you are never barren. You cling to (honour) the givers (of oblations).

He verily says (means) this, "Never do you harm (never are you malicious towards) the sacrificer".

"Oh mighty god! more and more, indeed, and ever more does the gift of you, the god, increase". (By saying),"More and more, indeed". This is what he verily says (means), "This our nourishment (prosperity)– please make it verily more and more for us. Increase it for us".

28. Then (he worships) with a *Ṛk* addressed to Savitṛ. Indeed Savitṛ (the Sun) is the begetter of the gods. Therefore do all these desires, produced by Savitṛ get fulfilled for him. (He chants), "May we meditate upon the superior effulgence of the divine Savitṛ, who will prompt our mental faculties!"

29. Then (he worships) with a *Ṛk* addressed to Agni. By that, at last he gives (himself) to Agni for protection. (He chants), "May your inaccessible chariot surround us (to protect) all around–the chariot by which you protect the givers (of oblations)". Indeed the sacrificers are the givers (of oblations). He verily says (means) this, "That your most inaccessible chariot with which you protect the sacrificers– with that protect us from everything (all around)".

30. He then utters the name of (his) son. (He says)"May(my) son continue this my task, this (my) virility." In that same manner does his son continue this task of his and this virility. If there is no son, then he should utter his own (name).

(First Brāhmaṇa Ends)

BRĀHMAṆA II

1. After performing the *Agnihotra,* he worships (the Agni) in the evening,

माशीर्वाव साशीर्वेवेयं तदनेनैवेतत्सर्वं पर्याप्नोति तस्मादनेनैवोपतिष्ठेतैतेनन्वाव[१] वयमुपचराम इति ह स्मासुरिराह ॥ १ ॥

अथ खलु प्रवत्स्यन्गार्हपत्यमेवाग्र उपतिष्ठतेऽथाहवनीयꣳ स गार्हपत्यमुपतिष्ठते नेर्य[२] प्रजां मे पाहीति प्रजाया हैष ईष्टे तत्प्रजामेवास्मा एतत्परिददाति गुप्तयेऽथाहवनीयमुपतिष्ठते शꣳस्य पशून्मे पाहीति पशूनाꣳ हैष ईष्टे तत्पशूनेवास्मा एतत्परिददाति गुप्तये ॥ २ ॥

अथ प्र वा व्रजति प्र वा धावयति स यत्र वेलां मन्यते तत्राप्य वाचं विसृजतेऽथ प्रोष्य पुनरेत्य यत्र वेलां मन्यते तत्राप्य वाचं यच्छति स यद्यप्यन्तरेण राजा स्यान्नैव तमुपेयात्स आहवनीयमेवाग्र उपतिष्ठतेऽथ गार्हपत्यं गृहा वै गार्हपत्यः प्रतिष्ठा वै गृहा गृहेष्वेवैतत्प्रतिष्ठायामन्ततः प्रतितिष्ठति ॥ ३ ॥

स आहवनीयमुपतिष्ठत आगन्म विश्ववेदसमस्मभ्यं वसुवित्तममित्यथोपविश्य तृणान्यपलुम्पत्यग्ने सम्राळभि द्युम्नमभि सह आयच्छस्वेत्यथ गार्हपत्यमुपतिष्ठतेऽयमग्निर्गृहपतिर्गार्हपत्यः प्रजावान्वसुवित्तम इत्यथोपविश्य तृणान्यपलुम्पत्यग्ने गृहपतेऽभि द्युम्नमभि सह आयच्छस्वेतीति नु स उपतिष्ठेत यो मन्त्रेणोपतिष्ठेत ॥ ४ ॥

स वै तूष्णीमेवोपतिष्ठेत यस्मिन्वाव ब्राह्मणो वा राजा वा मनुष्योन्वेव श्रेयान्वसेत्तन्वाव[३] स नार्हति वक्तुमेतन्मम त्वं गोपाय प्राहं वत्स्यामीत्यथैतँ[४] एतस्मिञ्छ्रेयाꣳसो देवा अग्नयो वसन्ति क उ अर्हत्येतान्वक्तुमेतन्मम यूयं गोपायत प्राहं वत्स्यामीति तस्मात्तूष्णीमेवोपतिष्ठेत स गार्हपत्यमेवाग्र उपतिष्ठेत ॥ ५ ॥

अथाहवनीयꣳ स गार्हपत्यमुपतिष्ठते तूष्णीमेव मनो वै देवा मनुष्यस्याजानन्ति तस्य गार्हपत्यो मन आजानाति प्रवत्स्यन्मा परि दामुपागादित्यथाहवनीयमुपतिष्ठते तूष्णीमेव तस्याहवनीयो मन आजानाति प्रवत्स्यन्मा परि दामुपागादिति ॥ ६ ॥

१. See Notes.

२. नर्य्य B.

३. न्वसेत्तं न्वाव Ca

४. त्यथैष Ca , M, My; see Notes.

(saying)"*Bhūḥ, Bhuvaḥ, Svaḥ*" (the earth, the ether, the sky). By that he enriches his speech with truth. With that (speech) enriched, he invokes blessings (thus), "May I with progeny, become one possessed of good progeny". Thus he hopes (prays) for progeny. He prays for heroic men by saying "(May I become) one possessed of heroes, with heroic men ". Saying, "(May I become) one possessed of good nourishment, with nourishing things", he prays for nourishment (abundance)"That long fire-worship also is, indeed, a prayer for blessing. This (short) one, too, is indeed that (same) prayer for blessing. Therefore, one gets all this (blessing) even with this (short prayer to Agni). Therefore one may worship verily with this– we serve (Agni) verily with this"–so said Āsuri, indeed.

2. Now when he is about to (go away on a journey) live away (from home), he first worships *Gārhapatya* only and afterwards (he worships) *Āhavanīya.* He worships *Gārhapatya* (chanting), "Oh one benign to men! please protect my progeny". For this (Agni) has power over progeny. Therefore he (the sacrificer) now makes over verily his progeny to him (Agni) for protection. Then he worships *Āhavanīya* (chanting), "Oh one worthy of praise! please protect my cattle". For, this (Agni) has power over cattle. Therefore does he (the sacrificer) now make over verily his cattle to him (Agni) for protection.

3. Then he either walks off or drives off. Reaching that (place) where he thinks the boundary to be, he lets out speech (breaks his silence). Having lived abroad and returning and reaching that (place) where he considers the boundary to be, he restrains his speech (observes silence). Even if a king should be within (his residence), he should not go upto him. He first worships *Āhavanīya* only and then (only) *Gārhapatya.* Indeed,the *Gārhapatya* is the home. The home is the (established) residential place, indeed. He verily thereby rests ultimately in the house itself, (which is) the resting place.

4. He worships the *Āhavanīya,* (chanting) "We have come to the All-knowing one who is the greatest finder (bestower) of wealth for us ".Then having sat down, he removes the blades of grass, (saying) "Oh Agni, the sovereign lord! give (us) wealth (lustre) and strength". Then he worships the *Garhapatya,* (saying), "This *Agni Gārhapatya* is the lord of the house. He is possessed of progeny and he is the greatest finder (bestower) of wealth". Then having sat down, he removes the blades of grass (saying),"Oh Agnì! master of the house! please bestow on us (wealth) lustre and strength". He who would worship with *mantras* should worship thus.

5. Indeed, he may worship silently.

Where there may be a Brāhmin ,a king or a noble(laudable) person, it is not proper indeed, for him (the head of the house) to say to him, "You please guard this (house) of mine, I shall be going on a journey. (I shall be living abroad)". And these the superior gods, the Agnis, dwell in this (place). Who then is fit to say to them, "You please protect this (house) of mine. I shall be living abroad". Therefore one may well worship silently. He first verily worships *Gārhapatya.*

6. Then (he worships) *Āhavanīya.* He worships the *Gārhapatya* silently indeed.

अथ प्र वा व्रजति प्र वा धावयति स यत्र वेळां मन्यते तत्प्राप्य वाचं विसृजतेऽथ प्रोष्य पुनरेत्य यत्र वेळां मन्यते तत्प्राप्य वाचं यच्छति स यद्यप्यन्तरेण राजा स्यान्नैव तमुपेयात्स आहवनीयमेवाग्र उपतिष्ठतेऽथ गार्हपत्यं गृहा वै गार्हपत्यः प्रतिष्ठा वै गृहा गृहेष्वेवैतत्प्रतिष्ठायामन्ततः प्रतितिष्ठति ॥ ७ ॥

स आहवनीयमुपतिष्ठते तूष्णीमेव तूष्णीमेवोपविश्य तृणान्यपलुम्पत्यथ गार्हपत्यमुपतिष्ठते तूष्णीमेव तूष्णीमेवोपविश्य तृणान्यपलुम्पति ॥ ८ ॥

स यद्यप्येताꣳ रात्रिꣳ सुक्रुद्ध इव स्याच्छ्व एव तद्भूते कुर्याद्वा वदेद्वैतदु ह वै गृहपतेः प्रोषुष आगताद्गृहाः समुत्रस्येव तिष्ठन्ति किमयमिह करिष्यति किं वा वदिष्यतीति स यदिह किञ्चित्करोति वा वदति वा तस्य हेश्वरो गृहाः प्रत्रसन्ति तस्य हेश्वरो गृ[५]हा विक्षोब्धो[६]रथ यो न किञ्चन करोति न किञ्चन वदति तस्य गृहा न प्रत्रसन्ति तस्य गृहा न विक्षोभन्त एष उ गृहाणामुपचारः ॥ ९ ॥

स उपतिष्ठते गृहा मा बिभीत मा वेपध्वमूर्जं बिभ्रत एमसि । ऊर्जं बिभ्रद्वः सुमनाः सुमेधा गृहानैमि मनसा मोदमानः । येषामध्येति प्रवसन्येषु सौमनसो बहुः । गृहानुपह्वयामहे तेनो जानन्तु जानतः । उपहूता इह गाव उपहूता अजावयः । अथो अन्नस्य कीलाल उपहूतो गृहेषु न इति ॥ १० ॥ इति द्वितीयं ब्राह्मणम् ॥

तृतीयं ब्राह्मणम्

प्रजापतिर्ह वा इदमेक एवास स हेक्षांचक्रे कथं नु प्रजायेयेति सोऽश्राम्यत्स तपोऽतप्यत स प्रजाः ससृजे ता अस्य प्रजाः सृष्टाः परा बभूवुस्तानीमानि वयाꣳसि पुरुषो वा अयं नेदिष्ठं प्रजापतेः स द्विपात्तस्माद्द्विपादो वयाꣳसि ॥ १ ॥

५. From गृहा upto प्रत्रसन्ति in TE.

६. See Notes on I-4-1-5.

For, the gods know the mind of man. The *Gārhapatya* knows his mind (and thinks), "(This person) who is going to live abroad has approached me the bestower". Then he worships the *Āhavanīya* verily silently. The *Āhavanīya* knows his mind (and thinks), "(This person) who is going to live abroad has approached me the bestower".

7. Then he either walks off or drives off, where he considers (it to be) the boundary, reaching that (place) he speaks (breaks his silence). Then having lived abroad and coming back again, reaching that (place) where he considers the boundary to be, he restrains his speech (undertakes silence). If there should be within (the house) even a king, he (the householder) should not go up to him (but) he approaches (worships) first only *Āhavaṇīya* and then the *Gārhapatya*. Indeed the *Gārhapatya* (Agni) is the home, the home is the established resting place. Thus he ultimately remains firmly established only in the home.

8. He worships the *Āhavanīya* silently, sitting only silently, he removes the blades of grass. Then he approaches (worships) the *Gārhapatya* silently. Sitting only silently, he removes the blades of grass.

9. Though he might be angry, as it were, this night (of his return home), only when the morrow has come may he do (anything) or say (anything), for this reason that the house remains afraid, as it were, of the master of the house who had been living away and who has returned the house (thinking), "What is this person going to do here? What is he going to say?" Whatever the master does here or says, his house fears, the house gets agitated; for he is the lord. (But) then, the house of that person who does nothing and says nothing does not fear, it does not get agitated. This is verily the observance (approach) with regard to the house.

10. He worhips (approaches the house saying), "Oh house! don't fear. Don't tremble. We come bearing strength. Bearing strength, with an auspicous mind and auspicous memory, rejoicing with the mind I come to you, the house. We invoke the house which one gets to (after) remaining away and in which are many who have auspicious minds (or, wherein are many gods). May that house understand us who understand it! Here are (invoked) invited the cows. Invited are the goats and sheep and invoked is food and water in our home "

(Second Brāhmaṇa Ends)

BRĀHMAṆA III

1. Prajāpati alone was here, indeed (in the beginning). He verily saw (thought), "How shall I be born?" (How can I reproduce?) He exerted himself. He performed penance. He created the creatures. Those creatures that were created by him languished (went away). They are these birds. Indeed man is the nearest to Prajāpati. He is a biped. Hence birds are bipeds.

स हेक्षां चक्रे यथा न्वाव पुरैळोऽभूवमेवमु न्वाँ अस्मीति स द्वितीयाः ससृजे ताः परैव बभूवुस्तदिदं क्षुद्रꣳ सरीसृपं यदन्यत्सर्पेभ्यस्तृतीयाः ससृजे ताः परैव बभूवुस्ते सर्पा इत्याहुरेता हत्वै द्वयीर्याज्ञवल्क्य उवाच त्रय्यस्तु पुनर्ऋचा भवन्ति ॥ २ ॥

सोऽर्चञ्छ्राम्यन्प्रजापतिः कथं नु मे प्रजाः सृष्टाः पराभवन्तीति स एतदेव ददर्शाँनिश्न-दतैव परा भवन्तीति स आत्मन्येवाग्रे स्तनयोः पय आप्याययांचक्रेऽथ प्रजाः ससृजे ता अस्य प्रजाः सृष्टाः स्तनावेवाभिपद्य ततः संबभूवुस्ता इमा अपराभूताः ॥ ३ ॥

तस्मादप्येतदृषिणाभ्यनूक्तं प्रजा ह तिस्रो अत्यायमीयुरिति या अमूः पराभूतान्यन्या अर्कमभितो विविश्र इत्यग्निर्वा अर्कस्तमिमाः प्रजा अभितो निविष्टा या इमा अपराभूता महद्ध तस्थौ भुवनेष्वन्तरिति प्रजापतिमेवैतदभ्यनूक्तं पवमानो हरित आविवेशेति दिशो वै हरितस्ता अयं पवमान आविष्टः सैषर्गेवैतदभ्यनूक्ता तदप्येतर्हि तथैव प्रजाः प्रजायन्ते यथा प्रजापतिः प्रजा असृजतेदꣳ हि यदैव स्त्रियाः स्तनावाप्यायेते ऊधः पशूनामथ यज्जायते तज्जायत एवꣳ ह्यग्रे प्रजापतिः प्रजा असृजत ॥ ४ ॥

तद्वा आहुः पय एवान्नमित्येतद्ध्यग्रे प्रजापतिरन्नमजनयतेति तद्वा आहुरन्नमेव प्रजा इतीदꣳ हि यासां पयोऽस्ति जाता एव तास्तनावेवाभिपद्यततः संभवन्ति यासु वै पयो नास्ति जातमेव ता अप्यादयन्ति तस्मादाहुरन्नमेव प्रजा इति स य एतेन हविषा प्रजाकामो यजत आत्मानमेवैतद्यज्ञं विधत्ते प्रजापतिं भूतम् ॥ ५ ॥

स एष आग्नेयोऽष्टाकपालो भवत्यग्निर्वै देवतानां मुखं प्रजनयिता तस्मादाग्नेयोऽष्टाक-पालो भवति ॥ ६ ॥

७. ऽभवमेवमन्वासीति TE; ऽभवमेवमु न्वा अस्मी P1, P2; ऽभूवमेवमु न्वाहासीति M.

८. अनशनतीव TE; अनश्नदतैव My; अनशनतीव Ca.; अनश्वदतैव M; see Notes.

2. He (Prajāpati) verily looked about (thought), "Even as I was alone formerly, so am I (now) verily (alone) " He created a second (batch of living beings). They too verily languished (went away). That is this vile (small) (species) reptile which is different from snakes. He created a third (batch of beings). They too verily languished. They (the people) say, "They are the serpents". Yājñavalkya said, "These are indeed of two kinds". But according to the *Ṛk*, they are of three kinds.

3. Worshipping and exerting himself, Prajāpati (thought). "How is it that my creatures that were created languish (perish)?" He discovered verily this, "They languish (because of) not eating (food)". He provided milk, even at first, in the two breasts in the body itself and afterwards created the creatures. Those creatures of this that had been created came to be found (well)(they survived), having taken verily to the breasts. They are these creatures that have not languished (that have not perished).

4. Therefore too, has this been repeated (said) by the *Ṛṣi* (Veda) (thus), "Three generations indeed, passed beyond". Those (generations) are those that perished, "The others settled around the Sun *(Arka)*. Surely Agni is *Arka*. These creatures which have not perished have settled around him (Agni) 'the great one' verily remained within the worlds". This has been said only with regard to Prajāpati. "The blower (purifier) entered into the directions (quarters)". The directions are indeed the quarters (regions). This blower (purifier) (the wind) has entered into them. This *Ṛk* itself has been recited with regard to this. It is (so) even now; creatures are born in the same manner as Prajāpati created the creatures. It is indeed this; when the two breasts of a woman and the udder of (cows) cattle are filled up (with milk), thereafter is born, what is born (the creature) (the offspring). It was verily thus that Prajāpati created the creatures at first.

5. About that they (people) say, Verily milk is food", "For Prajāpati created verily this (milk) as food". (People) say about it, "Indeed food itself is the creature (being)". It is this –those (creatures), even as they are born, live (exist) thereafter only resorting to the breasts of those who have milk. Those who have no milk, they too feed the just born (infant) (with other food) . Therefore they say, "Food itself is the creature". He who, being desirous of progeny, sacrifices with this oblation, thus makes himself verily this sacrifice which is Prajāpati.

6. This (offering) belonging to Agni is on eight potsherds. Indeed Agni is the mouth of the gods; he is the progenitor (of the gods). Hence is the offering to Agni on eight potsherds.

सौम्यश्चरुः सोमो वै रेतस्तदग्नौ प्रजनयितरि[९] सोमꣳ रेतः सिञ्चति तत्पुरस्तान्मिथुनं प्रजननं क्रियते ॥ ७ ॥

अथ सावित्रो द्वादशकपालो वा भवत्यष्टाकपालो वा सविता वै देवानां प्रसविता प्रजापतिर्मध्यतः प्रजनयिता तस्मात्सावित्रो द्वादशकपालो वा भवत्यष्टाकपालो वा ॥ ८ ॥

सारस्वतश्चरुः पौष्णश्चरुर्योषा सरस्वती वृषा पूषा तदु पुनरुपरिष्टान्मिथुनं प्रजननं क्रियत उभयतो ह वै मिथुनात्प्रजापतिः प्रजाः ससृज इतश्चोर्ध्वा इतश्चावाचीस्तथो वा एष एतदुभयतो मिथुनात्प्रजाः सृजत इतश्चोर्ध्वा इतश्चावाचीस्तस्मादेतानि पञ्च हवीꣳषि भवन्ति ॥ ९ ॥

अथातः पयस्याया एवायतनं मारुतस्तु सप्तकपालो भवति स यन्मारुतः सप्तकपालो भवति विशो वै मरुतो देवविशस्तां[१०] हेदमनिषिद्धा[११] इव चेरुस्ता ह प्रजापतिं यजमानमुपेत्योचुर्व्यु ते प्रजा मथिष्यामह इति या एतेन हविषा स्रक्ष्यसे न चेन्नोऽत्र भागं कल्पयिष्यसीति ॥ १० ॥

स हेक्षांचक्रे प्रजापतिः परा मे पूर्वाः प्रजा अभूवन्निमं[१२] उ चेद्वा इमा विमथ्नते ततो मे न किञ्चन परिशेक्ष्यत इति तत एभ्य एतं भागमकल्पयत्स स एष मरुतः सप्तकपालः स यत्सप्तकपालो भवति सप्त सप्त हि मारुतो गणः ॥ ११ ॥

सस्वतवद्ध्यः स्यात्स्वयꣳ हि ते तं भागमकल्पयन्त तदुत याज्यानुवाक्ये स्वतवत्यौ न विन्दति यदि याज्यानुवाक्ये स्वतवत्यौ न विन्देदपि मारुत्यावेव स्याताꣳ स एष प्रजानामेवाहिꣳसायै प्रजानाꣳ शान्तये क्रियते तस्मान्मारुतः सप्तकपालो भवति ॥ १२ ॥

९. प्रजनयितर्हि TE, My.

१०. देवविशं ता Ca, देवविशास्ता in M,D; see Notes.

११. अनिषेद्धा M; अनिषेधा Ca; अनिषिद्धा M.

१२. न्निमा उ TE.

7. Then is offered a *caru* (boiled rice) dedicated to Soma. Indeed Soma is the seed (semen). He (the sacrificer) pours Soma, that semen, into Agni the progenitor. Thereby is formed at the outset a productive pair.

8. Then there is (the offering of oblation) dedicated to Savitṛ, either on twelve potsherds or on eight potsherds. Indeed, Savitṛ is the begetter of the gods. (He is) Prajāpati (the lord of created beings), the intermediate progenitor. Therefore, the offering to Savitṛ is either on twelve potsherds or on eight potsherds.

9. (Then there is offered) a *caru* (boiled rice offering) to Sarasvatī (and there is) a *caru* for Pūṣan. Sarasvati is female, Puṣan is male. That again, is made into a later productive couple. Prajāpati indeed, created creatures from the two fold pair (union)–they (the creatures)that were before now and those that are later (in that will be) [they that are (straight) upward from there (the ground) and they that are (bent) downward]. Similarly does this (sacrificer) produce (beget) creatures from the two fold pair (union)–those that are upward and those that are downward. Therefore are these five offerings (made).

10. Thereafter verily (comes) the basis of curds: the offering to Maruts is on seven potsherds. (The reason) why (the offering) to Maruts is on seven potsherds (is that) the Maruts are Viś (common subjects), the subjects of the gods. They went about here, indeed, unchecked as it were. Having approached Prajāpati who was performing a sacrifice, they said, "If you do not allot a share to us in this (offering in the sacrifice) we shall destroy these, the creatures, which you are going to create with this oblation".

11. Prajāpati observed, "My former creatures have perished. If these (Maruts) destroy these (creatures to be created), then nothing will be left over for me". Then he allotted to them this share. This offering to Maruts is on seven potsherds. (The reason) why it is on seven potsherds (is that) indeed the host of Maruts is (in groups of) seven and seven (each).

12. That (share) should be for the self-strong (Maruts); for, they made (got) that share for themselves. But then, they (the priests) do not find the two (chants) for offering and subsequent address, related to the 'self-strong' (Maruts). If one can not find the two (chants) *Yājyā* and *anuvākyā* related to the 'Self-possessed ', then they (the two chants) may be the two addressed to Maruts (in general). This (offering) is made just for the sake of non-hurt to the creatures and for the sake of the tranquillity of the creatures. Therefore does the offering to Maruts become (one) on seven potsherds.

अथातः पयस्यैव पयसो वै प्रजाः संभूताः पयसः संभवन्ति तद्यत एव संभूता यतस्संभवन्ति तदेवाभ्य एतत्करोति तद्या एभिः पूर्वैर्हविर्भिः प्रजाः सृजते ता एतस्मात्पयस एतस्याः पयस्यायाः संभवन्ति तस्यां[13] मिथुनमस्ति योषा पयस्या रेतो वाजिनमेतस्माद्वै मिथुनाद्विश्वमसंमितमनु प्राजायत स यदस्या विश्वमसंमितमनु प्राजायत तस्माद्वैश्वदेवी ॥ १३ ॥

अथ द्यावापृथिव्य एककपाल एतैः[14] पूर्वैर्हविर्भिः प्रजापतिः प्रजापतिः प्रजास्सृष्ट्वा ता द्यावापृथिवीभ्यां परिजग्राह ता इमाः प्रजा आभ्यां द्यावापृथिवीभ्यां परिगृहीतास्तथो वा एष एतद्या एतैः पूर्वैर्हविर्भिः प्रजा सृजते ता द्यावापृथिवीभ्यां परिगृह्णाति तस्मा द्यावापृथिव्य एककपालः ॥ १४ ॥

अथात आवृदेव नोत्तरवेदिमुपकिरति सर्वमसद्विसृष्टमसद्वैश्वदेवमसदिति त्रेधा बर्हिः सन्नद्धं तत्पुनरेकधा भवत्येवꣳ हि प्रजननस्य रूपं प्रजननꣳ हीदं त्रेधा विहितꣳ हीदं प्रजननं पिता माता यज्जायते तत्तृतीयं तस्मात्त्रेधा बर्हिः सन्नद्धं तत्पुनरेकधा भवति प्र स्व उपसन्नद्धा भवन्ति ताः प्रस्तरं गृह्णाति प्रजननꣳ हीदं प्रजननꣳ हि प्रस्वः ॥ १५ ॥

आसाद्य हवीꣳष्यग्निं मन्थत्यग्निꣳ ह वै जायमानमनु प्रजापतेः प्रजा जज्ञिरे तथो वा एतस्याग्निमेव जायमानमनु प्रजा जायन्ते नवप्रयाजं भवति नवानुयाजं दशाक्षरा वै विराट् सैषा सम्पत्तामेवैतदुभयतो न्यूनां करोति प्रजननाय न्यूनाद्धीमाः प्रजाः प्रजायन्त उभयतो ह वै न्यूनात्प्रजापतिः प्रजाः ससृज इतश्चोर्ध्वा इतश्चावाचीस्तथो वा एष एतदुभयतो न्यूनात्प्रजाः सृजत इतश्चोर्ध्वा इतश्चावाचीस्तस्मान्नवप्रयाजं भवति नवानुयाजम् ॥ १६ ॥

त्रीणि समिष्टयजूꣳषि जुहोति ज्यायो हीदꣳ हविर्यज्ञाद्यं नवप्रयाजं नवानुयाजमित्यथो अप्येकमेव जुहुयाद्धविर्यज्ञो ह्येष तस्य प्रथमजो गौर्दक्षिणाग्र्यमिव हीदमिति स एतेनेष्ट्वा

१३. तस्या P1.

१४. एतैर्वै हविर्भि, Ca.

13. Now then, (comes the offering of) curds. Verily from milk did the creatures come to be. They exist on account of milk (subsisting on it). Therefore he (the sacrificer) offers to them that very thing from which they have sprung up and wherefore they exist. Thus the creatures which he (the sacrificer) produces with these former offerings they arise from this milk and from these curds. There is a couple in that (in the curds). The curds are female. The whey is the semen. From this pair indeed was then born the 'All' (universe-like). Because the 'all' (universe-like) was subsequently born of this (these curds), therefore that (the curds offering) is what has the Viśvedevas as its deity.

14. Then (there is the offering) to Heaven and Earth, on a single potsherd. Prajāpati, having created the creatures by means of these very oblations, enclosed them (between) with Heaven and Earth. In that (same) manner is that he (the sacrificer) encloses with Heaven and Earth the creatures which he produces by means of these foregoing offerings. Therefore (is this offering made) for Heaven and Earth on a single potsherd.

15. Then therefore, there is verily this procedure: He (the sacrificer) does not raise (use) the *uttaravedi* (the northern or extra altar), (He thinks), "Let everything be (complete); let the offering be (made); let it be sacred to the Viśvedevas ". The sacred grass *(barhis)* is tied into three (bunches) and that (the three) again becomes one (bigger bunch). Thus is indeed the form of procreation. This is verily procreation. This procreation is indeed made threefold (in three ways). (There is) the father, (there is) the mother, what is born —that is the third. Therefore (is) sacred grass tied in three ways (into three bunches). That again becomes a single (bigger bunch). They become tied together, in their individual characteristic. He (the sacrificer) takes them up as a *prastara* (spread around sacred grass). This is verily procreation; procreation is the individual characteristic.

16. After placing the sacrificial dishes (the things to be offered) (in their respective places), he churns the fire (produces the fire by churning). For, the offspring (creatures) of Prajāpati were born (immediately) after Agni as he was being produced (as he was coming into existence). In that very same manner, creatures (offspring) are born following verily the sacrificer's Agni that is born (that is being produced). There is a group of nine fore-offerings, (there is) a group of nine subsequent offerings. *Virāṭ* (the metre) has indeed ten syllables (per foot). This is the full wealth (fullness). That very thing (*Virāṭ*) he (the sacrificer) makes deficient (by one) on both sides, for the sake of production. Indeed these creatures arise from the deficient (material). Prajāpati created from (material) deficient on both sides, the creatures that are upward (straight) from here and that are downward (bent) from here. In that very same manner, indeed, does this (sacrificer) create creatures from (material) deficient on both

प्रजापतिर्येयं प्रजापतेः प्रजातिर्या विभूतिस्तद्बभूवैवं ह वाव प्रजायत एवं श्रियं गच्छति य एनेनैवं विद्वान्यजते ॥ १७ ॥ इति तृतीयं ब्राह्मणम् ॥

इति चतुर्थोऽध्यायः

sides-the creatures that are upward (straight) here and that are bent (downward) here. Therefore is it that there is group of nine fore-offerings and a group of nine after-offerings.

17. He offers three *'Samiṣṭa Yajus'*. (That would make the sacrifice well-performed). Because this (ritual) (consists of) a group of nine fore-offerings and a group of nine after-offerings, this is better than a *havir-yajña*. Yet, one may offer one oblation only (one *samiṣṭa yajus*). Indeed this (also) is a *haviryajña*. He who knowing thus, sacrifices with this (offering), is born (i.e. reproduces) verily and attains wealth (splendour), in the same manner, (attains the progeny and wealth) which accrued to Prajāpati on his thus performing this sacrifice.

(Third Brāhmaṇa Ends)

(Chapter Four ends)

पञ्चमोऽध्यायः

प्रथमं ब्राह्मणम्

वैश्वदेवेन ह वै प्रजापतिः प्रजास्ससृजे ता अस्य प्रजाः सृष्टा वरुणस्य यवं जक्षुर्वरुण्यो ह वा अग्रे यवस्तद्यन्वेव वरुणस्य यवं प्रादꣳस्तस्माद्वरुणप्रघासा नाम ॥ १ ॥

ता ह वरुणो जग्राह ता वरुणगृहीता अनत्य एव प्राणत्यः परिदीर्णाः शिश्यिरे च निषेदुश्च प्राणोदानौ हैवाभ्यो नापचक्रमतुरथ सर्वा अन्या देवता अपचक्रमुस्तयोर्ह हेतोर्न पराबभूवुः ॥ २ ॥

ताः प्रजापतिरेतेन हविषाभिषज्य[1]त्तद्याश्चैवास्य प्रजा जाता याश्चाजातास्ता उभयीर्वरुण-पाशात्प्रामुञ्चत्ता अस्यानमीवा अकिल्बिषाः प्रजाः प्राजायन्ताथ यदेष एतेन चतुर्थे मासि यजते नाहैवैतस्य प्रजास्तथा[2] वरुणो गृह्णाति याश्चत्वेवास्य प्रजा जाता याश्चाजातास्ता उभयीर्वरुणपाशात्प्रमुञ्चति ता अस्यानमीवा अकिल्बिषाः प्रजाः प्रजायन्ते तस्माद्वा एष एतेन चतुर्थे मासि यजते ॥ ३ ॥

तदद्वे वेदी द्वावग्नी भवत उभयत एवैतद्वरुणपाशात्प्रजाः प्रमुञ्चतीतश्चोर्ध्वा इतश्चावा-चीस्तस्मादद्वे वेदी द्वावग्नी भवत उत्तरस्यां वेदा उत्तरवेदिमुपकिरति न दक्षिणस्यां क्षत्रं वै वरुणो विशो मरुतः क्षत्रमेवैतद्विश उत्तरं करोति तस्मात् क्षत्रियमुपर्यासीनमधस्ताद्विश इमाः प्रजा उपासते ॥ ४ ॥

अथैतान्येव पञ्च हवीꣳषि भवन्त्येतैर्वै प्रजापतिः प्रजा असृजतैतैर्वेवैना एष एतदुभयतो वरुणपाशात्प्रजाः प्रमुञ्चतीतश्चोर्ध्वा इतश्चावाचीस्तस्मादेतानि पञ्च हवीꣳषि भवन्ति ॥ ५ ॥

अथैष ऐन्द्राग्नो द्वादशकपालः पुरोळाशो भवति प्राणोदानौ वा इन्द्राग्नी तयोर्वा अस्य हेतोः प्रजा न पराबभूवुः स यथा पुण्यं च[3]क्रुषे पुण्यं कुर्यादेवमेवैतत्प्राणोदानाभ्यामेवैत-त्प्रजा भिषज्यति प्राणोदानावेव प्रजासु दधाति तस्मादेष ऐन्द्राग्नो भवति ॥ ६ ॥

१. See Notes.

२. स्तथो V1.

३. चकृषे TE, My; see Notes.

Chapter Five

BRÂHMAṆA I

1. Indeed,Prajāpati created the creatures (progeny) by means of (an offering to) 'All Gods' (Viśvedevas). They, the created beings of this (Prajāpati), ate up the barley (corn) of Varuṇa.Originally, barley verily belonged toVaruṇa. Then, because they verily ate the barley of Varuṇa ,thence, indeed they are known as '*Varuṇapraghāsā*'.

2. Varuṇa, verily, captured them. Captured by Varuṇa ,they lay down and sat down, merely breathing in and breathing out, having been rent. Only the inhalation and exhalation of breath did not go out of them. Then all other faculties went out. Because of those two (breaths), they did not perish indeed.

3. Prajāpati treated them with this oblation. He released from Varuṇa's noose (bondage) both the kinds of creatures of his,–those which had been born and those that were (yet) unborn. His creatures were then born without disease and without evil (blemish). Because this (sacrificer) performs the sacrifice with this (offering) in the fourth month, Varuṇa does not seize his progeny at all in that manner. He releases both kinds of progeny from Varuṇa's noose–those that have already been born and those that are not (yet) born. Those children of his are born without disease and without blemish. Therefore indeed, does this (sacrificer) perform the sacrifice with this (offering) in the fourth month.

4. At that (sacrifice) there are two altars and two fires. From both sides, indeed, he (the sacrificer) releases the progeny (creatures) from Varuna's noose. Those that have been (born) before and those that are later (those that are straight (upward) here and those that look down-ward (that are bent here). Therefore are there two altars and there are two fires. On the northern altar he sweeps (scatters) the upper (northern) altar, he raises the upper altar and not on the southern (altar). Indeed Varuṇa is Kṣatra ((ruler or warrior) and the Maruts are the subjects. He thus makes verily the Kṣatra superior (at a higher level) to the common subject. Therefore these (common) people, the subjects, (remaining) below (at a lower level) wait upon the Kṣatriya(ruler) who is seated above.

5. Then there are verily these five oblations. Indeed by means of these did Prajāpati create the creatures. By these above does this (Prajāpati) release these (creatures). thus from Varuna's noose from both sides— those that are before now and those that are later. Therefore are there these five oblations.

6. Then there is (the offering of) this *puroḍāśa,* sanctified for Indra and Agni (together), on twelve potsherds. Verily the exhaled breath and the inhaled breath are Indra and Agni. Beacuse of them, indeed, his creatures (progeny) did not perish. This (offering to Indra and Agni) is just as one would do good

उभयत्रैव पयस्ये[4] भवतः पयसो वै प्रजाः संभूताः पयसस्सम्भवन्ति तद्यत एव सम्भूता यतः सम्भवन्ति तत एवैना एतदुभयतो वरुणपाशात्प्रजाः प्रमुञ्चतीतश्चोर्ध्वा इतश्चावाचीस्त-स्मादुभयत्र पयस्ये भवतः ॥ ७ ॥

वारुण्युत्तरा भवति वरुणो वा एना अगृह्णाद्वरुण्यादेवैतत्प्रत्यक्षं वरुणपाशात्प्रजाः प्रमुञ्चति मारुती दक्षिणाजामितायै न्वेव मारुती जामि हि कुर्याद्यदुभे वारुण्यौ स्यातामत उ ह वै प्रजापतेः प्रजा मरुतो दक्षिणतो जिघाꣳसांचक्रुस्तानेतेन भागेनाशमयत्तस्मान्मारुती दक्षिणा ॥ ८ ॥

तयोरुभयोरेव करीराण्यावपति किं वै प्रजापतिः प्रजाभ्यः करीरैरकुरुत कम्वेवैष एतत्प्रजाभ्यः कुरुते ॥ ९ ॥

उभयत्रैव शमीपलाशान्यावपति शं वै प्रजापतिः प्रजाभ्यः शमीपलाशैरकुरुत शम्वे-वैष एतत्प्रजाभ्यः कुरुते ॥ १० ॥

काय एककपालो भवति कं वै प्रजापतिः प्रजाभ्यः कायेनैककपालेनाकुरुत कम्वेवैष एतत्प्रजाभ्यः कुरुते ॥ ११ ॥

अथ पूर्वेद्युरतुषानिव यवान्कृत्वान्वाहार्यपचने मनागिवोपतप्य[5] यावन्तो गृह्यास्तावन्ति प्रतिपुरुषं करंभपात्राणि कुर्वन्त्येकेनातिरिक्तानि ॥ १२ ॥

मेषं च वा अपि मेषीं च कुर्वन्ति तयोर्यद्यनैळकीरूर्णा विन्देत्ताः प्रणिज्य[6] नि[7]ꣳश्लेषये-द्यद्यनैळकीर्न विन्देदपि कुशोर्णा एव निश्लेषयेत् ॥ १३ ॥

स यन्मेषी च मेषश्च भवत एष वै प्रत्यक्षं वरुणस्य पशुर्यन्मेषो वरुण्यादेवैतत्प्रत्यक्षं वरुणपाशात्प्रजाः प्रमुञ्चति मिथुनौ भवतो मिथुनादेवैतद्वरुणपाशात्प्रजाः प्रमुञ्चति यवमयौ

४. पयस्येव भवतः V1, Po.

५. मन एवोपतप्य M.

६. प्रणय्य TE.

७. निःश्लेष TE, C1, V1.

(in return) to one who has (already) done a good turn. He thus treats the creatures (progeny) verily with exhalation and inhalation. He places (infuses) exhalation and inhalation into the creatures. Therefore is this (offering) dedicated to Indra and Agni (together).

7. In both (fires) there are two (offerings of) curds. Indeed creatures originated from milk; they exist well because of milk. Therefore, where from they came into being and because of which they exist,–with that very thing, he releases these creatures thus on both sides from Varuṇa's noose–the creatures that are before this and that are (will be) after (those that are upright here and those that look downward here). Therefore there are two (offerings of) curds in both (fires).

8. The northern one (the one offered in the fire in the north) is dedicated to Varuṇa. Indeed Varuṇa captured these (creatures). He (the sacrificer) directly releases the creatures (progeny) thus from Varuṇa's noose, through,verily, the offering to Varuṇa. (The offering made in the south (fire) is dedicated to Maruts. (It is) verily for non-repetition (that) the offering to Maruts (is made).

For, if both (the offerings) were dedicated to Varuṇa, he (the sacrificer) would indeed be committing a repetition. Moreover, the Maruts wished to kill the creatures of Prajāpati, from the south. (Prajāpati) propitiated them with this share. Hence (in the fire in) the south (is made) the offering dedicated to Maruts.

9. Verily, on both of them (curds), he scatters *Karīra* fruits. Prajāpati indeed brought about happiness to the creatures with *Karīra* fruits. Thus, this (sacrificer too) verily brings about happiness to the creatures.

10. On both indeed, he puts *Śamī* leaves. Prajāpati verily brought about happiness to the creatures by means of *Śamī* leaves. This (sacrificer too) thus brings about happiness to the creatures.

11. There is an offering dedicated to Prajāpati, on one potsherd. Indeed, Prajāpati brought about happiness to the creatures by means of the offering dedicated to '*ka*' (Prajāpati) on a single potsherd. This (sacrificer too), thus brings about happiness to the creatures.

12. And on the previous day (first day), after husking and slightly roasting barley on the *Anvāhāryapacana (Dakṣiṇāgni,* on which subsequent offerings are cooked) they prepare as many vessels of *(Karambha)* a mixture of flour and curds as there are members of the (sacrificer's) family, one for each member, exceeding by one (and one more vessel).

13. They also prepare a (barley) ram and a (barley) ewe. If one can get the fibres of wool of a sheep other than *'Eḍaka'*, he should attach them (to the ram and ewe) after washing (the wool). If he cannot get (the fibres of wool) of any (sheep) other than *Edaka,* he may attach verily fibres of *Kuśa* (sacrificial grass).

भवतो यवꣳ हि जक्षुषीरगृह्णादुत्तरस्यां पयस्यायां मेषीमासादयति दक्षिणस्यां मेषमेवꣳ हि मिथुनं क्लृप्तमुत्तरतो हि स्त्री पुमाꣳसमुपशेते ॥ १४ ॥

सर्वाणि हवीꣳष्यध्वर्युरुत्तरस्यां वेदावासादयति मारुतीमेव प्रतिप्रस्थाता दक्षिणस्यामासाद्य हवीꣳषि संमृश्य ॥ १५ ॥

अथाध्वर्युराहाग्नये मथ्यमानायानुब्रूहीत्यग्निं मथित्वाहाग्नये समिध्यमानायानुब्रूहीत्युभौ त्वेवेध्मावभ्याधत्तोऽभ्याधायेध्मौ पूर्वावाघारावाघारयतः ॥ १६ ॥

अथाध्वर्युराहाग्निमग्नीत्संमृड्ढीत्यसंमृष्ट एवाग्निर्भवति संप्रेषितोऽथ प्रतिप्रस्थाता प्रतिपरैति स पत्नीमुदानयति तामुदानेष्यन्पृच्छति केन चरसीति वरुण्यꣳ ह वा एतत्स्त्री करोति यदन्यस्य सत्यन्येन चरति नेन्मेऽन्तः शल्या जुहवदिति निरुक्तमु ह वा एनः कनीयो भवति सत्यꣳ हि भवति सा यदि न प्रतिजानीते ज्ञातिभ्यो हास्या अहितं भवति ॥ १७ ॥

तां वाचयति प्रघासिनो हवामहे मरुतश्च रिशादसः । करम्भेण सजोषस इति यथा पुरोऽनुवाक्यैवमेषैतयैवैनानेतस्मै भागाय ह्वयति ॥ १८ ॥

तानि प्रतिपुरुषं यावन्तो गृह्यास्तावन्ति भवन्त्येकेनातिरिक्तानि प्रतिपुरुषमेवैतदेकेनैकेन या अस्य प्रजा जातास्ता वरुणपाशात्प्रमुञ्चत्येकेनातिरिक्तानि भवन्ति तद्या एवास्याजाताः प्रजास्ता एव तेन वरुणपाशात्प्रमुञ्चति ॥ १९ ॥

पात्राणि भवन्ति पात्रैर्ह्यशनमश्नन्ति यवमयानि भवन्ति यवꣳ हि जक्षुषीरगृह्णात् ॥ २० ॥

शूर्पेण जुहोति शूर्पेण ह्यशनं क्रियते पत्नी जुहोति मिथुनादेवैतद्वरुणपाशात्प्रजाः प्रमुञ्चति ॥ २१ ॥

८. See Notes.

14. That there are a ram and a ewe is because this ram is indeed a visible animal (to be offered) of Varuṇa (and) thus he (the sacrificer) obviously releases the creatures from Varuṇa's noose, because of its being dedicated toVaruṇa. The two are a pair. He releases the creatures from Varuṇa's noose, thus by the union (of the pair). The two are made of barley. For, he (Varuṇa) seized them (creatures) that had eaten barley. He (the sacrificer) places the ewe on the northern curds and the ram on the southern. Thus indeed is a (mating) pair formed. Verily to the north (left) of the man does the woman lie.

15. The Adhvaryu places all the dishes (oblations to be offered) on the northern altar; the pratiprasthātā (remains) having placed the oblation to the Maruts alone on the southern altar and having touched the dishes (of offerings).

16. Then the Adhvaryu says, "Speak (recite) for the Agni that is being churned". Having churned (and brought out) Agni, he says, "Recite for Agni who is being kindled". Both of them, indeed place two kindling sticks (firewood). Having placed (each one) the two kindling sticks,(the two)(Adhvaryu and Pratiprasthātṛ) pour out the first two libations (each one).

17. Then theAdhvaryu says,"Oh Agnīdh! Trim the fire well". (Yet) the fire remains verily despatched untrimmed. Then the Pratiprasthātṛ(who had been sent) returns. He fetches the wife (of the sacrificer). Before fetching her, he asks, "With whom do you move (sexually)?" That a woman who belongs to a different person moves with another (sexually), she verily commits (a sin) with regard to Varuṇa. If not (asked) (Varuṇa would think), she sacrifices to me with a pang within (her mind)". Verily, the sin that has been spoken out becomes less (lighter); it becomes the truth. If she does not speak out the truth (does not swear), harm befalls her relatives, indeed.

18. He then makes her recite, "We invoke the Maruts who are the devourers and eaters of enemies and who are delighted with the porridge (mixture of flour and curds)". This (expression) is just (in import) as is the prior invitation. With this, verily, does he invite these (Maruts) for this (their) share.

19. They (the dishes) are as many as there are members of the household (of the sacrificer); one for each member, exceeding by one. He thereby releases from the noose of Varuṇa his children (progeny) (already) born, each individual with one (dish) (for each). They (the vessels) are excessive by one, so that with that he releases from Varuṇa's noose verily those children which are(yet)unborn.

20. There are the vessels, for they eat food with (from) vessels. They (the dishes) are of barley, for he (Varuṇa) captured them (creatures) that had eaten the barley.

21. (She) makes the offering, with the winnow. For it is with the winnowing basket, indeed, that food is prepared. The (sacrificer's) wife makes the offering.

पुरा यज्ञात्पुराहुतिभ्यो जुहोत्यहुतादो वै विशो विशो वै मरुतस्तस्मात्पुरा यज्ञात्पुराहुतिभ्यो जुहोति यत्र ह वै तत्प्रजापतेः प्रजाः परिदीर्णाः शिश्रियरे च निषेदुश्च तदासां मरुतः पाप्मानं विमेथिरे तथो वा एतस्य प्रजानां मरुतः पाप्मानं विमथ्नते ॥ २२ ॥

स[९] जुहोति यद्ग्रामे यदरण्य इति ग्रामे वा ह्यरण्ये वैनः क्रियते यत्सभायां यदिन्द्रिय इति यन्मानुष इत्येवैतदाह यदाह यत्सभायामिति यदिन्द्रिय इति यद्देवत्रेत्येवैतदाह देवत्रा वा हि मानुषे वैनः क्रियते यदेनश्चकृमा वयमिदं तदवयजामहे स्वाहेति यत्किं च वयमेनश्चकृमेदं तस्मात्प्रमुच्यामह इत्येवैतदाह ॥ २३ ॥

अथैन्द्रीं मरुत्वतीं जपति यत्र ह वै तत्प्रजापतेः प्रजानां मरुतः पाप्मानं विमेथिरे तद्धेक्षांचक्रे प्रजापतिरिम उ ह मे प्रजा न विमथ्नीरन्निति ॥ २४ ॥

स ऐन्द्रीं मरुत्वतीमजपत् क्षत्रं वा इन्द्रो विशो मरुतः क्षत्रं वै विशो निषेद्धा निषिद्धा आँ[१०]सन्निति मो षू ण इन्द्रात्र पृत्सु देवैरस्ति हि ष्मा ते शुष्मिन्नवयाः । महश्चिद्यस्य मीळ्हुषो यव्या हविष्मन्तो[११] मरुतो वन्दते गीरिति ॥ २५ ॥

अथ वाचयत्यक्रन्कर्म कर्मकृत इत्यक्रन्हि कर्म कर्मकृतः सह वाचा मयोभुवेति सह हि वाचाक्रन्देवेभ्यः कर्म कृत्वेति देवेभ्यो हि कर्माक्रन्नस्तं प्रेत सचाभुव इति यदन्यत ओळ्हया सह भवति तस्मादाह सचाभुव इत्यस्तं प्रेतेति गृहा उ वा अस्तं जघनार्धो वा एष यज्ञस्य यत्पत्नी तामिदं प्राचीं प्रासीषदद्गृहा उ वा अस्तं तदेनां गृहेष्वेव प्रतिष्ठापयति प्रतिपराणीय प्रतिप्रस्थाता पत्नीमुदाद्रवति संमृजन्त्यग्नी[१२] उत्तरावाघारावाघारयतः ॥ २६ ॥

९. सा Ca., K. P1. P2.

१०. असन्निति Ca., (perhaps printing error)

११. हविष्मन्न मरुतो TE.

१२. मृजत्यग्नी TE. see Notes.

Thus she releases the children (progeny) from Varuṇa's noose, verily through the union (pair).

22. Prior to sacrifice, prior to the oblations, she makes the offering. For, indeed, the common subjects are not consumers of offerings; verily the Maruts are the common subjects (of gods). Therefore she offers before the sacrifice and before the oblations. Where then the creatures of Prajāpati lay down and sat themselves having been torn, there did the Maruts destroy their sin (hurt). Similarly, indeed the Maruts destroy the sin (harm) of the children of this (sacrificer).

23. She offers (saying), "What (sin was) commited in the village, what (was committed) in the forest", for sin is commited in the village and in the forest. (She says), "What (was commited) in the hall (in the society among the people) and what (was committed) in the senses". She verily says (means),"In the case of men", when she says, "What in the hall (in society)?"(By) "What in the senses" she verily says (means) this,"Towards the gods". Indeed a sin is committed towards the gods or towards men. (She says),"What sin we have committed here, we do expiate that- *svāhā*". She verily says (means) this, "What sin we have committed here, we are released from that".

24. He then mutters (the chant) addressed to Indra and referring to the Maruts, "When the Maruts verily destroyed the sin (hurt) of the creatures of Prajāpati", then Prajāpati observed, "These indeed, may not destroy my creatures".

25. He muttered (the chant) addressed to Indra and referring to the Maruts. Indra indeed is the Kṣatriya (ruler) the Maruts are the subjects. The ruler is the prohibiter (controller) of the subjects. (Prajāpati thought), "May they be prohibited (from hurting my creatures)"."Oh Indra! Let there be no fight for us in battles with gods. Indeed there is a sacrificial share (of oblations) for you, Oh strong one! whose glory of the bounteous one the word (of the sacrificer) adores abundantly".The Maruts (too) have (their share of) oblations (in the sacrifice).

26. Then he makes (her) recite, "Workers have done the work". Verily have the workers done the work. (She recites),"Its expression productive of delight". Indeed they did work, with expression (speaking). (She recites), "Having done the work for the gods". Verily they did the work for the sake of the gods. (She says), "Being together, go home". Wherefore she is now with one who has been brought from elsewhere. She hence says,"Those that are together", "Go home", (she says). The house indeed is (the place) where one hides himself (throws himself in) (place of rest). The wife is verily the hind (lower/base) part of the sacrifice. He has made her sit at the east. Indeed, the house is the resting place. Therefore, he establishes her indeed in the house. The Pratiprasthātṛ comes back (to his place), after leading the (sacrificer's) wife away. He trims the two

आश्राव्याध्वर्युर्होतारं प्रवृणीते सीदति होतोत्तरस्या वेदेर्होतृषदने प्रसूतः स्रुचावादायातिक्रम्याध्वर्युराश्राव्याह समिधो यजेति यज यजेत्येव चतुर्थे चतुर्थे समानयमानौ नव प्रयाजान्यजतः ॥ २७ ॥

अथाध्वर्युराहाग्नयेऽनुब्रूहीत्याग्नेयमाज्यभागमुभौ त्वेव चतुराज्यस्यावद्यतोऽतिक्रम्याश्राव्याग्निं यजेति वषट्कृते जुहोति ॥ २८ ॥

सोमायानुब्रूहीत्याह सौम्यमाज्यभागमुभौ त्वेव चतुराज्यस्यावद्यतोऽतिक्रम्याश्राव्याह सोमं यजेति वषट्कृते जुहोति ॥ २९ ॥

स यदिहैवाध्वर्युराश्रावयतीह वषट्क्रियतेऽथ कृतानुकर एव प्रतिप्रस्थाता क्षत्रं वै वरुणो विशो मरुतः क्षत्रायैवैतद्विशं कृतानुकरामनुवर्त्मानं करोति यद्धापि प्रतिप्रस्थाताश्रावयेत्प्रत्युद्यामिनीꣳ ह क्षत्रियाय विशं कुर्यात्तदप्रत्युद्यामिनीमेवैतत्क्षत्रियाय विशं करोत्यनुवर्त्मानं तस्मात्प्रतिप्रस्थाता नाश्रावयत्यथ पाणावेव बिभ्रत्प्रतिप्रस्थाता स्रुचा उपास्ते ॥ ३० ॥

अथैतैर्हविर्भिरध्वर्युः प्रचरत्यैन्द्राग्नेनान्तमेनाथ पयस्याभ्यां प्रचरिष्यन्तौ योऽयं मेषो मारुत्यां भवति तं वारुण्यामवदधाति यो[१३] मेषी वारुण्यां भवति तां मारुत्यामवदधाति ॥ ३१ ॥

स यदेवं विपरिहरन्ति क्षत्रं वै वरुणो वीर्यं पुमान्वीर्यमेवैतत्क्षत्रे दधाति विशो वै मरुतोऽवीर्या वै स्त्र्यवीर्यामेवैतद्विशं करोति ॥ ३२ ॥

१३. या TE, V1; या+उ=यो.

fires. The two (Adhvaryu and Pratiprasthātṛ) pour the two later libations (each, one).

27. Having called the attention (of Āgnīdhra), the Adhvaryu chooses the Hotṛ. The Hotṛ sits on the Hotṛ's seat at the northern altar. Having been prompted, the Adhvaryu takes up the two spoons, steps beyond and calls the attention (of the Āgnīdhra) and says (to the Hotṛ), "Offer the *Samidhs*", (pronounce the offering prayer for the kindling sticks). He says verily, "Offer", (at each offering). The two (Adhvaryu and Pratiprasthātṛ) bring together (the *ghee* from the spoons into the pouring spoon) at every fourth (offering). The two offer the nine fore-offerings.

28. Then the Adhvaryu says, "Speak for (call for) (utter the prayer of invitation) Agni" regarding the Agni's share of the *ghee.* Both indeed cut up (ladle out) the *ghee* four times. (The Adhvaryu) steps beyond, calls attention and then says , "Offer (worship) (utter the prayer of offering for) Agni". When, *Vaṣat* has been uttered he makes the offering.

29. He says, "Make the call for Soma", regarding Soma's share of the *ghee.* Both verily cut up (ladle out) the *ghee* four times. He (Adhvaryu) steps beyond, calls attention and then says, "Worship (offer) Soma (utter the prayer of offering for Soma)". When *Vaṣat* has been uttered, he makes the offering (pours the libation into the fire).

30. (The fact) that the Adhvaryu calls attention here itself (and) *Vaṣat* is uttered here and then pratiprasthātṛ is only an imitator of what has been done (by the Adhvaryu) (is due to this)- Indeed Varuṇa is Kṣatra (ruler), the Maruts are the subjects. Thus he (the sacrificer) makes the subject the imitator and follower for the Kṣatra. if the Pratiprasthātṛ should make the call for attention–one should make the subject go out to receive the ruler–this (call of Pratiprasthātṛ) makes the subject, the follower, verily as one not going out to receive the ruler. Therefore the Pratiprasthātṛ does not make the call for attention. The Pratiprasthātṛ, then, merely holding his breath, (remains nearby) waits upon (the Adhvaryu) with his spoon.

31. Then the Adhvaryu proceeds with this oblation with the one dedicated to Indra and Agni (together) being nearest. (As they are) about to proceed with the two curds (offerings), the two (Adhvaryu and Pratiprasthātṛ)–(one) (the Adhvaryu) places into the (northern) dish for Varuṇa and (barley) ram which is in the (southern) dish of the Maruts, and (the other) (Pratiprasthātṛ) places into (the curds dish) of Maruts the (barley) ewe which is on (the curds dish) of Varuṇa.

32. (The reason) why they transpose (the ram and ewe) thus (is that); indeed Varuṇa is Kṣatra, 'male' is 'virility'. Thus he puts verily virility into the Kṣatra.

अथाह वरुणायानुब्रूहीति तत्राप्यन्यतरेणावदानेन सह मेषमवदधात्यतिक्रम्याश्राव्याह वरुणं यजेति वषट्कृते जुहोति ॥ ३३ ॥

अथ प्रतिप्रस्थातुरुत्तरसिचमन्वारभ्याहाध्वर्युर्मरुद्भ्योऽनुब्रूहीति तत्राप्यन्यतरेणावदानेन सह प्रतिप्रस्थाता मेषीमवदधात्यध्वर्युरेवाश्राव्याह मरुतो यजेति वषट्कृते जुहोति ॥ ३४ ॥

अथाध्वर्युः कायेनैककपालेन प्रचरति कायेनैककपालेन चरित्वाहाग्नये स्विष्टकृतेऽनुब्रूहीति सर्वेषाꣳ हविषामध्वर्युरवद्यति मारुत्या एव प्रतिप्रस्थातातिक्रम्याश्राव्याहाग्निꣳ स्विष्टकृतं यजेति वषट्कृते जुहोति ॥ ३५ ॥

सादयित्वा स्रुचावध्वर्युः प्राशित्रमवद्यति प्राशित्रमवदायेळामवद्यति तदेवापि प्रतिप्रस्थात्रे स्रुचं प्रति[14]गृह्णाति तत्सोऽभ्यवदधात्युपहूयेळां मार्जयित्वाथाध्वर्युराहाग्नीत्समिधमाधायाग्निꣳ संमृड्ढि ब्रह्मन्प्रस्थास्याम इति पृषदाज्यꣳ स्रुचोरध्वर्युर्व्यानयते यदि प्रतिप्रस्थातुः पृषदाज्यꣳ स्यात्तत्स व्यानयेत यदि पृषदाज्यं न स्यादपि यदेवोपभृत्याज्यं तत्तर्हि व्यानयेतातिक्रम्याश्राव्याह देवान्यजेति यज यजेत्येव चतुर्थे चतुर्थे समानयमानौ नवानुयाजान्यजतः स यन्नवप्रयाजं नवानुयाजमित्युभयत एवैतन्न्यूनाद्वरुणपाशात्प्रजाः प्रमुञ्चतीतश्चोर्ध्वा इतश्चावाचीस्तस्मान्नवप्रयाजं भवति नवानुयाजम् ॥ ३६ ॥

१४. प्रगृह्णाति TE.

Indeed the Maruts are the subjects. Verily female is without virility. Thus he indeed makes the subject lacking in virility (strength).

33. Then he says, "Make the (invitation) call for Varuṇa". Then he places the (barley) ram (into the offering spoon) along with one of the two cutting up (of the *ghee*); stepping beyond and calling attention, he says, "Worship (recite the offering prayer for) Varuṇa". He offers (pours out the libation) after *Vaṣaṭ* has been pronounced.

34. Then touching the upper hem of (the garment of) the Pratiprasthātṛ the Adhvaryu says, "Make the invitation call for the Maruts". Then the Pratiprasthātṛ places the (barley) ewe, along with the other cutting up of *ghee*, (into the offering spoon). (But) Adhvaryu himself calls for attention and says, "Pronounce the offering prayer for the Maruts (worship of the Maruts)" when *Vaṣat* has been pronunced, he *(*Pratiprasthātṛ*)* pours out the oblation (into the fire).

35. Then the Adhvaryu proceeds with the oblation, on a single potsherd, dedicated to *(ka)* Prajāpati. Having performed (offered) with the (offering to) *ka*, on a single potshered, (he says) "Make the invitation call for *Agni-Sviṣṭakṛt* ". The Adhvaryu cuts up (portions) from all the offerings, but thc Pratiprasthātṛ (cuts up) only of the one dedicated to the Maruts. (The Adhvaryu) steps beyond, calls attention and says, "Worship (pronounce the offering prayer for) *Agni-Sviṣṭakṛt*". After the *Vaṣat* has been pronounced he pours out the libation (into the fire).

36. Placing down the two spoons, the *Adhvarya* cuts up the *Prāśitra*, having cut up the *Prāśitra*. he cuts up *Iḍā*. Then, indeed, does he hand it over to *Iḍā* Pratiprasthātṛ and hold up in the spoon. He places it down. Having invoked Idā and having washed up, Adhvaryu says, "Oh Agnīdh! placing the kindling stick, trim the fire". "Oh Brahman! we are going to start". The Adhvaryu pours the *ghee* mixed with sour milk (clotted ghee) into the two spoons. If the Pratiprasthātṛ has clotted *ghee* he too should put it (into the spoons). If he has no clotted *ghee*, then he should pour verily the *ghee* that is in the *upabhṛt* (secondary spoon). (The Adhvaryu) steps beyond, calls attention and says, "Worship (pronounce the offering prayer for) Gods", and (says) "Pronounce", "Pronounce" (at every offering). Pouring together (the *ghee*) at every fourth (offering), the two offer the nine after- offerings. That there is (a group of) nine fore-offerings and (a group of) nine after-offerings (is because) he verily on both sides, releases from the noose of Varuṇa (the creatures) before now and those after now (the creatures upright and the creatures bent down). Hence there is (an offering of) "nine fore-offerings" an (and offering of) "nine after-offerings".

सादयित्वा स्रुचो व्यूहतो व्यूह्य[१५] स्रुचः परिधीन्त्समज्य[१६] परिधीनभिपद्याध्वर्युराश्राव्या-
हेषिता दैव्या होतारो भद्रवाच्याय प्रेषितो मानुषाः सूक्तवाकायेति सूक्ता होता प्रतिपद्यत
उभावेवेमौ प्रस्तरावाददाते अनुप्रहृत्य प्रस्तरौ तृणे अपगृह्योपासाते अथाग्नीदाहानुप्रहरेत्यु-
भावेवानुप्रहरतः संवदस्वेत्यगादग्नीदगंच्छ्रवय[१७] श्रौषट् स्वगा दैव्या होतृभ्यः स्वस्तिर्मानुषेभ्य
इति शंयोर्होता प्रतिपद्यत उभावेवेमौ परिधीननुप्रहृत्य स्रुचः संप्रगृह्य स्फ्ये सादयतः
प्रतिपरेत्याध्वर्युः पत्नीः संयाजयत्युदेत्याध्वर्युः ॥ ३७ ॥

त्रीणि समिष्टयजूꣳषि जुहोति तूष्णीमेव प्रतिप्रस्थाता स्रुचं प्रगृह्णात्यथ ये वैश्वदेवेन
यजमानयोर्वाससी परिहिते स्यातां ते एवाप्यत्र स्यातामथास्या वारुण्याः पयस्यायाः
क्षामकर्षमिश्रमादाय तेनावभृथं[१८] यन्ति वरुण्यं वा इदं निर्वरुणतायै तत्र न साम गीयते न
ह्यत्र साम्ना कुर्वन्ति तूष्णीमेव परेत्यावभृथ निचुम्पुण निचेरुरसि निचुम्पुण । अव देवैर्देव-
कृतमेनोऽयासिषमव मर्त्यैर्मर्त्यकृतं पुरुराव्णो देव रिषस्पाहीति स्थालीमुपमारयति[१९]
स्नात्वान्ये वाससी परिधायोदेतः कामꣳ हैते यस्मै कामयेत तस्मै दद्यान्न हि दीक्षितवसने
स यथाहिस्त्वचो निर्मुच्येतैवं वरुण्यात्सर्वस्मात्पाप्मनो निर्मुच्योदैति केशश्मश्रूप्वाग्नी
समारोहयत उदवसाय ह्येतेन यजते नह्यवकल्पते यदुत्तरवेदावग्निहोत्रं जुहुयुर्गृहानागत्य

१५. व्युह्य Ca.
१६. न्त्समृज्य TE, P1, P2.
१७. See Notes.
१८. ततोऽवभृथं V1.
१९. मुपसादयति as alternate reading in TE only.

37. Having placed down the spoons, they (two) separate (them). Having separated the spoons, having anointed the enclosing sticks (with *ghee*) and having taken up the enclosing sticks and having called attention,the Adhvaryu says, "The divine Hotṛs are desired (called upon) for proclaiming success (of the ritual); the human(hotṛ)is called upon (desired) to recite the *Sūktas* (hymns). The Hotṛ takes up (recitation of) the hymns. These two(Adhvaryu and Pratiprasthātṛ) take up the two(sets of)spread out sacred grass. Having thrown the two (sets of) spread out sacred grass (into the fire) and removing two blades of grass (each-one), they (two) wait upon (the fire). Then the Agnīdh says, "Throw (into the fire)". Both throw each his blade of grass (into the fire). (Agnīdh says), "Talk cordially (to me)",(Adhvaryu asks),"Oh! Agnīdh! Has he gone?" (Agnīdh says), "He has gone "(Adhvaryu says). "Report (make them hear)– *'Śrauṣaṭ'* (hear), "Happy going for the divine Hotṛs; auspiciousness (well-being) to the humans (human Hotṛs)"–The Hotṛ pronounces *"Śam yoḥ"*. Both these(Adhvaryu and Pratiprasthātṛ)having subsequently thrown(offered) the enclosing sticks (into the fire) and having taken up the spoons together, place them on the wooden sword. Having returned (to his place),the Adhvaryu performs the *'Patnīsamyājas'* (offerings to gods along with their wives). Then the Adhvaryu, having got up.

38. Performs three *'Samiṣṭa-yajus'*.The Pratiprasthātṛ silently takes up the spoon. Now, those two garments that had been worn as they performed the Vaiśvadeva offerings,the very same should be (worn) here too (for the sacrificer and his wife). Thereafter, having taken up (the *havis*-food) mixed with the scanty (dried) scrapings of the curds dedicated to Varuṇa, they go to (the place of) expiatory bath. This (expiatory bath-*avabhṛta*) is related to Varuṇa (being performed) for release from Varuṇa. *Sāman* is not sung in it, for they do not (perform anything) at this (sacrifice) with *Sāman* (singing of *Ṛks*) at all. Having walked silently he throws the vessel into water, uttering, "Oh *avabhṛtha*!Oh swell flow! You glide along on great flow of water! I have removed with (the help of) gods the sin committed towards the gods; and with (the help of) men (have removed the sin committed towards men. Oh God! protect me from the injury from the fiercely (much)- howling (demon)". Having bathed and having donned two other cloths, they come up (to the bank). These two (garments worn while bathing) he may verily give to anybody to whom he likes (to give). For, they are not the two garments of one who has been initiated (*dīkṣita*). He comes out, released from all sins (committed)in relation to Varuṇa, just as a snake will be released from (its) slough. Having shaved off his hair and beard (leaving the tuft), he takes up (lifts) (withdraws) the two fires. For, after removing (completing) it he performs with this (other) sacrifice. Indeed it is not proper that they should perform *Agnihotra* on the *Uttaravedi* (the northern altar). Having come to the house and having churned (the fires), he performs the Full Moon offering. This sacrifice,viz., the *'Cāturmāsyas'* is verily broken (it

निर्मथ्य पौर्णमासेन यजत उत्सन्नो वा अयं यज्ञो यच्चातुर्मास्यानि क्लृप्तेनैवैतद्यज्ञेनान्ततः प्रतितिष्ठति ॥ ३८ ॥ इति प्रथमं ब्राह्मणम् ॥

द्वितीयं ब्राह्मणम्

वरुणप्रघासैर्ह वै प्रजापतिः प्रजा वरुणपाशात्प्रामुञ्चत्ता अस्यानमीवा अकिल्बिषाः प्रजाः प्राजायन्ताथैतैः साकमेधैरेतैर्ह वै देवा वृत्रं जघ्नुरेतैर्वेव व्यजयन्त येयमेषां विजितिस्तथो वा एष एतैः पाप्मानं द्विषन्तं भ्रातृव्यꣳ हन्ति तथो एव विजयते स वै द्व्यहमन्वहं यजते ॥ १ ॥

स पूर्वेद्युरग्नयेऽनीकवतेऽष्टाकपालं पुरोळाशं निर्वपत्यग्निꣳ ह वा अनीकं कृत्वा देवा उपप्रेयुः प्रातर्वृत्रꣳ हनिष्यन्तः स तेजोऽग्निर्नाव्यथत तथो वा[1] एष[2] पाप्मानं[3] द्विषन्तं भ्रातृव्यꣳ हनिष्यन्नग्निमेवानीकं कृत्वोपप्रैति तस्मादग्नयेऽनीकवतेऽष्टाकपालं पुरोळाशं निर्वपति ॥ २ ॥

अथ मरुद्भ्यः सान्तपनेभ्यो मध्यंदिने चरुं निर्वपति मरुतो ह वै सान्तपना मध्यंदिने वृत्रꣳ सन्तेपुः स सन्तप्तोऽनन्नै[4]व प्राणन्परिदीर्णः शिश्ये तथो वा एतस्य पाप्मानं द्विषन्तं भ्रातृव्यं मरुत एव सान्तपना मध्यंदिने सन्तपन्ति तस्मान्मरुद्भ्यस्सान्तपनेभ्यो मध्यंदिने चरुं निर्वपति ॥ ३ ॥

अथ मरुद्भ्यो गृहमेधिभ्योऽपराह्णे पर्णशाखया वत्सानपाकृत्य पवित्रवति संदोह्यैतं चरुꣳ श्रपयति सर्वो हि स चरुर्यत्र क्व च तण्डुलानावपन्ति मेधꣳ ह वा एतं देवा आत्मनि दधिरे प्रातर्वृत्रꣳ हनिष्यन्तस्तथो वा एष पाप्मानं द्विषन्तं भ्रातृव्यꣳ हनिष्यन्नात्मनि मेधं धत्ते स यत्क्षीरौदनो भवति मेधो वै पयो मेधस्तण्डुला उभयमेवैतन्मेधमात्मनि धत्ते ॥ ४ ॥

१. वा missing in M.

२. एष missing in Po.

३. एष एतं पाप्मानं in TE, M, My.

४. See Notes.

verily perishes). Only with this sacrifice (Full Moon sacrifice), that is regular (properly performed), he (the sacrificer) ultimately gets established.

(First Brāhamaṇa Ends)

BRĀHAMAṆA II

1. Prajāpati released the creatures from Varuṇa's noose indeed by means of '*Varuṇapraghāsas*'. Those creatures of his were born without disease and without blemish. Now with these *Sākamedhas* —indeed by means of the *Sākamedhas* did the gods kill Vṛtra. Verily with these only they attained this victory which victory is theirs. In that manner, indeed, does this (sacrificer) destroy his evil hateful enemy by means of these *(Sākamedhas)* and verily similarly conquers(becomes glorious). He indeed performs (this sacrifice) every day, for two days.

2. On the previous day (the first day) he offers an oblation *(Puroḍāśa)* on eight potsherds to *Agni-Anikavat*. For,the gods who would kill Vṛtra on the morning (of the morrow) went forward (towards Vṛtra), making Agni a sharp point (of weapon) (of making Agni the leader). That 'effulgence', Agni did not suffer (did not feel any pain). So also, this (sacrificer) too moves forward making Agni himself as a point (of weapon) (or a leader), in order to kill the evil hateful enemy. Therefore he offers a *puroḍāśa* on eight potsherds to *Agni-Anikavat.*

3. Then at mid-day he offers a *caru* (boiled rice) to the *Maruts—Sāntapanas*) (Maruts the scorchers). For indeed the Maruts, being scorchers, scorched Vṛtra. Having been scorched, merely breathing in and breathing out,breathing heavily he lay, torn all over. In the same manner do the scorching Maruts scorch, at midday, the wicked hateful enemy of this sacrificer. Therefore does he offer *caru*, at midday to the *Maruts-Sāntapanas.*

4. Then (he offers a *caru*)to *Marut-Gṛhamedhins* (Maruts theHouseholders) in the afternoon. Having removed the calves with a leafy turf and having drawn the milk into a vessel that has a purifying (device) (tuft of sacrificial grass), he heats this *caru* over a fire. All that is indeed a *caru* wherein they put rice grains (for cooking). About to kill Vṛtra on the (following) morning, the gods took (consumed) this nourishment within themselves. In that manner, indeed, this sacrificer (too) who is about to destroy his wicked hateful enemy, takes into himself nourishment in that he has milkfood. Indeed milk is nourishment; nourishment are grains of rice. He (the sacrificer) takes into himself verily this twofold nourishment.

तस्य द्वय्या[५]वृत्सैव वेदिस्तीर्णा भवति परिधीꣳश्चैव शकलाꣳश्चोपनिदधति स्रुवं चो [६]एव स्रुचं च सम्माष्टर्यथ द्वे पिशीले वा पात्र्यौ वा निर्णिज्य तयोरेतद्द्वैधौदनमुद्धरति तयोः सर्पिरासेचनं कृत्वा सर्पिरासिच्य तावादायोदाद्रवति स तामेव वेदिꣳ स्तीर्णामभिमृश्य परिधीन्परिधाय यावतः कामयते शकलाꣳ स्तावतोऽभ्यादधात्यासादयत्येतावोदनौ सीदति होता होतृषदने स्रुवं च स्रुचं चाभिपद्यमान आह ॥ ५ ॥

अग्नयेऽनुब्रूहीत्याग्नेयमाज्यभागꣳ सोऽस्य दक्षिणस्यौदनस्य चतुराज्यस्यावद्यत्यतिक्रम्याश्राव्याहाग्निं यजेति वषट्कृते जुहोति ॥ ६ ॥

सोमायानुब्रूहीत्याह सौम्यमाज्यभागꣳ सोऽस्योत्तरस्यौदनस्य चतुराज्यस्यावद्यत्यतिक्रम्याश्राव्याह सोमं यजेति वषट्कृते जुहोति ॥ ७ ॥

अथाह मरुद्भ्यो गृहमेधिभ्योऽनुब्रूहीति सोऽस्य दक्षिणस्यौदनस्य तत एवाज्यमुपस्तृणीते ततो द्विरवद्यत्यभिघारयति [७]प्रत्यनक्त्यवदाने अतिक्रम्याश्राव्याह मरुतो गृहमेधिनो यजेति वषट्कृते जुहोति ॥ ८ ॥

अथाहाग्नये स्विष्टकृतेऽनुब्रूहीति सोऽस्योत्तरस्यौदनस्य तत एवाज्यमुपस्तृणीते ततो द्विरवद्यत्यभिघारयति प्रत्यनक्त्यवदाने अतिक्रम्याश्राव्याहाग्निꣳ स्विष्टकृतं यजेति वषट्कृते जुहोतीळामेवावद्यति न प्राशित्रमेतन्त्वेकमयनम् ॥ ९ ॥

अथ द्वितीयꣳ सैव वेदि स्तीर्णा भवति परिधीꣳश्चैव शकलाꣳश्चोपनिदधति स्रुवं चो एव स्रुचं च सम्मार्ष्टि तथो एवैतं पवित्रवति सन्दोह्य चरुꣳ श्रपयत्यध्वर्य आज्यꣳ स्थाल्यामधिश्रयति तं यदा शृतं मन्यतेऽथैनमभिघार्योद्वासयति तमुद्वास्यानक्ति तꣳ सो[८]खमेवादायोदाद्रवति स तामेव वेदिꣳ स्तीर्णामभिमृश्य परिधीन्परिधाय यावतः कामयते

५. द्वयावृ B.

६. स्रुवं च स्रुचं TE, Co, T.

७. न प्रत्यन... TE, My, K, P1, P2, T, Pa, W, Ne.

८. सोषं in many Mss; ख and ष always interchanged and have not been noted every where.

5. For it there is a twofold method (two methods) of performance. The same altar is strewn with a covering (of sacrificial grass). They place the enclosing sticks and pieces (of wood) near it. He verily wipes clean the dipping spoon and the offering spoon. Having washed two small plates or two dishes, he takes this cooked rice in two parts in them. Having made a depression in those two (dishes) for pouring *ghee* and having poured *ghee* and having taken them (the two vessels) up, he rushes to that very altar. Having touched that altar covered (with sacrificial grass) and having placed the enclosing sticks around (the fire), he puts (into the fire) as many sticks as he likes. He places the (vessels of) two rice foods down. The Hotṛ sits on the Hotṛ's seat. Taking up the dipping spoon and the offering spoon (The Adhvaryu) says.

6. "Make the (invitation) call for Agni", with reference to Agni's share of the *ghee.* He cuts up (and takes) four times; of the *ghee* of the southern rice-food; having stepped beyond and having called attention, he says, "Worship (pronounce the offering prayer for) Agni". When *Vaṣaṭ* has been uttered, he pours the libation (into the fire).

7. He says, "Make the call (of invitation) for Soma", about Soma's share of the *ghee.* He cuts up (and takes) four times, of the *ghee* of the northern rice-food. Having stepped beyond and having called attention he says, "Worship Soma". When *Vaṣaṭ* has been pronounced, he makes the offering.

8. Then he says, "Make the call (of invitation) for *Marut-Gṛahamedhim*". He spreads (covers) the sourthern rice-food with the *ghee* from itself, makes two cuttings from it, sprinkles it with *ghee* but does not smear it over the two cut up (portions). Having stepped across and having called attention, he says, "Worship the *Marut-Gṛhamedhins*". He makes the offering after *Vaṣaṭ* has been pronounced.

9. Then he says, "Make the (invitation) call for *Agni-Sviṣṭakṛt*". He spreads (covers) the northern rice-food with the *ghee* from itself, makes two cuttings from it, sprinkles it with *ghee* (but) does not smear the two cut up (portions); having stepped beyond and having called attention, he says, "Worship *Agni-Sviṣṭakṛt*". When *Vaṣaṭ* has been pronounced, he makes the offering. He cuts up only *Iḍā* and not *Prāśitra*. (the fore-portion that belongs to *Brahman*). This, indeed, is one way (of performance).

10. Now the second (mode of performance);—
That very altar becomes covered (with sacrificial grass). They place the enclosing sticks and pieces (of wood) nearby. He wipes clean the dipping spoon and also the offering spoon. In the same way (as before) having milked in (a vessel) that has a purifier (bunch of sacred grass), he cooks the *caru.* Nearby he heats up the *ghee* in a pot. When he thinks it has been cooked, then he removes it after having sprinkled (*ghee* over) it. Having removed it, he smears it (with

शकलाꣳस्तावतोऽभ्यादधात्यासादयत्येतꣳ सोखमेवाध्वर्ध आज्यमासादयति सीदति होता होतृषदने स्रुवं च स्रुचं चाभिपद्यमान आह ॥ १० ॥

अग्नयेऽनुब्रूहीत्याग्नेयमाज्यभागꣳ सोऽस्याः स्थाल्याश्चतुराज्यस्यावद्यत्यतिक्रम्याश्राव्याहाग्निं यजेति वषट्कृते जुहोति ॥ ११ ॥

सोमायानुब्रूहीत्याह सौम्यमाज्यभागꣳ सोऽस्याः स्थाल्याश्चतुराज्यस्यावद्यत्यतिक्रम्याश्राव्याह सोमं यजेति वषट्कृते जुहोति ॥ १२ ॥

अथाह मरुद्भ्यो गृहमेधिभ्योऽनुब्रूहीत्युपस्तृणीत आज्यमथास्य चरोर्द्विरवद्यत्यभिघारयति [९]प्रत्यनक्त्यवदाने अतिक्रम्याश्राव्याह मरुतो गृहमेधिनो यजेति वषट्कृते जुहोति ॥ १३ ॥

अथाहाग्नये स्विष्टकृतेऽनुब्रूहीत्युपस्तृणीत आज्यमथास्य चरोः सकृदवद्यति द्विरभिघारयति न प्रत्यनक्त्यवदानमतिक्रम्याश्राव्याहाग्निꣳ स्विष्टकृतं यजेति वषट्कृते जुहोतीळामेवावद्यति न प्राशित्रम् ॥ १४ ॥

ते यावतो[१०] गृह्या हविराशाः स्युस्तेऽस्यौदनस्याश्नीयुरथो ऋत्विजोऽथो अन्ये ब्राह्मणा यदि बहु स्यादथेमामनिरशितामेव कुम्भीमपिधाय निदधति प्रातः पूर्णदर्वाय समवर्जन्ति[११] वत्साꣳस्तत्पशव आत्मनि मेधं दधते ॥ १५ ॥

यवाग्वैताꣳ रात्रिमग्निहोत्रं जुहोति निवान्याया वत्सं यमयन्ति प्रातः पितृयज्ञायाथ प्रातर्हुते वाहुते वाग्निहोत्रे यतरथा कामयेतास्या अनिरशितायाः कुम्भ्याः पूर्णदर्वमुपहन्ति पूर्णा दर्वि परापत सुपूर्णा पुनरापत । वस्नेव विक्रीणावहा इषमूर्जꣳ शतक्रतविति यथा पुरोऽनुवाक्यैवमेषैतयैवैनमेतस्मै भागाय ह्वयति ॥ १६ ॥

९. न प्रत्यन TE, My, K, P1, P2, T, Pa, W, N, Ne.

१०. यावन्तो TE.

११. See Notes.

ghee). Having taken it up along with the salt earth (smeared on the outer underside of the pot), he hastens (towards) the altar. Having touched that very altar that has been covered (with holy grass) and having placed the enclosing sticks around (the altar), he places (in the fire) as many pieces (of wood) as he likes. He places down this food with the vessel, with the (smeared) earth (on the outside bottom of the vessel). He places the (pot of) *ghee* down nearby. The Hotṛ sits on the Hotṛ's seat. (The Adhvaryu), taking up the dipping spoon and offering spoon, says,

11. "Make the (invitation) call for Agni", with reference to Agni's share of *ghee.* He cuts up (and takes four times from the *ghee* in the pot. Having stepped beyond and having called attention, he says, "Worship Agni". When *Vaṣaṭ* has been pronounced, he makes the offering.

12. He says, "Make the call (of invitation) for Soma", regarding Soma's share of the *ghee.* He cuts up (and takes) four times, of the *ghee* from the pot. Having stepped beyond and having made the call for attention he says, "Worship Soma". He makes the offering after *Vaṣaṭ* has been pronounced.

13. Then he says, "Make the call (of invitation) for *Marut-Gṛhamedhins*". He spreads *ghee* (in the offering spoon). Then he cuts up (and takes) two times of the *caru*. He sprinkles *ghee* (over it) and smears the two cut up portions (with *ghee*) (reanoints that part from where the cuttings have been made). Having stepped beyond and having called attention, he says, " worship the *Marut-Gṛhamedhins*". After *Vaṣaṭ* has been uttered, he makes the offering.

14. Then he says, "Make the call (of invitation) for *Agni-Sviṣṭakṛt*". He spreads *ghee* (in the offering spoon) and cuts up once from the *caru;* twice he sprinkles *ghee* (over it) (but) does not smear (does not anoint the part where from the cutting has been made) the cutting. Having stepped beyond and having called attention he says, "Worship *Agni-Sviṣṭakṛt*". When *Vaṣaṭ* has been pronounced he makes the offering. He cuts up only the *Iḍā* and not the *Prāśitra*.

15. As many members of the household as are (entitled) eaters of (the remainder of) the sacrificial food, may partake of this food; then the sacrificial priests and then other Brāhmins if there is much (food). Without its being made empty, they put the pot away after having covered it (with a lid). In the morning for the *'Pūrṇadarva'* (full-spoon) ritual, they gather the calves together. Thereby the cattle acquire nourishment in themselves (in their body).

16. This night he performs *Agnihotra* with rice gruel. In the morning they tie up the calf of a *'nivānya'* (cow suckling a calf other than its own), for (performing) the offering to the fathers (manes). Then in the morning, whether *Agnihotra* has been performed or not, (i.e. before or after the performance of *Agnihotra*), he cuts up a spoonful from this unemptied pot, whichever (portion) he pleases (saying), "Oh Spoon! Go away full. Come back well filled. Oh Indra

[१२]अथर्षभमाह्वयति स यदि रुयात्स वषट्कार एतद्वा इन्द्रस्य रूपं यदृषभस्य स्वेनैवैनमेतद्रू[१३]पेणैतस्मै भागायैतेन [१४]भागेन वृत्रस्य वधाय ह्वयति स यदि रुयादथ विद्यादा म इन्द्रो यज्ञमगन्त्सेन्द्रो मे यज्ञ इति यद्यु न रुयादपि ब्राह्मण एव दक्षिणत आसीनो ब्रूयाज्जुहुधीति [१५]सो एवैन्द्री वाक् ॥ १७ ॥

स जुहोति देहि मे ददामि ते नि मे धेहि नि ते दधे । निहारं निहरामि ते निहारं निहरामि मे [१६]स्वाहेति ॥ १८ ॥

अथ मरुद्भ्यः क्रीळिभ्यः सप्तकपालं पुरोळाशं निर्वपति मरुतो ह वै क्रीळिन इन्द्रं वृत्रꣳ हनिष्यन्तमागतमभितो महयन्तः परिचिक्रीळुस्तथो[१७] वा एतं[१८] पाप्मानं द्विषन्तं भ्रातृव्यꣳ हनिष्यन्तं मरुत एव क्रीळिनोऽभितो महयन्तः परिक्रीळन्ति तस्मान्मरुद्भ्यः क्रीळिभ्यः सप्तकपालं पुरोळाशं निर्वपति स यत्सप्तकपालो भवति सप्त सप्त हि मारुतो गणः ॥ १९ ॥ इति द्वितीयं ब्राह्मणम् ॥

तृतीयं ब्राह्मणम्

महाहविषा ह वै देवा वृत्रं जघ्नुस्तेनैव व्यजयन्त येयमेषां विजितिस्तथो वा एष एतेन पाप्मानं द्विषन्तं भ्रातृव्यꣳ हन्ति तथो एव विजयते ॥ १ ॥

१२. अथ ऋषभ M.

१३. पेणैतस्मै TE.

१४. भागेन TE.

१५. सा TE.

१६. स्वाहेति TE, P1, P2, B, Pa.

१७. स्तथा M.

१८. वा एष एतेन पाप्मानं M.

(of a hundred sacrifices) let us, (you and me) exchange (sell to each other) sustenance and strength as for price. This is verily just as is the *puronuvākya* (prayer of invitation). With this (call), indeed, he (the sacrificer) invites him (Indra) for this share.

17. Then they call up a bull. If he should bellow, that (bellowing) is the *Vaṣaṭkāra* (permissive utterance for offering). What is the form of the bull, this verily is the form of Indra. (Thus) he (the sacrificer) calls this (Indra) with his own form for (accepting) this share and for killing Vṛtra with this share. If (the bull) should bellow, he (the sacrificer) should understand, "Indra has come to my sacrifice. My sacrifice has Indra (is with Indra)".If (the bull) may not bellow, even then a Brāhmin(priest) seated to the south may say, "Perform the *Homa*". That verily is the expression (voice) of Indra.

18. He makes the offering (chanting),"Give to me, I give to you. Bestow on me, I bestow on you. I offer to you a present. You give me a present— *Svāhā*".

19. Then he makes an offering of *puroḍāśa* on seven potsherds to '*Marut-Krīḷins*' (Maruts—the sporters). Indeed Maruts are sporters. Praising him all around, indeed the Maruts sported around Indra who had come, who was going, to kill Vṛtra. In that same manner, the sportive Maruts praising him, sport around this (sacrificer) who is going to kill his evil hateful enemy. Therefore does he offer a *puroḍāśa* on seven potsherds to the sportive Maruts. (The reason) why it is on seven potsherds is that the host of Maruts (is in) groups of seven each.

(Second Brāhamaṇa Ends)

BRĀHMAṆA III

1. The gods killed Vṛtra verily by means of the *Mahāhavis* (the great oblation). By that indeed, did they attain this victory which is theirs. In that manner does this (sacrificer) too kill his wicked hateful enemy by means of this *(mahāhavis)* and similarly does he attain victory.

तस्यावृदुपकिरत्युत्तरवेदिं गृह्णाति पृषदाज्यं मन्थत्यग्निं नव प्रयाजा नवानुयाजास्त्रीणि समिष्टयजूꣳष्यथैतान्येव पञ्च हवीꣳषि भवन्ति ॥ २ ॥

स यदाग्नेयो भवत्यग्निना ह वा एनं तेजसा जघ्नुः स तेजोऽग्निर्नाव्यथत तस्मादाग्नेयोऽष्टाकपालो भवति ॥ ३ ॥

सौम्यश्चरुः सोमराजानो ह वा एनं जघ्नुस्तस्मात्सौम्यश्चरुर्भवति ॥ ४ ॥

अथ सावित्रो द्वादशकपालो वा भवत्यष्टाकपालो वा सविता वै देवानां प्रसविता सवितृप्रसूता ह वा एनं जघ्नुस्तस्मात्सावित्रो द्वादशकपालो वा भवत्यष्टाकपालो वा ॥ ५ ॥

सारस्वतश्चरुर्वाग्वै सरस्वती सा हैनमनुममादाभिपद्यंस्व[1] प्रहर जहीति तस्मात्सारस्वतश्चरुः ॥ ६ ॥

पौष्णश्चरुरियं वै पृथिवी पूषैषा हैवैनं प्रतिप्रददौ वधायैतया हैवैनꣳ संप्रत्तं[2] जघ्नुस्तस्मात्पौष्णश्चरुः ॥ ७ ॥

ऐन्द्राग्नो द्वादशकपाल एतेन ह वा एनं जघ्नुर्ब्रह्माग्निः क्षत्रमिन्द्रो ब्रह्म चैवैतत्क्षत्रं च सꣳरभ्य ते सयुजौ कृत्वा ताभ्याꣳ हैवैनं जघ्नुर्ब्रह्म चैवैतत्क्षत्रं च सयुजौ करोति तस्माद्ब्रह्म च क्षत्रं च सयुजौ ॥ ८ ॥

माहेन्द्रश्चरुरिन्द्रो वा एष पुरा वृत्रस्य वधादित्यथ वृत्रं जघ्निवान्यथा महाराजो विजिग्यान एवं महेन्द्र इति तस्मान्माहेन्द्रश्चरुर्महान्तमु चैवैनमेतत्करोति वृत्रस्य वधाय ॥ ९ ॥

वैश्वकर्मण एककपालो विश्वं वा एतद्देवानां कर्म कृतमासीत्सर्वं जितꣳ साकमेधैरीजानानां तथो वा एतस्य विश्वं कर्म कृतं भवति सर्वं जितꣳ साकमेधैरीजानस्य त एतेनेष्ट्वा

१. दाभिपद्यस्व TE; दाभिपद्यस्व K; दाभिपद्यस्व Ca.

२. संप्रवृत्तं P1, P2, H.

2. Its method (of performance) –He spreads the northern altar(with sacred grass).(He binds up the northern altar). He takes up (uses) clotted *ghee.* He churns the fire. There are (in this sacrifice) nine fore-offerings, nine after-offerings and three '*Samiṣṭa-yajus*'. Then there are these (following) five oblations.

3. That (the oblation) is one dedicated to Agni (because) they (the gods) killed him (Vṛtra) with Agni, with sharpness. That sharp Agni did not suffer (did not feel pain). Therefore there is (an oblation) dedicated to Agni, on eight potsherds.

4. (There is) a *caru* (offering) dedicated to Soma. (The gods), verily having Soma as their king, killed him (Vṛtra). Therefore there is a *caru* (offering) dedicated to Soma.

5. Then there is (an offering) dedicated to Savitṛ on twelve potsherds or on eight potsherds. Indeed Savitṛ is the producer (inspirer) of the gods. Produced (inspired) by Savitṛ, indeed did they kill this (Vṛtra). Therefore there is (an offering) dedicated to Savitṛ, of twelve potsherds or of eight potsherds.

6. (Then there is offered) a *caru* dedicated to Sarasvatī. Indeed speech is Sarasvatī. She verily cheered him (Indra) up (saying), "Attack, strike, kill". Hence (the offer of) a *caru* dedicated to Sarasvatī.

7. (Then there is an offering of) a *caru* dedicated to Pūṣan. Verily this earth is Pūṣan (the nourisher). Indeed she surrendered him for killing. They (gods) killed this (Vṛtra) who was given up by this (earth). Therefore (is offered) a *caru* dedicated to Pūṣan.

8. (The oblation) dedicated to Indra and Agni (together) is on twelve potsherds. For indeed by means of that they killed this (Vṛtra);Agni isBrāhmin (the priest). Indra is Kṣatra (ruler). Having excited Brahman and Kṣatra and having made them close together, through those two, they (gods) indeed killed this (Vṛtra). Thus does he (the sacrificer) make Brahman and Kṣatra (be close) together. Hence are Brahman and Kṣatra together.

9. There (is offered) a *caru* dedicated to *Mahendra* (Indra the Great). This (god) was verily Indra before the killing of Vṛtra.Then he killed Vṛtra. Just as (a king) (after) conquering (becomes) a great king *(Mahārāja),* so also (Indra became) *Mahendra* too. Therefore is a *caru* dedicated to *Mahendra.* Thereby he (the sacrificer) makes this (Indra) great (strong) for killing Vṛtra.

10. (Then, there is an oblation offered) dedicated to Viśvakarman, on a single potsherd. This action of gods who performed the *Śākamedha* sacrifices was made complete (comprehensive), by which all was conquered. So also all work becomes done and everything (becomes conquered) for one who performs the

देवा येयं देवानां जितिर्या श्रीस्तद्बभूवुरेवꣳ ह वाव जयत्येवꣳ श्रियं गच्छति य एनेनैवं विद्वान्यजते ॥ १० ॥ इति तृतीयं ब्राह्मणम् ॥

॥ इति पञ्चमोऽध्यायः ॥

Sākamedha sacrifice. He who knowing this performs a sacrifice thus with this *(Sākamedha)*, verily conquers and attains splendour, which conquest and what splendour those gods attained after having performed with this *(Sākamedha)* (sacrifice).

(Third Brāhmaṇa Ends)

(Chapter Five ends)

षष्ठोऽध्यायः

प्रथमं ब्राह्मणम्

महाहविषा ह वै देवा वृत्रं जघ्नुस्तेनैव व्यजयन्त येयमेषां विजितिरथ यानेवैषां तस्मिन्त्संग्रामेऽघ्नꣳस्तानेव पितृयज्ञेन समैरयन्त पितरो वै त आसꣳस्तस्मात्पितृयज्ञो नाम ॥ १ ॥

तद्वसन्तो ग्रीष्मो वर्षा एते ये व्यजयन्ताथ शरद्धेमन्तः शिशिरस्त उ ते यान्पुनः समैरयन्ताथ यदेष एतेन यजते नाहैवैतस्य कंचन घ्नन्तीति देवा अकुर्वन्निति त्वेवैष एतत्करोति तानु च हैवैतदवति यान्देवाः समैरयन्त स्वानु च पितॄञ्छ्रेयाꣳसं लोकमुपोन्नयति[1] यदु चैवास्यात्मनोऽचरणेन हन्यते मीयते तदु चैवैतेन पुनराप्याययति[2] तस्माद्वा एष एतेन यजते ॥ २ ॥

स वै पितृभ्यः सोमवद्भ्यः षट्कपालं पुरोळाशं निर्वपति सोमाय वा पितृमते षड्वा ऋतव ऋतवो वै पितरस्तस्मात्षट्कपालो भवति ॥ ३ ॥

अथ पितृभ्यो बर्हिषद्भ्यः पूर्वेद्युरन्वाहार्यपचने धानाः कुर्वन्ति तासामर्धाः पिꣳषन्त्यर्धा इत्येवापिष्टा भवन्ति ता उ पितृभ्यो बर्हिषद्भ्यः ॥ ४ ॥

अथ पितृभ्योऽग्निष्वात्तेभ्यो निवान्याया दुग्धे सकृदुपमथित एकशलाकया मन्थो भवति सकृद्ध्येव पराञ्चः पितरस्तस्मात्सकृदुपमथितो भवति ॥ ५ ॥

तद्यं[3] एव सोमेनेजानास्ते पितरः सोमवन्तोऽथ येऽनीजानाः सोमेन दत्तेनैव पक्वेन लोकं जयन्ति ते बर्हिषदोऽथ ये ततो नान्यतरच्चन यानग्निरेव दहन्त्स्वदयति तेऽग्निष्वात्ता एते वाव त्रयाः पितरः ॥ ६ ॥

अथ खलु प्राचीनाववीती भूत्वा जघनेन गार्हपत्यं दक्षिणासीनः सव्यं जान्वाच्यैतꣳ षट्कपालं पुरोळाशं गृह्णाति स तत एव दक्षिणा तिष्ठन्नवहन्ति दक्षिणैव दृषदुपले उपधत्ते

१. न्नयन्ति TE, T.

२. प्याययते M.

३. तद्यत एव Co.

Chapter Six

BRĀHMAṆA I

1. The gods killed Vṛtra verily by means of (the offering of) *Mahāhaviṣ* (the great offering). By that, indeed, they attained this victory which is theirs. By means of the *Pitṛ-yajña* (sacrifice to the fathers), they impelled (brought) back to life among them whom they (the Asuras) had killed in that battle. They became the fathers *(Pitṛs)* indeed. Hence it is known as *Pitṛ-yajña*.

2. Now, spring, summer, the rains– these (seasons) are in which they conquered; autumn, snow and winter–these are those in which they (the gods) impelled (back to life). (The reason) that one performs this sacrifice (is so that the Asuras) do not (may not) kill any one at all related to this (sacrificer). He verily performs it because the gods performed (it). Also he pleases indeed, those whom the gods brought (back to life) and he also leads his own *Pitṛs* to a higher (better) world. Whatever belonging to him, is destroyed or hurt by his (own) non-performance, that also he verily fills up (compensates) by this. Therefore indeed does this (sacrificer) perform this sacrifice.

3. He verily offers to the *Pitṛ-Somavats* (the manes associated with Soma) a *puroḍāśa* on six potsherds or (he does it) for Soma (associated with *Pitṛs)*. Six indeed are the seasons. The seasons are verily the *Pitṛs*. Therefore (is offered the *puroḍāśa)* of six potsherds.

4. Then on the previous (first) day, they prepare fried (barley) grains on the *Anvāhāryapacana (Dakṣiṇāgni)* for (offering to) the *Pitṛ-Barhiṣads* (the fathers seated on the holy grass). Half of them, they grind . Only the other half remains unground; they (the unground grains) are verily for the *Pitṛ-Barhiṣads*.

5. Then for the *Pitṛ-Agniṣvāttas* (the fathers placed in fires) –when the milk of a cow suckling a calf other than its own is once stirred with single splinter, it becomes *'mantha'* (the stirred up). Indeed the *Pitṛs* passed away only once. Therefore is it stirred up once (only).

6. There those fathers who have sacrificed with Soma, they are the *Pitṛs* associated with Soma (*Somavantaḥ*). And those who, without sacrificing with Soma, win the world (of gods) by merely offering cooked (sacrificial food) they are the *Pitṛ-Barhiṣads* (seated on the sacrificial grass). Those who are neither *(Somavats* nor *Barhiṣads)* but whom Agni himself consumes (tastes), burning (them) they are *Agniṣvāttas* (placed in the fires). These are indeed the three kinds of *Pitṛs*.

7. Then, having worn the sacred thread in the *Prācīnāvīti* position (over the right shoulder and under the left arm), being seated behind the *Gārhapatya* and facing south, having bent the left knee, he takes up (the rice for preparing) this *puroḍāśa* (to be sanctified) on six potsherds. From there itself standing facing

दक्षिणार्धे गार्हपत्यस्य षट्कपालान्युपधत्ते स[४] यदेतां दिशꣳ सचन्त एषा हि पितॄणां दिग्दक्षिणेनैवान्वाहार्यपचनं चतुःस्रक्तिं वेदिं करोत्यवान्तरदिशोऽनु स्रक्तीः करोत्यवान्तरदिशो हि पितरः ॥ ७ ॥

तन्मध्येऽग्निꣳ समादधाति पुरस्ताद्वै देवाः प्रत्यञ्चो[५] मनुष्यास्तस्मादेभ्यः प्राङ् तिष्ठन्जुहोति सर्वत एव पितरोऽवान्तरदिशो हि पितरः सर्वतो हीमा अवान्तरदिशस्तस्मान्मध्येऽग्निꣳ समादधाति ततः प्राक्स्तम्बयजुर्हरति ॥ ८ ॥

अथ पूर्वं परिग्राहं परिगृह्णातीममेवाग्रेऽथेममथेमं लिखति हरति यत्तत्र हर्तव्यं तदुत्तरं परिग्राहं परिगृह्य प्रोक्षणीरासादयतीध्माबर्हिरुपसादयन्ति स्रुचः सम्मार्ष्टि नात्र पत्नीꣳ सन्नह्यति नेत्पत्नीं पितृषु दधानीत्यथाज्यानि ग्रहीष्यन्यज्ञोपवीती भवति ॥ ९ ॥

तदाहुर्द्विरुपभृति गृह्णीयाद्द्वौ ह्यनुयाजाविति तद्वष्टावेव कृत्वो गृह्णीयान्नेद्यज्ञस्य विधाया अयानीत्याज्यानि गृहीत्वा प्रोक्षिष्यन्पुनः प्राचीनाववीती भवति ॥ १० ॥

स इध्ममेवाग्रे प्रोक्षत्यथ वेदिमथास्मै बर्हिः प्रयच्छन्ति तदुपमूले दितं भवत्यग्रमिव वै देवानां मध्यमिव मनुष्याणां मूलमिव पितॄणां तस्मादुपमूले[६] दितं भवति तत्प्रोक्ष्योपनिनीय न प्रस्तरं गृह्णाति सकृद्ध्येव पराञ्चः पितरः सन्नहनमनुविस्रꣳस्यापसलवि त्रिः परिस्तृणन्पर्येति स तत एवैतावन्मात्राणि प्रस्तरभाजनं परिशिनष्टि तैरु पुनः सह प्रसलवि त्रिः पर्येति स याꣳस्त्रयान्पितॄनन्ववैति तेभ्य एवैतत्पुनरपोदेतीममभि स्वं लोकं दक्षिणैव परिधीन्परिदधाति दक्षिणैतं प्रस्तरमासादयति नान्तर्गृह्णाति विधृती सकृद्ध्येव पराञ्चः पितरः ॥ ११ ॥

४. स goes with उपधत्ते.

५. See Notes; मनुष्याꣳ in all Mss.

६. मूल दितं Ca.

south he thrushes (the rite). He places the *Dṛṣad* and *Upala* (the twostonesused for grinding) on the south itself. He places the six potsherds on the southern portion of the *Gārhapatya.* That they take to this direction (south) is (because) this is verily the quarter of the manes. Indeed south of the *Anvāhāryapacana (Dakṣiṇāgni)* he builds up a square altar. He makes the corners (of the altars) towards the intermediate quarters. For the intermediate quarters are the manes.

8. In its midst, he lays down the fire. From the east the gods (come) to men in the west. Therefore he (man) offers to these (gods), (himself) standing (facing) east. All around (in all the directions) (everywhere) are the *Pitṛs.* Indeed the intermediate quarters are the manes. All around (on all sides) are there intermediate quarters. Therefore he lays down the fire in the middle.

Then he takes away (throws) the bunch of stumps of sacred grass to the east.

9. Then he takes up (makes) the first enclosure (of the altar), this (side) first, then this and then this. (He) scratches (draws lines). (He) removes what has to be removed there (the dust). Then taking up (making) the next (second) enclosure, he places (in it) the (vessels of) sprinkling water. They place the firewood (sticks) and *barhis* (the sacrificial grass) near it. He wipes the spoons clean. Here he does not involve his wife (for the ritual), thinking, "If not, I may be placing (her) amidst the *Pitṛs*". He then wears (changes his sacred thread to) *yajñopavīta* position (over his left shoulder and under his right arm) in order to take up (before taking up) the *ghee.*

10. About that, they say, "He should take (ladle out) twice in the *'upabhṛt'* for there are two after-offerings (in this sacrifice), thinking, "If not, I may depart from the procedure of the sacrifice". Having taken up the *ghee,* he again wears the sacred thread in *prācīnāvīta* position before sprinkling (water).

11. First he verily sprinkles the fire wood (with water), then the altar. Then they hand over the sacrificial grass to him. That (bunch) of sacrificial grass has been cut near the root, for the top verily is of gods, the middle verily for men and the bottom (root) verily of the manes. Therefore, it is cut near the root. Having sprinkled it (with water) and having taken it very close, – he does not take hold of the *prastara,* for the fathers have departed once for all–and having untied the knot, he moves thrice, from right to left (in the *apasavya* manner (around the altar) spreading (the sacrificial grass) thrice from right to left. He reserves from that (bunch of sacred grass) itself as much as would serve as *prastara* bunch with them, he again moves thrice from left to right (in the *pradakṣiṇā* manner (around the altar). Those three (groups of) *Pitṛs* whom he follows (first), away from them verily he comes towards this, his own world. He lays down the enclosing sticks (with their tops) towards the south only. He places the *prastara* (with their tips) towards the south. He does not take the two *(vidhṛtis* in between (the *barhis* and the *prastara*). For, the fathers have passd away once for all (once only).

तज्जुहूमासादयत्यथोपभृतमथ ध्रुवामथ पुरोळाशमथ धाना अथ करम्भमासाद्य हवीꣳषि सम्मृश्य सर्वे यज्ञोपवीतिनो भवन्तीत्याद्यजमानश्च ब्रह्मा च पश्चात्परीतः पुरस्तादग्नीत् ॥ १२ ॥

तेनोपाꣳशु चरन्ति तिर इव वै पितरस्तिर इवैतद्यदुपाꣳशु परिवृते चरन्ति तिर इव वै पितरस्तिर इवैतद्यत्परिवृतम् ॥ १३ ॥

अथाहाग्नये समिध्यमानायानुब्रूहीति स एतामेकाꣳ सामिधेनीं त्रिरन्वाहोशन्तस्त्वा निधीमह्युशन्तः समिधीमहि । उशन्नुशत आवह पितॄन्हविषे अत्तव इति स यदेकामन्वाह सकृद्ध्येव पराञ्चः पितरः ॥ १४ ॥

अथावाहयत्यग्निमग्न आवह सोममावह पितॄन्त्सोमवत आवह पितॄन्बर्हिषद आवह पितॄनग्निष्वात्तानावह देवाँ३[७]आज्यपां आवहाग्निꣳ होत्रायावह स्वं महिमानमावहा च वह जातवेदः सुयजा च यजेत्याघारावाघार्याध्वर्युराश्राव्य न होतारं प्रवृणीते नेद्धोतारं पितृषु दधानीति सीद होतरित्येवाह सीदति होता होतृषदने प्रसूतः स्रुचावादायातिक्रम्याध्वर्युराश्राव्याह समिधो यजेति सोऽपबर्हिषश्चतुरः प्रयाजान्यजति प्रजा वै बर्हिर्नेत्प्रजाः पितृषु दधानीति तस्मादपबर्हिषश्चतुरः प्रयाजान्यजत्याज्यभागाभ्यां चरित्वा हविर्भिः प्रचरिष्यन्तः सर्वे प्राचीनाववीतिनो भवन्तीत्याद्यजमानश्च ब्रह्मा च पुरस्तात्परीतः पश्चादग्नीत् ॥ १५ ॥

तदुताश्रावयन्त्योꣳ३ स्वधेत्यस्तु स्वधेति प्रत्याश्रावणꣳ स्वधा नम इति वषट्कारस्तद्धासुरिरुवाचाश्रावयेयुरेव प्रत्याश्रावयेयुर्वषट्कुर्युर्नेद्यज्ञस्य विधाया अयानीति स द्वे पुरोऽनुवाक्ये अन्वाहैकया वै देवान्प्रच्यावयति द्वाभ्यां पितॄन्त्सकृद्ध्येव पराञ्चः पितरस्तस्माद्द्वे पुरोऽनुवाक्ये अन्वाह ॥ १६ ॥

७. देवां३ see Notes on pluta.

८. वयन्त्यो३ꣳ see Notes on pluta.

12. Then he lays the *'juhū'*, then the *'upabhṛt'*, then the *'dhruvā'* then the *puroḍāśa,* then the fried grains and then the mixture of flour and curds (in this order). After thus having placed (them in this order) and after thus having touched the oblations, all wear their sacred threads in the *'upavīta'* position. From here, the Agnīdh moves round to the east (of the fire) and the sacrificer and Brahman go round to the west.

13. Therefore do they perform this, in a low (muffled) voice; for verily the manes are invisible (concealed) as it were. This, viz., what is in a low voice (muffled) is verily, concealed as it were. They perform it in an enclosed space. The *Pitṛs* are verily invisible (concealed), as it were. This, what is enclosed, is verily as if concealed (invisible).

14. Now he says, "Make the (invitation) call for Agni who is being kindled". He *(*Hotṛ*)* recites thrice this one *Sāmidhenī* (kindling chant),"Being Desirous, we place you. Being desirous let us kindle you. Being desirous, bring here the desirous fathers for the oblations, to eat (the oblation)". Why he recites (only) one chant (is because) indeed the fathers have passed away only once (once for all).

15. Then he invokes Agni to convey (the gods and *Pitṛs)* (saying), "Oh Agni, fetch Soma, fetch the *Pitṛs Somavats,* fetch the *Pitṛ-Barhiṣads,* fetch the *Pitṛ Agniṣvattās,* fetch the Gods the consumers of *ghee,* fetch Agni for the function of Hotṛ ,bring here your own greatness; Oh Jātavedas!(Oh knower of all that is born!) fetch, do surely fetch here,"The good sacrificer, you please offer the sacrifice". So saying, having sprinkled *ghee* twice and having called attention the Adhvaryu-he does not ceremoniously choose the Hotṛ,(as he thinks), "If not,I may be putting the Hotṛ amidst the *Pitṛs* ".–merely says, "Oh Hotṛ! please sit down". The Hotṛ sits on the Hotṛ's seat. Being permitted (prompted) the Adhvaryu,having taken up the two spoons and having stepped beyond and called attention says, "Worship (utter the offering prayer for) *Samidhs* (kindling sticks)". He makes the four fore-offerings excluding the one to *Barhis.* "For the *Barhis* is indeed progeny."If not, I might be putting the progeny (my off-spring) amidst the *Pitṛs*".–(thus he thinks). Therefore does he offer the four fore-offerings omitting the one to *Barhis.* Having proceeded with the (offering of) two *ghee*-shares, before performing the *havis* offerings (as they are going to perform *havis* offerings to *Pitṛs),*all put on the *prācināvīta* position of the sacred thread. From here, the Brahma and the sacrificer move round to the east and Agnīdh to the west (of the fire).

16. Moreover, they call attention *(Śrauṣaṭ),* as, "Om 3 *Svadhā*. The response call is,"Let there be *Svadhā*", (in the place of) *Vaṣat* utterance, there is *"Svadhā namaḥ"* (obeisance). About that Āsuri said, "Verily they must call attention, (with *āśrāvaya* as usual). They must make the response call-*(astu śrauṣaṭ* as usual)".They must utter *Vaṣaṭ* (they should think)."If not, I shall be deviating

अथाह पितृभ्यः सोमवद्भ्योऽनुब्रूहीति सोमाय वा पितृमत उपस्तृणीत आज्यमथास्य पुरोळाशस्यावद्यति तेनैव सह धानानां तेन सह करम्भस्य तत्सकृदेवावदधाति द्विरभिघार्य प्रत्यनक्त्यवदानानि नातिक्रमतीत एवोपोत्थायाश्राव्याह पितॄन्त्सोमवतो यजेति वषट्कृते जुहोति ॥ १७ ॥

अथाह पितृभ्यो बर्हिषद्भ्योऽनुब्रूहीत्युपस्तृणीत आज्यमथासां धानानामवद्यति तेनैव सह करम्भस्य तेन सह पुरोळाशस्य तत्सकृदेवावदधाति द्विरभिघार्य प्रत्यनक्त्यवदानानि नातिक्रामतीत एवोपोत्थायाश्राव्याह पितॄन्बर्हिषदो यजेति वषट्कृते जुहोति ॥ १८ ॥

अथाह पितृभ्योऽग्निष्वात्तेभ्योऽनुब्रूहीत्युपस्तृणीत आज्यमथास्य करम्भस्यावद्यति तेनैव सह पुरोळाशस्य तेन सह धानानां तत्सकृदेवावदधाति द्विरभिघार्य प्रत्यनक्त्यवदानानि नातिक्रामतीत एवोपोत्थायाश्राव्याह पितॄनग्निष्वात्तान्यजेति वषट्कृते जुहोति ॥ १९ ॥

अथाहाग्नये कव्यवाहनायानुब्रूहीति तत्स्विष्टकृद्भाजनꣳ हव्यवाहनो वै देवानां कव्यवाहनः पितॄणां तस्मादाह कव्यवाहनायानुब्रूहीत्युपस्तृणीत आज्यमथास्य पुरोळाशस्यावद्यति तेनैव सह धानानां तेन सह करम्भस्य तत्सकृदेवावदधाति द्विरभिघार्य न प्रत्यनक्त्यवदानानि नातिक्रामतीत एवोपोत्थायाश्राव्याहाग्निं कव्यवाहनं यजेति वषट्कृते जुहोति ॥ २० ॥

from the procedure for sacrifice. He (the Hotṛ) recites two prayers of invitation; with one he indeed makes the gods move down and the *Pitṛs* with two. Indeed the fathers have passed away only once (once for all). Therefore, indeed, does he recite two invitation- prayers.

17. Then he (Adhvaryu) says, "Make the call of invitation for the *Pitṛ-Somavats. (Pitṛs* associated with Soma) or for *Soma Pitṛmat* (Soma associated with *Pitṛs).* He spreads (a layer of) the *ghee* (on the spoon), then makes a cutting of the *puroḍaśa* and then together with it some of the fried grains and along with it some of the porridge (mixture of flour and curds); thus he puts all at once (in the *juhū).* Having sprinkled *ghee* on it twice, he pours (a little) *ghee* again (into wherefrom he has taken) into the cut parts of sacrificial food. He does not walk beyond. Here itself. having risen and having made the call for attention, he says, "Worship (recite the offering prayer) *Pitṛ- Somavats*". He makes the offering after *Vaṣaṭ* has been pronounced.

18. Then he says, "Make the invitation call for *Pitṛ-Barhiṣads* ". He spreads (a little) *ghee* (in the spoon) and then takes off a portion of these fried grains and then along with it, of the (mixture of flour and curds) porridge and along with that, of the *puroḍāśa*–he puts all that once (simultaneously) (into the spoon). Having sprinkled it with *ghee* twice, he anoints the cut off portions of the offerings (remaining in the dishes). He does not move beyond. Getting up here itself and having called attention, he says, "Worship the *Pitṛs Barhiṣads*". He makes the offering when *Vaṣaṭ* has been uttered.

19. He then says, "Make the invitation call for *Pitṛs Agniṣvātta-s*". He spreads (a little) *ghee* (in the spoon). Then he makes a cutting of the porridge, along with it, then, of *Puroḍāśa* and then along with it of fried grains. That he puts (into the spoon) only once. Having sprinkled *ghee* on it twice, he anoints the cut off parts (of the oblations in the dishes). He does not move beyond. Here itself after getting up and having called attention, he says, " worship the *Pitṛs Agniṣvātta-s*". When *Vaṣaṭ* has been uttered, he makes the offering.

20. Then he says, "Make the invitation prayer for *Agni Kavyavāhana*". That is what takes the place of *Sviṣṭakṛt.* For the Gods he is *Havyavāhana* (bearer of oblations for gods) (and) for the manes he is *Kavyavāhana* (bearer of oblations to *Pitṛs*). Hence does he say, "Make the call of invitation for *Kavyavāhana*". He spreads (a little) *ghee* (in the spoon). Then he makes a cutting of the *puroḍāśa* and then along with it, of the fried grains and then with it of the porridge; (all) that he puts (in the spoon) at once (once only). Having sprinkled *ghee* twice (on it)–he does not anoint with *ghee* the cut off portions (of the oblations in the dishes) and he does not move beyond– and getting up from there itself and having called attention he says, "Worship *Agni Kavyavāhana*". He makes the offering after *Vaṣaṭ* has been pronounced.

स यन्नातिक्रामति सकृद्ध्येव पराञ्चः पितरोऽथ यत्सकृत्सकृदवद्यति सकृद्ध्येव पराञ्चः पितरोऽथ यद्यतिषङ्गमवद्यत्यृतवो वै पितर ऋतूनेवैतद्यतिषजत्यृतूत्सन्दधाति ॥ २१ ॥

अथेळा तदुतैतमैव[९] मन्थꣳ होतुः पाणावादधति तꣳ होतोपहूयावजिघ्रति तमग्नीधे प्रयच्छन्त्ति[१०] तमग्नीदवजिघ्रति तं ब्रह्मणे प्रयच्छन्त्ति[११] तं ब्रह्मावजिघ्रति तद्धासुरिरुवाच यथैवेळां प्राशित्रमितरस्य यज्ञस्यावद्यन्तीत्येवमेव समवद्येयुरवत्वेव जिघ्रेयुर्न प्राश्नीयुः प्राश्यं खलु वै तस्य यस्याग्नौ जुह्वतीत्युपहूयेळां मार्जयित्वा ॥ २२ ॥

अथ यतरो दास्यन्भवति यद्यध्वर्युर्वा यजमानो वा स उदपात्रमादायापसलवि त्रिरभिषिञ्चन्पर्येत्यसाववनेनिक्ष्वेति यजमानस्य पितरमसाववनेनिक्ष्वेति यजमानस्य पितामहमसाववनेनिक्ष्वेति यजमानस्य प्रपितामहं यथाशिष्यतोऽवनेजयेदेवमेतत् ॥ २३ ॥

अथास्य पुरोळाशस्यावद्यति तत्सव्ये पाणौ कुरुते धानानामवद्यति तत्सव्ये पाणौ कुरुते करम्भस्यावद्यति तत्सव्ये पाणौ कुरुते स येमामवान्तरदिशमनु[१२]स्रक्तिस्तद्ददात्यसावेतत्त इति यजमानस्य पित्रेऽथ येमामवान्तरदिशमनुस्रक्तिस्तद्ददात्यसावेतत्त इति यजमानस्य पितामहायाथ येमामवान्तरदिशमनुस्रक्तिस्तद्ददात्यसावेतत्त इति यजमानस्य प्रपितामहायाथ येमामवान्तरदिशमनुस्रक्तिस्तत्पाणी निमृष्टेऽत्र पितरो मादयध्वं यथाभागमावृषायध्वमित्यत्र पितरो यथाभागमश्नीतेत्येवैतदाहैतदु स्वान्पितॄनेतस्माद्यज्ञान्नान्तरेत्युदञ्चो निष्क्रम्य सर्वे यज्ञोपवीतिनो भवन्ति ॥ २४ ॥

९. तदुतैतमेव M, Ca, My, Po.

१०. प्रयच्छति M.

११. प्रयच्छति M.

१२. See Notes.

21. (The reason) that he does not move beyond (the fire) is that the fathers have passed away only once (once for all). And (the reason) that he cuts up only once each time (from the sacrificial dishes) is that the fathers have passed away only once (once for all). And that he cuts up keeping (them) together is that the seasons are the *Pitṛs* thus he keeps together the seasons themselves. He unites the seasons.

22. Now then (about) *Iḷā* — Then they place this same in the palm of Hotṛ. Having addressed (invoked) it, the Hotṛ smells it. They give it to Agnīdh. The Agnīdh smells it. They give it to the Brahman. The Brahman smells it. About this Āsuri said, "Just as they cut up *Iḷā* and *Prāśitra* of any other sacrifice, in the same manner they should cut up; they should only smell (but) should not consume (it)".Indeed (a part) of that which they offer in the fire is to be consumed. Thus having invoked *Iḷā* and having wiped (it)---.

23. Now, whoever (of the two)is going to present, whether it is the Adhvaryu or the sacrifiçer, he, having taken the vessel of water and having moved round (the altar) from right to left, sprinkling (water),should wash (pour out water for) the father of the sacrificer, saying, "(Name of the father in the vocative!) Wash (yourself)", (then) the grandfather of the sacrificer, saying, "(Name of the grandfather in vocative!) Wash yourself" and then the great grandfather of the sacrificer, saying, "(Name of the great grandfather in vocative!) Wash yourself". —This is just in the manner one would pour out water for washing for those (guests) who were going to take food.

24. Then he cuts up (a part) of the cake that he keeps in his left plam. He cuts up (a portion) of the fried grains; he keeps in his left palm. He cuts up a portion of the porridge; that he keeps in his left palm. He presents it there in that intermediate direction towards which is this corner (of the squarish altar) (in the north-western part) (in the fire) to the father of the sacrificer, saying, "(Name of the father in vocative)! This is for you" (And) then he presents (in that intermediate direction towards which is this corner (in the south-western part) to the grandfather of the sacrificer, saying, "(Name of the grandfather in the vocative)! This is for you". And then he presents it there in that intermediate direction towards which is this corner (in the south-eastern part) to the great grandfather of the sacrificer, saying, "(Name of the great grandfather in vocative!) This is for you". And then, there towards which is this corner (north east) he cleanses his two palms saying, "Oh fathers! Take delight here. Act like bulls towards your particular shares". Here he verily says (means), "Eat according to your share". This is (done) so that he does not exclude his fathers from this sacrifice. Having gone out (of the shed) northward, all wear their sacred threads in the *Yajñopavīta* way (over the left shoulder and under the right arm).

त आहवनीयमुपतिष्ठन्ते देवान्वा एष उपावर्तते य आहिताग्निर्दर्शपूर्णमासाभ्यां यजतेऽथेदं पितृयज्ञेनाचारिषुः[१३] स यानेव देवानुपावृत्तो भवति तेभ्य एवैतन्निह्नुते तस्मादैन्द्री-भ्यामुपतिष्ठन्त इन्द्रो ह्याहवनीयोऽक्षन्नमीमदन्त ह्यव प्रिया अधूषत। अस्तोषत स्वभानवो विप्रा नविष्ठयामती योजान्विन्द्र ते हरी।सुसंदृशं त्वा वयं मघवन्वन्दिषीमहि। प्र नूनं पूर्णबन्धुर स्तुतो यासि वशां३[१४] अनु योजा न्विन्द्र ते हरी इति ॥ २५ ॥

अथ गार्हपत्यं मनो न्वाहुवामहे[१५] नाराशꣳसेन स्तोमेन। पितॄणां च मन्मभिः। आ न एतु मनः पुनः क्रत्वे दक्षाय जीवसे। ज्योक् च सूर्यं दृशे। पुनर्नः पितरो मनो ददातु दैव्यो जनः। जीवं व्रातꣳ सचेमहीति पितृयज्ञेन वा इदमन्वाचारिषुस्तत्पुनर्जीवानभिपद्यन्ते[१६][१७] तस्मादाह जीवं व्रातꣳ सचेमहीति ॥ २६ ॥

अथ यतरो ददाति यद्यध्वर्युर्वा यजमानो वा सोऽभिप्रपद्य जपत्यमीमदन्त पितरो यथाभागमावृषायिषतेतित्याशिषुः पितरो यथाभागमित्येवैतदाहाथोदपात्रमादाय पुनः प्रसलवि त्रिरभिषिञ्चन्पर्येत्यसाववनेनिक्ष्वेति यजमानस्य पितरमसाववनेनिक्ष्वेति यजमानस्य पितामहमसाववनेनिक्ष्वेति यजमानस्य प्रपितामहं यथा जक्षुषोऽवनेजयेदेव-मेतत्स यत्पुनः प्रसलवि त्रिरभिषिञ्चन्पर्येति स याꣳस्त्रयान्पितॄनन्ववैति तेभ्य एवैतत्पुनरपो-दैतीममभि स्वं लोकम् ॥ २७ ॥

अथ नीविमुद्वृह्य नमस्करोति पितृदेवत्या वै नीविर्यज्ञ उ वै नमो यज्ञियानेवैतत्पितॄन्क-रोति षट्कृत्वो नमस्करोति षड्वा ऋतव ऋतवो वै पितर ऋतुष्वेवैतद्यज्ञं प्रतिष्ठापयति

१३. यज्ञेऽन्वाचरिषुः V1, TE, H.

१४. वशां३ Ca., see Notes pluta.

१५. त्वा Ca.

१६. इदमन्वाचारिष्यत्तत्पुन as alternate reading in TE.

१७. वानपिपद्यन्ते Ca.

25. They stand by (worship) the *Āhavanīya.* Indeed, this person who, having established his fires, sacrifices with the New Moon and Full Moon sacrifices, returns to the gods. But then, they have (just now) proceeded with the sacrificer to the manes. He keeps this (concealed) from those gods themselves to whom he returns. Therefore they worship with two (chants) addressed to Indra. Indeed Indra is the Āhavanīya–"(Our) dear persons (friends) have eaten; they have rejoiced. They have shaken"(they shook their dear bodies,(in satisfaction). (They shook off their enemies). The wise, who have their own imagination, have extolled (you) with the newest (praise). Oh Indra! Verily yoke your two horses which are (like) thoughts (in speed). "Oh great one! May we adore (make obeisance to) you who are very good looking. Praised (thus) do you go forth with your chariot filled (with equipment)–according to our desires. Verily yoke your two horses".

26. Then (they come to) the *Gārhapatya* (and worship it) –"We invoke the mind indeed with the string of verses of *Nārāśaṁsa* (that praise man) and with the hymns of the manes. May the mind come back to us for wisdom, dexterity and life, for us to see the Sun for long! May the divine being, Oh father! Give us out mind again! May we be linked (associated) with the living group. Verily have they performed this with a sacrifice to the manes. From that they again get back to the living beings. Therefore does he say, "May we be associated with living beings".

27. Then whoever of the two, whether the Adhvaryu or the sacrificer, he, having gone up (towards the fire), mutters, "The fathers have taken delight. They have acted like bulls towards their particular shares". He verily says (means) this, "The fathers have eaten according to their (individual) share". Then having taken up the water–vessel, he moves round (the altar) from left to right thrice, sprinkling water. (Saying) "(Name in vocative)!" "Wash yourself" (he pours water for washing) to the sacrificer's father, and to the sacrificer's grandfather saying, "(Name in vocative!) Wash yourself" and to the sacrificer's great grandfather saying, "(Name in vocative!) Wash yourself" This is just as one would make those who have eaten, wash (themselves). But that he moves round (the altar) thrice from left to right sprinkling (water) (means) he returns towards this, his own world, from verily those three *Pitṛs* whom he has been following.

28. Then loosening the tuck of his garment (at his navel), he performs prostration. For the navel tuck has indeed the manes as its divinity. Indeed the obeisance is sacrifice. Thus he makes the *Pitṛs* worthy of sacrifice. He prostrates himself six times. Verily six are the seasons; the seasons are the manes. He thus establishes this sacrifice; indeed, in the seasons. He says, "Oh fathers! Give us homes". This indeed is his prayer for blessing of this ritual. Verily the manes have power over the homes. Therefore does he say, "Oh fathers! Give us

गृहान्नः पितरो दत्तेत्याहैषो हैतस्याशीः कर्मणो गृहाणामु ह वै पितर ईशते तस्मादाह गृहान्नः पितरो दत्तेत्यथ सर्वे यज्ञोपवीतिनो भवन्तीत्याद्यजमानश्च ब्रह्मा च पश्चात्परीतः पुरस्तादग्नीत्सीदति होता होतृषदने ॥ २८ ॥

अथाध्वर्युः संप्रेष्यत्यग्नीत्समिधमाधायाग्निꣳसंमृड्ढि ब्रह्मन्प्रस्थास्याम इति स्रुचावादाय प्रत्यङ्ङतिक्रम्याध्वर्युराश्राव्याह देवान्यजेति सोऽपबर्हिषौ द्वावनुयाजौ यजति प्रजा वै बर्हिर्नेत्प्रजाः पितृषु दधानीति तस्मादपबर्हिषौ द्वावनुयाजौ यजति ॥ २९ ॥

सादयित्वा स्रुचौ व्यूहति व्यूह्य[१८] स्रुचौ परिधीन्त्समज्य परिधीनभिपद्याध्वर्युराश्राव्याहेषिता दैव्या होतारो भद्रवाच्याय प्रेषितो मानुषः सूक्तवाकायेति सूक्ता होता प्रतिपद्यते नायं प्रस्तरमादत्तेऽथाग्नीदाहानुप्रहरेति नायं किञ्चनानुप्रहरति संवदस्वेत्यगादग्नीदगंच्छ्रावय[१९] श्रौषट्स्वगा दैव्या होतृभ्यः स्वस्तिर्मानुषेभ्य इति शं योर्होता प्रतिपद्यत उपस्पृश्यायं परिधीन्त्स्रुचौ संप्रगृह्य स्फ्ये सादयत्यथ बर्हिरनुसमस्यति तत्र हाप्येके हविरुच्छिष्टमनुसमस्यन्ति तदु तथा न कुर्याद्यथोच्छिष्टमग्नौ जुहुयादेवꣳ ह तत्तस्मात्तदपो वैवाभ्यवहरेयुः[२०] प्राश्नीयुर्वैनत् ॥ ३० ॥ इति प्रथमं ब्राह्मणम् ॥

द्वितीयं ब्राह्मणम्

महाहविषा ह वै देवा वृत्रं जघ्नुस्तेनैव व्यजयन्त येयमेषां विजितिरथ यानेवैषां तस्मिन्त्संग्राम इषव आर्च्छꣳ[१]स्तानेवैतच्छल्यान्व्यवृहन्त तान्निरहरन्त यत्त्र्यम्बकैरयजन्ताथ यदेष एतेन यजते नाहैवैतस्य कंचनेषुर्ऋच्छतीति देवा अकुर्वन्निति त्वेवैष एतत्करोति या उ चैवास्य प्रजा जाता याश्चाजातास्ता उभयी रुद्रियात्प्रमुञ्चति ता अस्यानमीवा अकिल्बिषाः प्रजाः प्रजायन्ते तस्माद्वा एष एतेन यजते ॥ १ ॥

१८. व्युह्य Ca.

१९. दगंछ्रावय TE, K, P1, P2; see Notes.

२०. वैवाभ्यवह Ca., M, T, V1; वैवाभ्यवह TE.

१. आर्च्छं स्ताने Ca.

homes". Thereafter, all wear their sacred threads in the *upavīta* position. From here, the sacrificer and the Brahman go round (around the altar) to the west and the Agnīdh (moves) (around the altar) to the East. The Hotṛ sits on the Hotṛ's seat.

29. Then the Adhvaryu prompts, "Oh Agnīdh! putting the kindling sticks (in the fire), trim the fire". "Brahman, we are going to start". Having taken the two spoons, having crossed to the western side and having called attention, the Adhvaryu says, "Worship (pronounce the offering prayer for) the gods". He offers two after-offerings, omitting the *Barhis*. Indeed progeny is *Barhis*. (Thinking). "If not, I might be putting the progeny admidst the manes". Therefore he performs (only) the two after-offerings avoiding the *Barhis* (offering).

30. Placing the two spoons, he separates them. Having separated the two spoons, having anointed (with *ghee*) the enclosing sticks, having taken up the enclosing sticks, and having called attention (for *Śrauṣaṭ*) the Adhvaryu says, "The divine Hotṛs have been desired (called upon) to pronounce auspiciousness (welfare). The human (Hotṛ) has been prompted (desired) for the recitation of hymns". The Hotṛ takes up (recites) the hymns. This person (the Adhvaryu) does not take up the *'prastara'* (spread out bunch of sacrificial grass).

Then the Agnīdh says, "Put it (into the fire) after". The Adhvaryu does not put anything after. Then the Agnīdh (says), "Speak cordially". The Adhvaryu (asks), "Has he gone, Oh Agnīdh!" (Agnīdh says) - "He has gone". (Adhvaryu says) "Make (the gods) hear". (The Agnīdh says) *"Śrauṣaṭ"* (may the gods hear). "May there be a good-going to the divine Hotṛs. May there be well-being for the humans (human Hotṛs). The Hotṛ recites, *"Śaṁyoḥ"*. The Adhvaryu, having touched the enclosing sticks and gathering together the spoons, places (the spoons) on the wooden sword. Then he throws after the sacrifical grass (into the fire). Even there, some throw thereafter, the remaining sacrificial food (too) (into the fire). But one should not do it so. For it is indeed just like one offering the 'left out' in the fire. Therefore they may either take this (remaining *havis*) to (throw it into) the water or they may eat it".

(First Brāhmaṇa Ends)

BRĀHMAṆA II

1. Indeed the gods killed Vṛtra by means of *Mahāhaviṣ* (the great oblation). Thereby only, they won this victory which is theirs. Whomsoever among them the arrows (of the Asuras) reached (hit) those very darts they (the gods) uprooted (and) removed them in that they sacrificed with the *Tryambaka* chants. Now, that this (sacrificer) sacrifices with this (*Tryambaka* chant offering) he does verily (with the thought) that no arrow (trouble) (will) reach any one belonging to him or that the gods performed (it). Whatever progeny of his has been born and

ते वै रौद्रा भवन्ति रुद्रस्य हीषुरेककपाला भवन्त्येकदेवत्या असन्निति[2] यावन्तो गृह्यास्तावन्तः प्रतिपुरुषं भवन्त्येकेनातिरिक्ताः प्रतिपुरुषमेवैतदेकेनैकेन या अस्य प्रजा जातास्ता रुद्रियात्प्रमुञ्चत्येकेनातिरिक्ता भवन्ति या एवास्याजाताः प्रजास्ता एव तेन रुद्रियात्प्रमुञ्चति ॥ २ ॥

अथ खलु यज्ञोपवीती भूत्वा जघनेन गार्हपत्यमुदङ्ङासीन एतान्गृह्णाति स तत एवोदङ्ङ्तिष्ठन्नवहन्त्युदीच्यावेव दृषदुपले उपधत्त उत्तरतो गार्हपत्यस्य कपालान्युपधत्ते स यदेतां दिशꣳ सचन्त एषा हि तस्य देवस्य दिक्तेऽक्ताः स्युरित्याहुरक्तꣳ हि हविरिति तद्वनक्ता एव स्युरभिमानुकौ[3] ह रुद्रः पशून्त्स्याद्यदज्ज्युस्तस्मादनक्ता एव स्युः ॥ ३ ॥

तान्त्समुद्वास्यैकस्यां पात्र्यामन्वाहार्यपचनादुल्मुकमादायोदञ्चः परेत्य जुह्वत्येषा हि तस्य देवस्य दिक्पथि जुह्वति पथा ह वै यदेषश्चरति चतुष्पथे यथा ह जांघितं[4] प्रज्ञातमवसानमेवꣳ हास्य चतुष्पथः पलाशस्य पलाशेन मध्यमेन जुहोति ब्रह्म वै पलाशस्य पलाशं मध्यमं ब्रह्मणैव तज्जुहोति स सर्वेषामेव समवद्यत्यतिरिक्तस्यैव नावद्यति ॥ ४ ॥

स जुहोत्येष ते रुद्रभाग इति सह स्वस्राम्बिकया तं जुषस्व स्वाहेत्यम्बिका ह वै नामास्य स्वसा तया तयास्यैष सह भागः स यदस्यैष स्त्रिया सह भागस्तस्मात्त्र्यम्बका नामाथ योऽयमतिरिक्तो भवति तमेवमुत्तरत आखुकरीष उपकिरत्येष ते रुद्र भाग आखुस्ते पशुरिति तमस्मा आखुमेव पशुमनुदिशति तमस्यास्ये दधाति तथेतरान्पशून्न हिनस्ति तद्या एवास्याजाताः प्रजास्ता एवैतेन रुद्रियात्प्रमुञ्चति तिर इव वै तद्यदुपकीर्णं तिर इव गर्भा अजातास्तस्मादुपकिरति ॥ ५ ॥

२. An archaic form for आसन्.

३. मानुषो TE.

४. जांधितं Ca.; जाधितं V1; see Notes.

those that are (as yet) unborn, both of them be released from Rudra's power. They, his children, are born without disease and without blemish. Therefore indeed does he sacrifice with this.

2. They (those offerings) are verily dedicated to Rudra–for it was indeed Rudra's arrow (from which they are saved)– They are of a single potsherd (each), for they have a single deity. They are as many as are numbers of the household (of the sacrificer)– one for each (member)-exceeding with one. He releases from Rudra's power his children that have been born. Verily individually each with a single (separate)(offering), they (the offerings) are excessive by one. By means of that (extra offering) he delivers verily those children of his that are (as yet) unborn, from the power of Rudra.

3. Then having become, *Yajñopavītin* (wearing the sacred thread over his left shoulder and under the right arm), being seated facing north behind the *Gārhapatya,* he takes up these offerings (the rice needed to prepare the offerings). There itself, standing (facing) north, he threshes them. He places (keeps) the two mile-stones verily (towards the) north. To the north of the *Gārhapatya* does he place the potsherds. That they take to the north is because this is the quarter of that god. "They (the offerings) may be smeared (with *ghee*)"–they say, for the *havis* is anointed. But they should verily be unanointed, for, if they anoint (the offerings), Rudra would be insidious towards the cattle (of the sacrificer). Therefore, they should verily be unanointed.

4. Having removed them (from the potsherds) into a single vessel, having taken out a firebrand from the *'Anvāhāryapacana'* and then having walked to the north, they make the offering. For this is the direction of that god. They make the offering on the road; for that god moves about along the road. They offer in the cross road (where four roads radiate), as it is well-known as his congenial resting place. So indeed is the cross road for him. He (the sacrificer) makes the offerings with the middle leaflet of the *Palāśa* (tree). Verily, the middle leaflet of the *Palāśa* is Brahman Therefore he offers verily with Brahman itself. He makes a cutting of all (the oblations) only, he does not make a cutting of the extra one.

5. He offers (chanting), "Oh Rudra! This is your share". "Please accept it, along with Ambikā your sister– *Svāhā* ". Indeed his sister is known as Ambikā. This share is his, along with her. As this is a share for him along with a female, therefore is it called Tryambakā. Then, the thing (oblation) that is in excess, he scatters (buries) thus in the north, on the molehill (earth from the mole hill), (chanting), "Oh Rudra! This is your share; the mole is your animal". He (the sacrificer) indicates the mole (itself as animal) (victim to be offered) to him (Rudra). He places it in his (Rudra's) north. Thereby, he (Rudra) does not harm other animals. Thereby, his those children who are (as yet) unborn, verily them does he release by means of this (offering) from the power of Rudra.

अथ पुनरेत्य जपत्यव रुद्रमदीमह्यव देवं त्र्यम्बकम्। यथा नो वस्यसस्करद्यथा नः श्रेयसस्करद्यथा नो व्यवसाययात्। भेषजमसि भेषजं गवेऽश्वाय पुरुषाय भेषजम्। सुगं मेषाय मेष्या इत्याशिषमेवैतदाशास्ते ॥ ६ ॥

अथापसलव्यूरूनुपाघ्नानाः परियन्ति त्र्यम्बकं यजामहे सुगन्धिं पुष्टिवर्धनम्। उर्वारुकमिव बन्धनान्मृत्योर्मुक्षीयमामृतादित्याशिषमेवैतदाशास्ते तद्धि शमिव यो मृत्योर्मुच्यातै नामृतात्तत्रापि कुमार्यः परीयुर्भगस्य भजामहा इति या ह वा अस्य सा स्वसाम्बिका सा ह वै भगस्येष्टे तासामु तासां जपस्[५]त्र्यम्बकं यजामहे सुगन्धिं पतिवेदनम्। उर्वारुकमिव बन्धनादितो मुक्षीय मामुत इति ज्ञातिभ्यस्तदाह यदित इति मामुत इति पतिभ्यस्तदाह पतयो हि स्त्रियाः प्रतिष्ठात एतेनैव जपेन पुनः प्रसलवि परियन्ति प्रसलवि नः कर्मानुसन्तिष्ठाता इति ॥ ७ ॥

अथेमान्यजमान उदस्यति यावद्गौर्नोदाप्नुयात्तावदात्मभ्य एव तच्छल्यान्निर्मिमते[६] तान्विलिप्सन्त उपस्पृशन्ति भेषजमेव तत्कुर्वतेऽथ द्वयोर्मूतकयोरुपनह्योभयतः कुपस्य वा वेणोर्वा प्रतिषज्य यदि तत्र वृक्षं वा स्थाणुं वा वल्मीकं वा विन्देत्तत्प्रतिषजेदेतेन रुद्रावसेन परो मूजवतोऽतीहीत्यवसेन वा अध्वानं यन्ति तदेनमेतेनैवावसेनावर्जति यत्रास्य चरणं तदन्यत्र ह वा अस्य चरणं परो मूजवतस्तस्मादाह परो मूजवतोऽतीहीत्यवततधन्वा पिनाकावस[७] इत्यहिंꣳसन्नः शिवः शान्तोऽतीहीत्येवैतदाह कृत्तिवासा इति निष्वपयत्येवैनं तत्स्वपन्हि न कञ्चन हिनस्ति ते दक्षिणं पार्श्वमन्वावर्तन्ते तेऽनपेक्षमाणा आयन्ति तेऽप

५. जप Ca., M, My, V1.

६. निर्मिमीत TE, Co, P1, P2.

७. See Notes.

Indeed this thing that is scattered (buried) is as if concealed. Concealed, as it were, are the unborn embryos. Therefore does he scatter (bury).

6. Then having returned (to his own seat) he mutters, "We have offered to Rudra and to god Tryambaka, so that he may make us wealthier and that he may make us determined (in our purpose). You are the medicine; medicine for the cow, the horse and medicine for men; welfare for the ram and the ewe" he verily prays for this blessing thus.

7. Then they go round (the altar) from right to left beating their thighs; (saying), "We worship Tryambaka the fragrant one, the increaser of nourishment (prosperity). May I be released from death like the cucumber from its stalk, but let me not be dissociated from immortality. He verily prays for this blessing. This is verily happiness for one who will be released from death but not from immortality. Even there; maidens may go round saying, "May we resort to (share in) happiness".That Ambikā who is the sister of this (Rudra), she verily has power over happiness for them (the maidens). Hence is their muttering,"We worship Tryambaka, of fine fragrance, the one who bestows husbands. May we be released from here like the cucumber from the stalk, but not from there". By "from here" she says (means) "from my relatives". By "not from there" she says (means) "from the husbands". Verily the husbands are the (firm) support for a woman. Therefore, indeed, do they (sacrificer and others) go round (the altar) from left to right again, muttering the same *mantras*, and saying, "Our ritual may be rightly performed".

8. Then the sacrificer throws up these (remnants of the offerings) as far (high) as a cow (the earth) may not get it. From themselves (their own bodies) they forge his (Rudra's)darts. (Again) desiring to get them (back), they touch them; they verily make it a medicine. Then, having packed it into two baskets, having attached them on both sides of a beam (of a balance) or a bamboo, (on his going northward), if he finds there a tree, a post or an ant hill, he should fasten them there, (saying),"Oh Rudra! With this provision (for journey) go beyond the Mūjavat (mountains). Indeed they (people) go on travel with provisions. Hence, he sends away this (Rudra) verily with this provision, towards where his journey is. Here his (Rudra's) journey is beyond Mūjavats. Therefore he says, "Go beyond Mūjavats". "With your bow let loose (unstrung)". Oh bearer of Pināka!" He verily says (means) this, "Not hurting us, being auspicious, tranquil, go away". "One wearing hide", he verily makes him (Rudra) fall into sleep, for, one who is sleeping does not hurt any one. They turn to the right side. They come without looking about. They touch water; for they have performed this (ritual) relating to Rudra. The waters are 'abatement' (of impurity or evil). Verily they are 'abatements'. They reach (back) by the same (way) by which they go out. Having shaved off his hair (leaving the tuft) and beard, he takes up(withdraws)the two fires. Verily after having shifted does he

उपस्पृशन्ति रुद्रियेण वा इदमचारिषुः शान्तिरापः शान्त्य एव ते येनैव निष्क्रामन्ति[8] तेन प्रपद्यन्ते केशश्मश्रूप्त्वाग्नी समारोहयत उदवसाय ह्येतेन यजते नह्यवकल्पते यदुत्तरवेदावग्निहोत्रं जुहुयुर्गृहानागत्य निर्मथ्य पौर्णमासेन यजत उत्सन्नो वा अयं यज्ञो यच्चातुर्मास्यानि क्लृप्तेनैवैतद्यज्ञेनान्ततः प्रतितिष्ठति ॥ ८ ॥ इति द्वितीयं ब्राह्मणम् ॥

तृतीयं ब्राह्मणम्

अक्षीयँ[1] ह वै सुकृतं चातुर्मास्ययाजिनः संवत्सरँ हि जयति तं वै त्रेधा विभज्य यजते त्रेधा विभज्य प्रजयति सर्वं वै संवत्सरोऽक्षीयँ[2] वै सर्वं तेन हास्याक्षीयँ[3] सुकृतं भवत्यथो हर्तुरेवैतद्भवति स ऋतुर्भूत्वा देवानप्येत्यक्षीयं[4] वै देवानां तेन हैवास्याक्षीयँ[5] सुकृतं भवति तस्माद्वाव चातुर्मास्यैर्यजते ॥ १ ॥

यच्छुनासीरीयेण यजते या वै श्रीर्देवानाँ साकमेधैरीजानानां विजिग्यानानामासीत्तच्छुनमथ यः संवत्सरस्य प्रजितस्य रसस्तत्सीरँ सा याचैव श्रीर्देवानाँ साकमेधैरीजानानां विजिग्यानानामासीद्यश्च संवत्सरस्य प्रजितस्य रसस्तमुभयं परिगृह्य तमात्मनि कुरुते तस्माद्वाव शुनासीरीयेण यजते ॥ २ ॥

८. निष्क्रामति TE, B.

१. अक्षयँ M; अक्षय्यँ should be the correct form; invariably अक्षीय an. archaic form is used for अक्षय्य.

२. रोक्षयं M.

३. स्याक्षयँ M.

४. त्यक्षयँ M.

५. स्याक्षयँ

sacrifice with this (fire). It is not proper that they should perform *Agnihotra* in the northern altar. Having reached home and having churned (the fires) he sacrifices with the Full Moon offering. The sacrifice, viz. 'the *Cāturmāsyas* (the seasonal sacrifices) is broken up (detached). He (the sacrificer) ultimately remains firm (well established) only by means of this regular (well performed) sacrifice.

(Second Brāhmaṇa Ends)

BRĀHMAṆA III

1. Indeed, the merit of the person performing the *Cāturmāsyas* (the seasonal sacrifices) is imperishable. He conquers the year. He performs that sacrifice, dividing it into three; he conquers, dividing (the year) into three. The year verily means 'all'. 'All' is imperishable. Thereby, his merit becomes imperishable. And moreover, by this he verily becomes the season. Having become the season, he merges in the gods. What belongs to the gods is imperishable. By that verily his merit becomes imperishable. Therefore, indeed, does he sacrifice with the seasonal sacrifices.

2. That he sacrifices with the *Śunāsīrīya* (offerings) is because; the splendour that is of the gods who had performed the sacrifice with the *Sākamedha* (offerings) and who were victorious, that is (called *Śuna*). And what is the essence of the conquered year – that is *Sīra* . That splendour which was of the gods who had performed sacrifice with *Sākamedha* (offerings) and who were victorious and the essence of conquered year – taking up both of them, makes them his own (takes them both into himself). Therefore, indeed, does he sacrifice with *Śunāsīrīya* (offering).

तस्यावृन्नोत्तरवेदिमुपकिरति न पृषदाज्यं गृह्णाति नाग्निं मन्थति पञ्चप्रयाजास्त्रयोऽनुयाजा[६] एकः॑ समिष्टयजुः ॥ ३ ॥

अथैतान्येव पञ्चहवींःषि भवन्त्येतैर्वै प्रजापतिः प्रजा असृजतैतैर्वेव वरुणपाशात्प्रामुञ्चदेतैर्देवा वृत्रमघ्नन्नेतैर्वेवैष एतया च श्रीर्देवानाः॑ साकमेधैरीजानानां विजिग्यानानामासीद्यश्च संवत्सरस्य प्रजितस्य रसस्तमुभयं परिगृह्य तमात्मनि कुरुते तस्मादेतानि पञ्चहवीःषि भवन्ति ॥ ४ ॥

अथ शुनासीरीयो द्वादशकपालः पुरोळाशो भवति स बन्धुः शुनासीरीयस्य यमवोचामाथ वायव्यं पयो भवति पयो वै प्रजा जाता अभिसञ्ज्ञानते विजिग्यानं मा प्रजाः श्रियै[७] यशसेऽन्नाद्यायाभिसञ्ज्ञानान्ता[८] इति स यद्वायव्यमयं वाव वायुर्योऽयं पवत एष ह वा इदं प्रप्याययति यदिदं[९] वर्षति वृष्टादोषधयो जायन्त ओषधीर्जग्ध्वापः पीत्वा तस्यैष उभयस्य रसस्सम्भवत्येष हीदं जनयति[१०] तस्माद्वायव्यम् ॥ ५ ॥

अथ सौर्य एककपालः पुरोळाशो भवत्येष ह वै सूर्य इमाः सर्वाः प्रजा अभिगोपायति साधुना त्वदसाधुना त्वदेष उ एवैना विदधाति साधौ त्वदसाधौ त्वदेष मा विजिग्यानं प्रीत इति साधुनाभिगोपायात्साधौ विदधदिति तस्मात्सौर्य एककपालः पुरोळाशो भवति ॥ ६ ॥

तस्याश्वः श्वेतो दक्षिणा[११] तस्य रुक्मः पुरस्तात् तद्ध्येतस्य रूपं य एष तपति यद्यश्वं न विन्देदपि गौरेव श्वेतः स्यात् ॥ ७ ॥

स य उत्स्रक्ष्यमाणः स्याद्यत्रैव साकमेधैर्यजेत तत एव यदा कामयेताथ शुनासीरीयेण यजते यद्वाव त्रिः संवत्सरस्य यजते तेनैव संवत्सरमाप्नोति रात्रिभिर्हैक आपिपयिषन्ति यद्यु

६. ऽनुयाजौ as alternate reading in TE.

७. श्रिये Ca.

८. See Notes.

९. यदिदं किं च वर्षति Ca., M.

१०. जनयते Ca., TE.

११. दक्षिणा तद्ध्येतस्य in all Mss, except M,B, My; see Notes.

3. Its mode (of performance) - He does not prepare the *Uttaravedi* (the northern altar). He does not take up clotted *ghee.* He does not churn the fire. There are (in the ritual) five fore-offerings, three after-offerings and a single *Samiṣṭa-yajus* .

4. And there are indeed these five (regular) oblations. Verily with these Prajāpati created the creatures. By means of this, verily, did he release (them) from the noose of Varuṇa. By means of this, the gods killed Vṛtra. This (sacrificer) having taken up the two verily by means of his (sacrifice), takes them into himself (makes them his own) – the two,viz., the spelndour which was of the gods who had sacrificed with *Sākamedha* (offerings) and who were victorious and the essence that was of the year that had been won. Therefore, there are these five oblations.

5. Now, the *Śunāsīrīya* (offering) is a *puroḍāśa* on twelve potsherds. What we have stated is an explanation of *Śunāsīrīya.* There is (an offering of milk dedicated to Vāyu. It is milk indeed that beings (just) born understand. "May the creatures recognize (understand/take to) me for (their) prosperity, glory and food" -so (he thinks) (and offers that) which is dedicated to Vāyu. This verily is Vāyu who blows (purifies). This Vāyu indeed conceals whatever rain falls here. From the rains, plants spring up. (On the cattle) eating plants and drinking water, this (milk) the essence of both, is produced. Verily this (Vāyu) produces this. Therefore is (it) (an offering) to Vāyu.

6. Then, there is (an offering of) a *puroḍāśa* on a single potsherd dedicated to the Sun (Sūrya). Verily this 'Sūrya' protects all creatures, by good and by bad (means). He himself puts them under (some) a good (thing) and under (some) bad (thing). He (the sacrificer) (thinks), "Being pleased, may (the Sun) protect me with a good (means)–one who has attained victory; may he put me under a good (thing)". Therefore is there a *puroḍāśa* on a single potsherd, dedicated to ' Sūrya '.

7. For that (ritual) the fee is a white horse. That verily is the form of this (Sūrya) who scorches. If one cannot get a horse, there may be indeed a white bull (as fee).

रात्रिभिरापिपयिषेद्यदेव पुरस्तात्फाल्गुनस्योद्दृष्टं तदेतेन शुनासीरीयेण यजेत स तत एव दीक्षेत तं[१२] नानीजानं फाल्गुनोऽभिपर्येयात्पुनः प्रयोग इव ह स यदेनमनीजानं फाल्गुनोऽभिपर्येयादिति नूत्स्रक्ष्यमाणस्य ॥ ८ ॥

अथाभिप्रयुञ्जानस्य पूर्वेद्युः पौर्णमास्याः शुनासीरीयेण यजेताथ वैश्वदेवेनाथ पौर्णमासेनेत्[१३]युवविप्रयुञ्जानस्य ॥ ९ ॥

अथ वा अतो निवर्तनस्यैव सर्वतोमुखो ह वा असावादित्यस्तस्मादेषोऽन्नाद एष ह वा इदं नि[१४]र्दहति यदिदं किं च शुष्यति सर्वतोमुखोऽयमग्निर्यतोह्येव कुतश्चाग्नावभ्यादधति तत एव दहत्यथायमन्यतोमुखः पुरुषः स एतत्सर्वतोमुखो भवति यन्निवर्तयते स एवमन्नादो भवति यथैतावन्नादौ तदु होवाचासुरिरपि तन्नाद्रियेत यन्निवर्तनमिति किं तत्र मुखस्य यदपि सर्वाणि लोमानि वपेतेति यद्वा एतेन यज्ञेन यजते तेनैव सर्वतोमुखो भवति तेनान्नाद इति ॥ १० ॥ इति तृतीयं ब्राह्मणम् ॥

चतुर्थं ब्राह्मणम्

तद्य[१]दाहुः साकमेधैर्ह वै देवा वृत्रं जघ्नुरिति सर्वैर्ह वाव चातुर्मास्यैर्देवा वृत्रं जघ्नुस्सर्वैर्वेव व्यजयन्त येयमेषां विजितिः ॥ १ ॥

अथ देवाश्च ह वा असुराश्चोभये प्राजापत्या अस्पर्धन्त त एतस्मिन्नेव यज्ञे प्रजापतौ पितर्यस्पर्धन्त संवत्सरोऽस्माकमयꣳ स्यादस्माकमयꣳ स्यादिति ॥ २ ॥

१२. तन्नानीजानं TE.

१३. त्युवभिप्र Ca. M, TE; see Notes.

१४. निर्द्धयति B; निर्धयति Ca., H, P1; P2; see Notes.

१. यद्यदाहुः B.

8. He, who is going to discontinue it, he later performs with *Śunāsīrīya* (offering) when he likes, there itself where he may sacrifice with *Sākamedha* (offerings). As he sacrifices thrice in a year, – by that itself he secures the year. Some (a few) desire to obtain (the year) by means of the nights. If one should desire to acquire through the nights, he may perform with this *Śunāsīrīya* (offering) only when before the *Phālguṇa* (before the Full Moon of *Phālguṇa* month) (the New Moon) has been seen (up in the sky). He should take up (the vow of) consecration even then. The *Phālguṇa* (Full Moon) may pass him by as he is not sacrificing. It will be like a performance (to be) done again if the *Phālguna* (Full Moon) should pass him by when he is not sacrificing. Such (is the procedure) for one who is going to leave it off (discontinue the seasonal offerings).

9. Now for one who is performing (the seasonal offerings)—He should perform with *Śunāsīrīya* offering on the previous day (first day) of the Full Moon and then perform with *Vaiśvadeva* (offering to the 'All-gods') and then with the Full Moon (offering). Thus for one who performs.

10. Now, verily regarding the shaving (off the head of the sacrificer) —
Indeed the yonder Sun faces all around (in every direction). Therefore is he indeed, the consumer of food. Whatever dries up here that this (Sun) verily sucks up. This Agni (also) is one with faces all around, wherefore, he burns up (whatever thing) they put anywhere (in the fire in any direction). Now this person (sacrificer) has his face somewhere else (face only in one direction). By this he becomes 'facing everywhere' in that he shaves his head (turns his head around in shaving). Thus he becomes a consumer of food, just as these two (the Sun and the fire) are consumers of food. In that matter, Āsuri said, "One need not care for (adopt) that shaving (of the head). Even if one may shave all the hair, what does it matter to the face?" "Only by the fact that he sacrifices with this sacrifice does one become 'one having faces all around' and by that (does he become) the consumer of food".

(Third Brāhmana Ends)

BRĀHMAṆA IV

1. Regarding what they say, "Indeed the gods killed Vṛtra by means of the *Sākamedha* (offerings)", verily by means of all the *Cāturmāsya* sacrifices did the gods kill Vṛtra and by means of all (*Cāturmāsya* sacrifices), indeed, did they attain this victory which is theirs.

2. Then (once), the gods and the Asuras, both sprung from Prajāpati, contended. They contended for their father Prajāpati, in this very sacrifice, thinking, "In a year he will be ours; he will be ours".

ते होचुर्देवा असुरैस्संयत्ताः केन राज्ञा केनानीकेन योत्स्याम इति स होवाचाग्निर्मयैव राज्ञा मयानीकेनेति तेऽग्निनैव राज्ञाग्निनानीकेन चतुरो मासः प्राजयꣳस्तद्ब्रह्मणा च पर्यगृह्णत त्रय्या च विद्यया ॥ ३ ॥

ते होचुः केनैव राज्ञा केनानीकेन योत्स्याम इति स होवाच वरुणो मयैव राज्ञा मयानीकेनेति ते वरुणेनैव राज्ञा वरुणेनानीकेनापराꣳश्चतुरो मासः प्राजयꣳस्तद्ब्रह्मणा च पर्यगृह्णत त्रय्या च विद्यया ॥ ४ ॥

ते होचुः केनैव राज्ञा केनानीकेन योत्स्याम इति स होवाचेन्द्रो मयैव राज्ञा मयानीकेनेति त इन्द्रेणैव राज्ञेन्द्रेणानीकेनापराꣳश्चतुरो मासः प्राजयꣳस्तद्ब्रह्मणा च पर्यगृह्णत त्रय्या च विद्यया तमेवꣳ सर्वꣳ संवत्सरꣳ संवृज्य देवा असुराणाꣳ साकमिन्द्रेणैधन्त स यत्साक-मिन्द्रेणैधन्त तस्मात्साकमेधा नाम ॥ ५ ॥

स यद्वैश्वदेवेन यजतेऽग्निनैव तद्राज्ञाग्निनानीकेन चतुरो मासः प्रजयति त्र्येणी शलली भवति लोहः क्षुरस्तेन निवर्तयते त्रय्या विद्याया रूपं त्र्येणी शलली ब्रह्मणो रूपं लोहः क्षुरोऽग्निर्हि ब्रह्म लोहित इव ह्यग्निर्लोहित इव लोहः क्षुरस्तद्ब्रह्मणा च परिगृह्णीते त्रय्या च विद्यया ॥ ६ ॥

अथ यद्वरुणप्रघासैर्यजते वरुणेनैव तद्राज्ञा वरुणेनानीकेनापराꣳश्चतुरो मासः प्रजयति त्र्येणी शलली भवति लोहः क्षुरस्तेन निवर्तयते त्रय्या विद्याया रूपं त्र्येणी शलली ब्रह्मणो रूपं लोहः क्षुरोऽग्निर्हि ब्रह्म लोहित इव ह्यग्निर्लोहित इव लोहःक्षुरस्तद्ब्रह्मणा च परिगृह्णीते त्रय्या च विद्यया ॥ ७ ॥

अथ यत्साकमेधैर्यजत इन्द्रेणैव तद्राज्ञेन्द्रेणानीकेनापराꣳश्चतुरो मासः प्रजयति त्र्येणी शलली भवति लोहःक्षुरस्तेन निवर्तयते त्रय्या विद्याया रूपं त्र्येणी शलली ब्रह्मणो रूपं लोहः क्षुरोऽग्निर्हि ब्रह्म लोहित इव ह्यग्निर्लोहित इव लोहःक्षुरस्तद्ब्रह्मणा च परिगृह्णीते त्रय्या च विद्यया तमेवꣳ सर्वꣳ संवत्सरꣳ संवृज्य साकं देवैरिन्द्रेणैधते ॥ ८ ॥

यद्वैश्वदेवेन यजतेऽग्निरेव तद्भवत्यग्नेः सायुज्यꣳ सलोकतां जयत्यथ यद्वरुणप्रघासैर्य-जते वरुण एव तद्भवति वरुणस्य सायुज्यꣳ सलोकतां जयत्यथ यत्साकमेधैर्यजत इन्द्र

3. They, the gods said, "Engaged in conflict with the Asuras, with whom asking and with whom as leader shall we fight? Agni said, "(You may fight) with me as king and with me as your leader". For four months they conquered verily with Agni as king and Agni as leader. They encompassed it with Brahman and the three fold learning (the three Vedas).

4. (Then) they said, "With whom verily as king and with whom as leader shall we fight?". Varuṇa said, ("You will fight) Verily with me as king and with me as leader". They conquered another four months, with verily Varuṇa the King and Varuṇa the leader. That they enclosed with Brahman and the threefold learning.

5. (Then) They said, "With whom verily as king and with whom as leader shall we fight?" Indra said, "(You will fight) verily with me as king and with me as leader". With Indra verily as king and with Indra as leader, they won another four months. That they encompassed with Brahman and the threefold learning. Having thus appropriated the entire year of the Asuras, the gods prospered along with Indra. Becasue they prospered along with Indra, hence (the sacrifices) are known as *Sākamedhas*.

6. In that he sacrifices with Vaiśvadeva, he verily conquers four months with Agni himself as his king and Agni as leader. (In shaving) there is a porcupine's quill with spots in three places. The razor is copper. With that he has the shave. The three-spotted quill of the porcupine is the form of the threefold knowledge. The copper razor is the form of Brahman. Indeed Agni is Brahman. Red-like is Agni. The copper razor is red-like. Therefore he (the priest) encompasses him with Brahman and threefold learning.

7. Then, as he sacrifices with *Varuṇapraghāsa* (offerings), he wins another four months with verily Varuṇa as his king and Varuṇa as the leader. There is the porcupine quill that has three spots; the razor is copper. With that he has the shave. The three-spotted porcupine quill is the form of the threefold knowledge. The copper razor is the form of Brahman. Verily Agni is Brahman. Indeed Agni is red-like. The copper razor is red-like. Thus he encompasses him with Brahman and three fold learning.

8. As he sacrifices with *Sākamedha* (offerings), he wins the other four months with Indra himself as his king and with Indra as the leader. There is the porcupine quill, having three spots; (there is the) copper razor. With that he has the shave. The three spotted porcupine quill is the form of the threefold learning. The copper razor is the form of Brahman. Agni verily is Brahman Red-like is Agni. The copper razor is red-like. Thus he (the priest) encompasses with Brahman and with threefold learning. Having thus appropriated the entire year, along with the gods, along with Indra, he (the sacrificer) prospers.

एव तद्भवतीन्द्रस्य सायुज्यꣳ सलोकतां जयत्यथ यच्छुनासीरीयेण यजते वायुरेव तद्भवति वायोः सायुज्यꣳ सलोकतां जयति स यस्मिन्नृतौ चातुर्मास्ययाज्यमु लोकमेति स एनमृतुः परस्मा ऋतवे प्रयच्छेति[२] परः परस्मै तमेवमृतवः संप्रदायं परममैव[३] स्थानं परमं लोकं गमयन्ति[४] तस्मादाहुश्चातुर्मास्ययाजिनं नानुविन्दन्तीति परमꣳ ह्येव स लोकं परमां जितिं जयतीति ॥ ९ ॥ इति चतुर्थं ब्राह्मणम् ॥

॥ इति षष्ठोऽध्यायः ॥

॥ इति एकपात्काण्डं समाप्तम् ॥

—::०::—

२. प्रयछंति P1, P2, B.

३. परममेव P1, P2, H.

४. गमयति P1, P2.

9. In that he sacrifices with *Vaiśvadeva* (offerings), he thereby verily becomes Agni himself. He wins intimate union with Agni and residence in the same world as Agni; then as he sacrifices with *Varuṇapraghāsa* (offerings), thereby he verily becomes Varuṇa himself; he wins intimate union with Varuṇa and residence in the same world as Varuṇa. Then, as he sacrifices with *Sākamedha* (offerings), thereby he verily becomes Indra himself; he wins intimate union with Indra and residence in the same world as Indra. Then, as he sacrifices with *Śunāsīrīya* (offerings), thereby he becomes Vāyu himself; he wins intimate union with Vāyu and residence in the same world as Vāyu. In whatever season the performer of *Cāturmāsya* sacrifices goes to the yonder world that season hands him over to another season, that other one to yet another one (and so on). Thus the seasons, handing him over (from one to another), make him reach the supreme (highest) status and the supreme (highest) world. Therefore, they say, "They do not find the performer of the *Cāturmāsya* sacrifices; for he verily conquers the very highest (supreme) world, the highest (supreme) conquest "

(Fourth Brāhmaṇa Ends)

(Chapter Six ends)

(EKAPĀT KĀNDA ENDS)

PĀṬHAVIMARŚA

1.1.1 इत्थाच्च इत्थाच्च means 'By this and that process'. इतश्च meaning 'from hither and thither' goes better with ततस्तत which comes later and hence preferred.

1.1.2 The indicating of the *pluta svara* by adding the numeral '3' (as in this case यत्राग्नी 3), though relevant for the Saṁhitā text need not be given in the *Brāhmaṇa* where *Bhāṣika svara* is used even for Saṁhitā portions quoted. But true to oral tradition the *pluta* is being indicated.

1.1.3 In MD the reading is मिथुन्याभिः स्याम्. Caland's reading मिथुन्येना स्याम् would involve अ in the middle and in that case it can be only एन and not एना. The reading एनाः is preferred in the accusative with an instrumental sense.

1.1.3 विन्दत्यप्सु though found only in TE is given as an alternative, since it can be justified on the basis of the dictum जात्येकवचन, it is preferred.

1.1.4 ऊषा is preferred to उषा since the former justifies the formation of ऊषर and so ऊषा though archaic is accepted.

1.1.7 Caland's reading तदेनान्यथा is untenable since the reference is to प्रतिष्ठां and not to असुरान्.

1.1.9 If there is *sandhi,* it should be श्वश्श्रेयसं and if not श्वः श्रेयसम् Since none of the Mss support either, श्वः श्रेयसम् in *sandhi* is preferred which would be least objectionable.

1.2.1 द्वमिव an archaic usage for द्वि. M perhaps tried to correct it as त्वं.

1.2.7 Same as I.1.1.9.

1.2.12 Caland's reading आददे is not acceptable since earlier and later usages like आदधाति are found. Moreover, the root धा covers both दान and धारण.

1.2.12 नक्षत्रमाहास्य given as alternate reading due to the possibility of splitting नक्षत्रं-आ-हा-अस्य and the letter आ can go with भवति.

1.3.8 यदैवैनं adopted by Caland is not correct. It implies आ in-between, which does not fit in when there is आ in अदधोत.

1.3.8 Same as I. 1.1.9.

1.4.2 Caland's reading सर्वत्याय is not preferred because if it is भावार्थ it should be सर्वत्यत्वाय.

1.4.5 अपराद्धि is in feminine gender meaing अपराध.

1.4.23 प्राञ्चमवर्जीत-वर्ज् in the tenth conjugation should become वर्जयति. अ in negative sense is rarely found with a root and even then it will have a कुत्सितार्थ which does not fit in here. Hence we are obliged to amend it on the basis of the MD reading प्राञ्चं प्रमुञ्चति. For translation purpose the text is construed as आवर्जयति.

2.1.9 उपाववर्त is archaic, वृत being *ātmanepada* आववर्त in *parasmaipada* is not possible. Pāṇini mentions a root वृतु meaning 'speaking' in the 10th conjugation *parasmaipada,* but it does not make sense here.

2.1.12 विराड्डीयं is preferred since it can split into विराट्-हि-इयं. In त्रिष्टुब्भीयं later also this हि is there.

2.2.1 शास् in the second conjugation meaning disciplining or controlling, is used. Here in the context of संज्ञपन the root शस् to squeeze would have been more appropriate, in which case it should be विशसन्ति. We can only presume that शास् is used in the sense of शस् as roots can have multiple meanings.

2.2.5 This perhaps means ब्राह्मणानां शुश्रूषा उ अनूचानां.

2.2.8 Though many Mss support the reading यमिदमिमाः as adopted by Caland, there is much confusion in respect of gender and hence we amend it as यदिदमिमाः.

2.3.14 यन्तु preceded by वि should be वियन्तु. Here the usage व्यन्तु is archaic.

2.4.4 In MD also it is ओषंधय and Sāyaṇa explains it as ओषं पक्वं कृत्वा धय, so ओषं is correct.

3.1.2 The construction is तथा अर्थान् विसृज्यन्ते. The prefix अनु governing the accusative in प्रजा is repeated here with अर्थान्, so Caland's preference for अर्थानाम् is not acceptable though it is supported by most of the Mss.

3.1.8 उदन्त means अन्तोन्मुखं यदा भवति. Here it means just before it is fully boiled.

3.1.10 ततोत्वन्तरेण preferred by Caland would split as तत-उ-तु-अन्तरेण, here उ can be taken to mean 'only'. But तु does not serve any purpose. So ततोन्वन्तरेण is accepted.

3.1.12 Except VI which reads यश all Mss read यज्ञं. The former would have been better since fame is sought after most. For want of support from Mss the VI reading is given as alternative.

3.2.1 अश्नानि इति means a statement of intention. 'Let me eat'—thus saying. अश्नाति a positive statement does not need इति.

3.2.4 अजामहा—अज् is in *parasmaipada* but used in *ātmanepada*. It is archaic.

3.2.9 परिचक्षोतो adopted by Caland has conjunctional difficulties; same case with परिचक्षात in L with the added problem of the absence of the *upadhmānīya* with the following प. So परिचक्षाथो is accepted as the simplest form found in M and TE.

3.2.10 सन्धरि in the seventh case meaning mediation is preferred to शन्तरि meaning peace-maker, since the latter assumes अन्तर्भावित णिच् in the sence of प्रेरणा.

3.3.4 लभाध्वै for लभध्वे and अश्नाथ for अश्नीथ are archaic usages.

3.4.3 TE and some other Mss read ययन्वेकस्य which does not make sense. ययान्वेकस्य supported by My. splits into यया नु-एकस्य. Caland's conjectural reading यान्वेकस्य is not warranted.

3.4.3 असत्सेन्न-Here असत् means आस. Then we have सा-इत्-नु and नु is used in इव sense as in मृगन्न भीमं..

3.4.4 एदानमेव-Here it splits as अ-इ-दान; अ used in the sense of वा 'or' and इ is a *sambodhana*.

3.4.9 स्वदयति + इह as well as स्वदयति वा in the sense of एव both are possible. So are retained as alternate readings.

3.4.13 In TE reading अग्नये वीहि alone is from the *mantra* text. In अग्नेवीहि, the entire expression is from the *mantra* part. In the former अग्नये goes with जुहोति.

3.4.14 पश्चो एव—पश्च-उ-एव in view of एव the intervening उ becomes redundant. Still it is better. Alternative पश्च एव is not acceptable since it should be पश्चैव and not disjuncted.

4.1.1 एदग्निं—अ-इद्-अग्निं here the prepositions अ and इद् go with तिरोभूतम्. The reading एतदग्निं in one Ms can be explained as एषचासावग्निश्च. Hence retained as an alternate reading.

4.1.5 द्वेष्टोः is formed by applying the Vedic termination टोस् and would mean 'will get angry with' द्वेषाय भवति.

4.2.1 प्रतिष्ठितैतेनन्वाववयम् can be split as प्रतिष्ठिता-एतेन-नु-आ-व-वयम्. Here आ goes with the following verb उपचराम. व is in the sense of प्रसिद्धि.

4.2.5 अथैत though found only in one Ms is preferred because अथैष in singular does not fit in with later plural usages upto वसन्ति.

4.3.3 All the readings have some defect or the other. अनश्नदतैव in My. seems to be least objectionable if अत + एव forming अतैव is considered as an archaic *sandhi*.

4.3.10 देवविशं ता is the reading in most of the Mss. But the plural ता is inexplicable. The MD reading विशस्ताः has no such problem since विश is an adjectival noun and qualifies the pronoun ताः and also fits in with अनिषिद्धा.

5.1.3 अभ्यषज्यत् should be the correct form. अडागम is dropped perhaps on the rule that *āgamas* are optional.

5.1.6 There is no other word in the second person in the context. So चक्रुषे preferred to चकृषे.

5.1.20 जक्षुषीः is an accusative plural and goes with प्रजाः. Subject सा is understood from अस्याः.

5.1.26 Here the *Pratiprasthātā*, *Yajamāna* and *Patnī* are all engaged in cleaning. So plural is correct. मृजत्यग्नी in TE is grammatically untenable.

5.1.37 The question here is 'किं अगात्' (Did he go?). The reply should be 'Yes, he has gone'. Corresponding to the verbal usage in the question the normal reply should be अगात्. In all the Mss as well as in MD the reading is अगं. So we retain it as an archaic usage. च्छ्र or छ्र after अंग is also questionable. It should have been अगंश्छ्रावय .

5.2.3 अनन्नेव प्राणान्- The word प्राणान् is by way of explaining the previous word. Otherwise it will be a repetition.

5.2.15 समवर्जन्ति. The root is वृज् वर्जने and as such it should be संवर्जन्ति. Since no Ms has a variant reading, it has to be accepted as an archaic usage.

6.1.8 प्रत्यञ्चो मनुष्याः found in all Mss. does not go with पुरस्ताद्वै देवाः nor with तस्मादेभ्यः प्राङ् which follows. If it were an adverbial usage it should be प्रत्यङ्मनुष्यान्. In MD this reading is justified by अभि following it. Therefore, here we are reluctantly obliged to amend it as प्रत्यङ्-मनुष्यान्. . .

6.1.24 Sāyaṇa in MD while explaining the word चतुःस्रक्ति almost in the same context interprets it as the four-cornered *āhavanīya* altar. Here अनुस्रक्ति appears in four places. स्रक् has the (गत्यर्थ) sense of moving. अनु might have been used in the sense of अभि (proceeding towards) and goes well with दिशं. स्रक्तिः with a *visarga* (in all Mss.) precludes the sense given by Sāyaṇa; that of a corner. It means here only गमनं as a verbal noun.

6.2.8 पिनाकावस may mean 'One doned with *Pināka* bow', or it may be हे ! पिनाक ! आवस when पिनाक means पिनाकिन्.

6.3.5 सञ्ज्ञानानान् ताः should be the correct accusative plural. Here one ना is omitted and is perhaps archaic.

6.3.9 नेत्युवविप्रयुञ्ज्ञानस्य-न-इति-उ-अवि should be नेत्वविं. It may be a scribal error that has come to stay due to break in oral tradition.

6.3.9 निर्धयति is also possible. निर्दहति is preferred in view of the same दहति coming later.